# EYES AND EARS

LETTERS OF LIFE, LOVE, AND ESPIONAGE
IN WWII GERMANY 1938-1956

SUSAN KANDT PETERSON

Mountain Page Press
HENDERSONVILLE, NC

Copyright © 2020 Susan Kandt Peterson
Published 2022 by Mountain Page Press

ISBN
978-1-952714-42-9 (paperback)
978-1-952714-43-6 (eBook)

All rights reserved.
No part of this publication may be reproduced, stored in a retrieval system, distributed or transmitted in any form or by any means (electronic, mechanical, photocopying, recording, or otherwise) without prior written permission from the author.

For information, contact the publisher at:
Mountain Page Press
www.MountainPagePress.com

Edited by Brenda Dammann
Designed by Meghan McDonald
Cover photo provided by Susan Kandt Peterson

This is a work of creative non-fiction. All of the events in this memoir are true to the best of the author's memory. Some names and identifying features have been changed to protect the identity of certain parties. The views expressed in this memoir are solely those of the author. The author makes reasonable efforts to present accurate and reliable information in this book; The author is not responsible for any errors in or omissions references or websites listed or other information contained in this book, nor is the author responsible for the timeliness of the information contained on those websites or external references.

# DEDICATION

History is written by the stories we tell. All of our stories are important. They are built on the origins of those who came before us, connecting us to universal truths about ourselves and about the world. This book is dedicated to my parents with love and gratitude. May their history help us reflect on our own, and the stories we will tell.

# INTRODUCTION

On July 27th, 1938, two young Americans sailed on the SS *New York* for Germany. Bill Kandt, a law student at the University of Kansas, and his new bride, Lois, eagerly accepted the chance for him to be an exchange student at Tübingen University. Having grown up with German parents and grandparents, Bill spoke fluent German. A German student would, in exchange, come to K.U.

Lois and Bill boarded a train in their hometown of Independence, Kansas, ready for knowledge and adventure beyond their small-town confines. Educated yet unworldly, they absorbed the marvels of New York City then drifted past the Statue of Liberty and left America's shores.

These were my parents, and they were traveling into a Germany perched on the cusp of historical events. Hostility toward the outside world – and especially toward Americans – was growing.

The downfall of the German republic had been underway for over five years, beginning when Adolph Hitler was appointed chancellor of Germany in January of 1933. Less than two months later – when Germany's first concentration camp was opened to house political prisoners – the Nazi party passed an act which laid the legal foundation for Hitler's dictatorship. By July, new legislation declared the National Socialist Workers (Nazi) party the only party in Germany. This law, "The Law to Remove Stress from the People and State," gave Hitler the right to pass legislation without approval of the parliament. It also gave the Nazis permission to completely ignore the civil and human rights previously guaranteed by the German constitution.

On June 30 of 1934, Hitler consolidated his power by murdering hundreds of his own political rivals in a purge called "The Night of the Long Knives." A few days later, the German president died, and Hitler merged the roles of chancellor and president to become supreme leader.

Oppression of the Jewish people began in 1935 with the passage of the Nuremberg Laws, which stripped Jews of German citizenship and barred them from marrying or having relations with Germans or German-related blood. Losing citizenship rights meant Jews could not vote and effectively rendered them stateless. The government then began removing Jews from contact with other Germans, progressively taking away their civil rights and making it easier to convince the public that Jews were less than human. By 1937 and 1938, Jewish property had to be registered. Jewish businesses were seized and bought at bargain prices by non-Jewish Germans. Jewish doctors could no longer treat non-Jews and Jewish lawyers could no longer practice law. All had to have a recognizable Jewish name, with Jewish men using "Israel" as their middle name and Jewish women using "Sarah." Germans had to carry identity cards, but Jews had theirs stamped with a red "J."

They could not get a valid passport for travel between countries nor acquire visas to leave Germany. Later versions of the Nuremberg Laws were amended to include black people and Roma, or Gypsies, in the same category as Jews.

In March of 1938, German troops had marched into Austria to annex the German-speaking nation for the Third Reich, sending alarm around the globe. This was the evolving situation in Germany as my parents undertook their journey.

Years after World War II, my older brother Jim and I grew up hearing stories told about our parents' year in Germany and their travels to other countries. Only occasionally did Dad recount a story from his wartime years in the Counter Intelligence Corps. As children, we were too young to comprehend foreign countries across the globe. We didn't know what questions to ask. We didn't live in a pre-war or a war-torn country, so it had no relevance for us. Our 1950s and 1960s history classes didn't teach about World War II; it was a war still being unraveled, in need of distance. And time changed the retelling. The stories we heard were memories of memories, told years after their creation and through different voices.

There is much truth to the statement that one does not get to know one's parents until they are gone. I could only wish I had known mine as young adults, as peers unencumbered by life. Then, I struck gold. Through the gift of my mother's diary and thick bundles of old letters tied with string, I was introduced to my parents before they were Mommy and Daddy, Mom and Dad, and grandparents Judge Bill and Loma. No longer were my memories of frail, aging parents in need of care; with these letters, my parents were transformed into young, active, adventuresome, inquisitive people, with dreams and goals and a deeply unshakable love for one another.

I unwrapped my gift slowly, reading first the letters they wrote home from Europe, then the war letters, and – lastly – those written by my father upon his return to Germany in 1956. I learned that they, like all of us, were the ripening fruit of their time, nurtured by the world in which they lived. As their own political knowledge expanded, I witnessed their struggle to understand the citizens of a nation who were surrendering themselves to a false and dangerous ideology.

I learned, in spite of what I'd been told, that they both felt the fear of war and that, yes, my father was sometimes in danger. And I learned that my father later had reservations about going back again to a country – the country from which his ancestors hailed – which had so disappointed him.

Parents, with all of their merits and flaws, don't stop giving to us in their lifetimes. But what a wonderful gift it was that mine, even in their absence, kept on giving.

My husband and I traveled to Germany in 2014. Mom and Dad were no longer alive, and I regret not having done it sooner. Tübingen is a beautiful college and university town on the Neckar River which charmed us as it had them. We were able to find the building that housed the pensione where Mom and Dad lived in Tübingen before they moved to Stuttgart to work for the American Consulate processing visas for Jews seeking asylum in America. The building stands now, attractively, as a publishing house. Mom and Dad had two adjoining rooms, and as Dad wrote, "The bedroom looks like it was tossed into the air and wedged between this and the adjoining building."

*Eyes and Ears*

We gazed up at that room, which indeed did look like it was tossed into the air and comfortably wedged between a larger and smaller building.

As I typed my mother's letters for this manuscript, I chuckled at times, her naivete inexplicable but somehow charming. However, I also cringed at some of her statements about Jews coming to America. I felt embarrassed, and my first protective impulse was to omit them. However, I couldn't. I only wished that I had read her letters and educated myself more while she and Dad were alive.

I want to ask them questions that haunt me now. I didn't grow up in an antisemitic home. So why her biased comments? It is apparent that my mother had great empathy for the Jewish population while in Germany. At the American Consulate, she daily read their pleas requesting visas to leave the country and go to America. She saw them waiting in the halls and on the steps. Did she write things that would appease the German government should her letters be opened? Was that the reason? Or was her fear a product of her time?

In the late 1930s, there was no television in American homes. Certainly, there was no internet or cell phones. Newspapers, magazines, and radio broadcasts were the media sources that Americans relied upon. America was at the end of the Great Depression. But in 1937, the economy took another sharp downturn and unemployment grew. In 1939 rain finally brought the Dust Bowl to an end, but its economic devastation persisted. Antisemitism rose along with a fear of foreigners taking jobs from Americans. Many private clubs would not allow Jews to become members, and there were colleges and hotels who would not accept them.

Non-whites, people who looked different, or people who practiced different religions were often viewed with skepticism, just as Irish Catholics and Italians had once been. Jim Crow laws enforcing racial segregation still flourished in many sectors of the country. There were no anti-lynching laws. Almost two million Mexican immigrants and Mexican Americans, mostly laborers and farm workers, were deported during the Great Depression in the belief it would free up jobs for others.

After the devastating losses of World War I, Americans had no desire to become involved in European affairs. Reports of Jewish businesses and synagogues being burned and Jews beaten on Kristallnacht outraged many Americans and there were public protests. And yet, public sentiment faded. America was trying to get back on her feet. Worries at home outweighed events overseas. It wasn't until an attack on Pearl Harbor on December 7, 1941 that American neutrality quickly turned to patriotism.

Perhaps it is no different today. We hear about genocide and other atrocities happening in other countries. We learn of dictators who abuse and kill their own people. The stories sober and sadden us. And yet, they are in a land far, far away…until we are directly affected.

"Looking back," Dad later wrote, "that year in Germany had great value for us. It caused us to introspect our own way of life. By contrast, it taught us better to know the value of human freedom."

As a District Court Judge in Wichita, Kansas, Dad authored the words above the entrance on the new Sedgwick County

Courthouse in 1960: "A Free and Independent Court for a Free and Independent People."

No doubt, Dad's years of service as a Special Agent in the United States Army Counter Intelligence Corps (Army CIC) during World War II reinforced his beliefs. And, too, like most in America, he was a product of immigration. He and my mother clearly understood the need to fight for the preservation of freedom, at home and abroad.

Dad had strong feelings about immigration. I remember, even as a child, his telling me how meaningful it was to witness naturalization proceedings, and the emotions he felt. In 1955 he gave the principal address in the United States District Court Number One, in Wichita, Kansas to a group of new Americans. After having talked at length about the meaning of freedom, he said the following:

> *Perhaps the most vital human factor of citizenship in any nation is that nation's concept of personal freedom. The glory of its civilization and the strength of its ideals must be measured ultimately by the realistic application of its concept of personal freedom of the individual, and not only upon its citizens, but upon all men everywhere. The individual, in all of his dignity, is still the fundamental unit of our society. The pressure for freedom grows and the exhilarating influence of freedom expands. Yet in the days of our time, we are experiencing once again how personal freedom may be lost. Challenged by false doctrine, we feel again the need to define and relearn our basic concept of freedom. During the crisis, our comprehension becomes blurred by frustration and confusion. Sometimes it seems our passion for freedom becomes dissipated by the terrible tensions of friction, suspicion, and*

*fear. And sometimes it seems that the price for maintenance is too exacting and that we are neglecting our heritage. But these are surface impressions merely. We are simply examining and re-examining ourselves and our position with freedom while the immigrant seeks entrance to our land.*

*We are pleased to receive new citizens among us. You can challenge us with new truths and new ideas. You can bring to us new talent and new spirit. You can fire our imaginations, enliven our adventures, attack our weaknesses, bolster our strengths, criticize and improve our institutions, and stimulate our ideals. You can remind us that we must live in equality in order to maintain equality; and that, in order to preserve freedom, we must understand freedom. This you can do openly and freely, for you are now America's first-generation citizens of freedom, citizens of the United States.*

In 1956, Dad had the unique opportunity to return to Germany at the invitation of the West Germany government, where his story came full circle. He and Mom had lived in a pre-war Europe under the threat of Hitler and the Nazi regime. As a soldier and counterintelligence agent, he witnessed the death and devastation wrought by a tyrannical man and his collaborators. Ten years later, he was once again "eyes and ears" in a country whose people were rebuilding a new foundation of hope atop the ravages of a warped propaganda.

This is not a novel. There is no building climax, nor a satisfactory resolution to that climax. Instead, it is a glimpse, through letters, into the lives of two people who happened to spend remarkable years, at a remarkable time, in a remarkable country that changed the world forever: World War II, the deadliest conflict in human history.

*Eyes and Ears*

Susan Kandt Peterson

## Itinerary
## Lois Woods Kandt and William (Bill) Carl Kandt
### July 25, 1938 - August 3, 1939

Independence to Lawrence, Kansas
Chicago
New York
USS York to Cherbourg, Southampton, to Hamburg Germany
Berlin, Germany
Halle, Germany
Tübingen, Germany
Zürich, Switzerland
Como, Italy
Milan, Italy
Genoa, Italy
Pisa, Italy
Isle of Elba, Italy
Rome, Italy
Florence, Italy
Venice, Italy
Innsbruck, Germany
Munich, Germany
Stuttgart, Germany
Tübingen, Germany
Freudenstadt, Germany
Stuttgart, Germany

## Susan Kandt Peterson

Paris, France
Heidelberg, Germany
Freiburg, Germany
Basel, Switzerland
Lucerne, Switzerland
Zurich, Switzerland
Stuttgart, Germany
Carl Schurz trip through Germany
Amsterdam, Holland
Stuttgart, Germany
Passau, Germany
Vienna, Austria
Budapest, Hungary
Belgrade, Yugoslavia
Sofia, Bulgaria
Bucharest, Romania
Istanbul, Turkey
Athens, Greece
Rhodes, Italy (Ceded to Greece after WWII)
Trieste, Italy
Stuttgart, Germany
Tübingen, Germany
Heidelberg, Germany
Brussels, Belgium
London, England
Southampton, England
SS *New York* to New York City
Washington DC
Lawrence to Independence, Kansas

July 25-27, 1938
New York

Dear Mother and Dad,

    We arrived in New York by way of the Michigan Central Railroad. We've been busy ever since. John and Margaret Clement met us and we went to their apartment. We had our first subway ride. Last night we went to the Music Hall in Rockefeller Center and saw a movie and a spectacular stage show. Then we walked up Broadway to Times Square. The huge buildings and too numerous signs were overwhelming. We were just terribly impressed. We took a boat trip around Manhattan Island. We went to the Battery and we walked up Wall Street and saw the financial district. Our necks are still sore. We had our dinner at a funny little oriental cafe called The Son of the Sheik. The food was good in spite of being so different. We saw our first Broadway play, the Pulitzer Prize play, *Our Town*. This morning we packed for sailing and went to 5th Avenue in the afternoon. We had dinner at Child's. I had ham because I thought it might be my last for a while. We saw the hotel from which the boy leaped yesterday. The next day, everyone on the streets were saying, "So long," "Don't jump off a ledge."

Lois and Bill Kandt onboard
SS *New York*, July 1938

Well, today is the day! We are so excited. Margaret and John went to the boat to see us off. We went to our third-class cabin and then saw the rest of the boat. It was quite a thrill pulling out and watching the skyline and the Statue of Liberty pass by. I had a queer feeling about leaving the U.S. for a year.

Love,
Lois


July 28-August 4, 1938
SS *New York*

Dear Mother and Dad,

As we are now nearing land, I must settle down and get some letters ready for mailing. We've had a perfectly delightful voyage in spite of sometimes having to take to our bunks due to rough water. Our cabin in third class is small but with ample room.

*Eyes and Ears*

We have met so many grand people onboard. All of the members of the exchange group are lots of fun and a congenial group. Also, there are girls from Wellesley. They are just traveling and having fun. There are several married couples. Everyone is fun and all clean and wholesome looking. As one first class passenger said after looking over third class, "Well, they are clean anyway." That has been our byword.

It is impossible to describe the food, so wonderful it is. Every meal is a banquet. Sirloins are 2" thick. Our service is really something with much silver and attention. And you've never tasted wine until you have Rhineland wine. Monday night the captain had the exchange group for cocktails. His quarters are very elegant. He served caviar, pressed chicken livers, and all sorts of deluxe things that I don't like.

Every night we've had some sort of entertainment with movies or dancing. There was a concert in the dining room one evening. A first-class orchestra played and an opera singer sang for us. Last night we had a costume ball. Bill went as a clown and I as a Japanese girl. It was fun to see what types of costumes impressed the Germans as compared to the Americans. We played shuffleboard for the first time and each evening, dancing, singing, and beer. The beer doesn't have the bitter taste that we drink in America. Tonight, we are having our farewell dinner. I must stop now and will write more later.

Our farewell dinner, what an affair! Everything was festooned up and very fancy. In the afternoon there was a children's party. They all looked so cute in their little paper hats. In the evening we struck rough water and I went to bed. It was a mistake. Bill had fun and went to first class.

We just came in sight of land, but it is so foggy that visibility is poor. We are to arrive at Cherbourg, France at 4:30 in the morning. Tomorrow we go up the English Channel. I hope that it isn't too rough because they say it is very interesting. You see ships from every country there. We reach Hamburg around noon, the day after tomorrow.

Cherbourg to Southampton to Dover. I tried hard to sleep through Cherbourg, but the anchor seemed to drop over our cabin. I have never heard such noise. We were in Southampton by noon. The chalk cliffs of Dover were very impressive with the green pastureland all around. In the evening we had fun with Red, from Brooklyn. He is 13 years old. To bed early for a change.

Love,
Lois

*Eyes and Ears*

Write to:
Anslandsstelle
Exchange Student
Tübingen University
Tübingen, Germany

August 7, 1938
Hamburg, Germany

Dear Mother and Dad,

Well, we have been on German soil for two days now and it is very thrilling. Hamburg is a city of almost 1½ million people. It is a port town which makes it very cosmopolitan. We will buy our bikes in the morning. Six of us will be starting out. Emily and I feel we won't be able to keep up with the boys so we will probably be slower.

Baths are very expensive. We indulged yesterday and will take cat baths for a while. On our arrival we had a lovely banquet given by the University of Hamburg. The restaurant is the oldest in the city, operated since 1674. We had Rhine wine served with our dinner instead of water. Everyone here is so friendly. You ask them to tell you where a place is, and they will walk with you to show you.

I hate to tell you but so far, your American propaganda has been "all-wet." Oranges are sold on fruit stands about every corner and at the same price as in the US. Yesterday we bought oranges, red plums, and pears. Also, butter is served with every meal and we have cream in our coffee. Germany is really as clean as people said.

Yesterday we visited the Hagenbeck Zoo, the largest and most famous in the world. It was just beautiful. Today at dinner we are going to the home of Claus Holthausen, the boy who was at KU as an exchange student.

Love,
Lois

August 8

We had a wonderful time yesterday visiting with Claus' family. Claus was away. They are one of the old families here and have an interesting house and background. The home is 4 stories high and they have many servants. We had dinner at noon and then they showed us many interesting parts of the city. There is a statue of Bismarck about the size of the Statue of Liberty. Last night we had supper, typically German. Each of us had two poached eggs. We had our first champagne, served in a most delightful way. You took a small peach and punched lots of holes in it with a fork. When the peach becomes saturated, it begins to dissolve in the liquid and then you eat the peach. We dared only indulge in two such affairs.

In her later years, Mom said, "After his time as an exchange student at KU, Claus wanted to see California, so we arranged for him to stay with Bill's sister. When he was found spending so much time at the shipyards, he became suspect and was sent home." In 1992, Dad corresponded with an old KU and CIC friend. In that letter he stated, "Claus Holthausen, KU's German exchange student in 1936, did not want to see me the last time I was in Germany. He apparently was picked up by the CIC sometime during the war because he carried a little book containing the names and addresses of the many Americans he had known, including mine. He was a Nazi spy all the time he was here."

We called on the American Consul, registered, and attended to many details and got our youth hostel cards. Then we bought our bicycles. They are equipped with lights, racks, packs, etc., for 52.50 marks, about $12 our money. They are lovely, black trimmed with blue. Everyone thinks that if you are from America, you are rich. But if you shop carefully, you can buy at reasonable prices.

They say Hamburg is about as open and free as any city in Germany. Very little is said of Hitler so far and we have heard only Heil salutes. Most of the people seem to be genuinely in favor of the present set-up. They all seem very interested and all ask if Roosevelt is running for the third term.

   Last night we went to a beautiful spot on the Elbe. It is huge with outside tables and a grand concert orchestra. It accommodates over a thousand people. Never have I seen more beautiful flowers since we have been here. We rode the subway three times. It is much slower than in New York. We enjoyed talking about *Gone with the Wind* with two Germans and three Englishmen.

Love,
Lois

Mom and Dad had to make the last part of the trip to Tübingen via train, due to the terrain. Prior to that, they bicycled between towns to see the countryside and villages.

                                        August 14, 1938
                                        Berlin, Germany
Dear Mother and Dad,

   It was Hamburg to Berlin or bust and we did it with comparatively little effort on our bicycles. We stopped at a lovely new youth hostel. These are built to accommodate the German youth in training. The beds are straw mattresses but not so very uncomfortable. On Wednesday we had lunch at a lovely hotel in a village. We always

eat outside under the
trees and cool wind.
We had lovely thick
steaks. Then we cycled
for about an hour and
slept in a beautiful
pine tree forest for
45 minutes.

We slept at a
quaint village inn,
called a gasthaus. It
was clean but very old and the food was good. A
mean old dog bit Bill on the ankle but it wasn't
deep. The dog was not at all mad, just protective. On Thursday, we started against a strong
east wind. There are so many hills, cycling can
be difficult. A nice German boy rode with us.
I fell off my bike and got a good skinned knee
and bruised hip. It didn't hurt, though. We had
a chicken dinner at a lovely little town called
Ludwigslust. When we reached Perelburg, the youth
hostel was full, so we stopped at a fancy hotel.
Emily and I had a room with a big, white canopy
over the bed and four big windows. Bill and Duane
had the room next to us and it was just as nice.
Duane and Emily are not married. They met as
friends and decided to ride bikes with us. The
next day Emily and I went out for breakfast and
we were royally stung for being Americans. Then
we shopped for a picnic lunch. Everyone is so
interested in us and so helpful. There are cheese

Duane, Bill, Lois and Emily,
Hamburg, August 1938

shops, bread and pastry shops, meat shops and fruit stores. We ate in another lovely woods. We were riding along and saw a tall, old building in a village and rode up to it and found out it was a castle over 300 years old and the land had been in the same family for over 700 years.

We stopped at Kryist at the youth hostel. The hostel is not fancy and quite unorderly because a troop of soldiers just left. There were many jolly German youths around, and we had a good time. A funny thing happened at the hostel. I called out for Bill and about 15 youth boys came running! We have a hard time establishing our marriage here because they only wear yellow gold bands about twice as large as ours on their right hands, and on the left, when engaged.

Saturday, we rode for 56 kilometers and two German high school boys rode with us and they helped a lot. The traffic became so heavy that we took the train to Berlin. We cycled to the youth hostel and it was full. There are so many things going on here. We found a nice little hotel and the four of us are here. Our hotel has a balcony and we can stand out and look up and down the street. We had a bath, which is something these days. I ate my very first kraut and sausage. I have never had so much pep. The exercise is good for us and I am so brown I could pass for a full blood Indian.

*Eyes and Ears*

Berlin is older and does not have the light, airy appearance of Hamburg. If a building is more than five or six stories high, it is noticeable. Two nice high school boys who had been riding with us helped us find our way around. The German people are so polite and will go to no end of trouble to help. We mailed our clothes from Hamburg and thought they would be here today, but we can't get them until Monday. The only dress I have is my little full skirt, the $1.95 print one. It has been raining so I can cover up with my trench coat. Poor Duane has only his Bavarian shorts.

Bill and I walked and walked and saw many statues, the University of Berlin, and many museums. Eating our dinner, we saw our first German drunk. They have no ability to care for them.

We never know any news as the German papers use too many words that Emily and I can't understand. We are always surprised when we hear of something happening. They are preparing for a big parade or something here, but we haven't found out what it is yet. This afternoon there is a big sports meet at the Olympic Stadium which we may go to. America has quite a few boys here to take part.

Love,
Lois

**Youth hostels** had been in existence many years prior to the Nazi Party and were used for young hikers and outdoor enthusiasts. However, by the mid-1930s, hiking from hostel to hostel was an illegal act as it was considered bourgeois. Hikers were ostracized as unpatriotic, antisocial leeches. Self-discovery was no more.

After 1933, when the Nazi party seized power, the Reich absorbed and consolidated youth institutions. By 1936, all Aryan children between the ages of ten and seventeen were required to join the Hitler Youth, where young men and women were encouraged to abandon their individuality in favor of the Aryan collective. The Hitler Youth combined sports and outdoor activities with National Socialism ideology. Similarly, the League of German Girls emphasized collective athletics deemed less strenuous to the human body and better geared to prepare them for motherhood. It trained young people through rigorous drills and exercises that pitted individuals against nature, or against each other.

Via this system, the Nazis set up an entire generation of youth for indoctrination into their ideology. Young men were trained for war. Most children grew up with antisemitism, Nazi propaganda, swastikas, and a love of the German Führer, saying, "Heil Hitler!" with arm raised many times a day. Youth leaders frequently encouraged children to report their parent's disloyal statements about the Nazi Party.[i]

*Eyes and Ears*

August 19
Halle, Germany

Dear Mother and Dad,

We left Berlin yesterday by train for Tübingen because of the mountains and stopped over for a couple of days in Halle. A nice young man, Herr Zimmerman, helped us find our way around. He had dinner with us that night. It is a town of 100,000 and has the appearance of being much older than anything we have seen. Hans Martin, who was at KU last year, is in school here and we had a nice time with him the next day. We went to a little sidewalk cafe and had coffee and macaroons with whipped cream. Then we walked around and saw the university, the marketplace, and Woolworths. Hans came back after he was excused from a meeting. He had on an all-black uniform. They were having a Hitler Youth sports event and the town was very crowded. Hans was very helpful in explaining the various uniforms. Hans is a member of the SS. They are a select group which has to meet certain physical requirements, like being over six feet tall, and must be able to take part in sports events. The girls they marry must also meet certain requirements.

**The SS, or Schutzstaffel**, was originally established as Adolf Hitler's personal bodyguard unit. It would later become both the elite guard of the Nazi Reich and Hitler's executive force. They were prepared to carry out all security-related duties without regard for legal restraint. The SS had to swear a personal oath to Hitler by men who perceived themselves as the "racial elite" of the Nazi future. Beginning in 1933, the SS operated concentration camps to hold Jews, Roma (gypsies), homosexuals, political dissidents, and – eventually – Catholics and the disabled. Some of the concentration camps were later to become extermination camps. The SS was specifically charged with the leadership of the "Final Solution," the murder of European Jews.[ii]

```
In Berlin, Bill saw the Olympic Stadium and
the American German track games. The four fliers
who flew to New York and back sat directly in
front of him. They were introduced to the crowd.
Berlin is simply full of statues, museums, and
all sorts of historical places. While at the war
memorial for the heroes of 1914-1918 we saw the
changing of the guard. They really did the goose
stepping then and clicking of heels. In Hamburg
we saw very few
uniforms but in
Berlin almost every
third person wears a
uniform.

We went through
the Frederick
Wilhelm I Palais.
We had to shuffle
around in funny
felt shoes. It was
very impressive.
```

SS Officers, Berlin, August 1938

We had our farewell dinner at the Viktoria Cafe, with cold chocolate soup with miniature almond macaroons in it, ham with tomatoes and pickles, ox tongue, and a ham omelet, meat patties with potatoes, cucumber salad with fruit, and pastry for dessert.

The German beds are certainly funny. The mattresses are all like ours only there is a separate little piece which goes under the pillow to raise the head and shoulders more. Then the pillows are huge and feathery and light. I always have to take the extra mattress piece off. And then, instead of having a single top sheet, they enclose a light, feather mattress affair in a sheet and that is your cover. In this kind of weather, it is too chilly to sleep without some cover and yet the feather affair is too warm. There are no blankets or spreads. Very few places have running water, so I juggle around pitchers and washbasins.

Bill went to get his first German haircut.

We now plan to go to Tübingen and get settled. Then we can make more definite plans. Starting September 1 for ten days is the Nazi Congress at Nuremberg. We would like to attend but it is now too late to get a room anywhere near unless you have political pull.

Love,
Lois

Susan Kandt Peterson

August 24, 1938

Dear Folks,

At last I have found a schrieb [sic] machine and with it the inspiration to write what has taken place with Lois and myself since we watched the Statue of Liberty disappear from view. Much water has flowed under the bridge or under the boat since that time, and many things of interest have happened to us. The sea voyage was most delightful. Several times during the trip we passed other ships on the horizon which was a welcome sight. I have never before seen ocean waves, so I was quite impressed. We saw many flying fish and at every port the graceful seagulls were as thick as flies.

On the boat were other exchange students and we had a jolly time. One evening several of us stole up to first class and drank beer in a swanky bar there. We met a funny Englishman and had a hilarious night of it. We tried coming back the next night, but the stewards were watching for us and wouldn't let us in, said we were too noisy. Best of all I enjoyed standing in the prow of the ship and watching the restless waves roll by.

One evening we found engraved invitations from the captain inviting the exchange group to his cabin for cocktails and for the first time I tasted caviar. Nothing particularly thrilling to eat fish eggs, but the party was lovely.

The first port was Cherbourg. We heard the anchor and chains rolling over our cabin as the anchor slipped into the sea. It sounded like the ship was tearing in two. The boat reached Southampton several hours later and we had our first close view of England. Several passengers and their cars were unloaded here and we crossed the English Channel into the North Sea. We passed the White Cliffs of Dover and they were imposing against the grey of the morning. In a few hours we reached Cuxhaven, the German port. There were many people on deck and they all gave the Nazi salute as the band played the German national anthem. It took about three hours to reach customs where we were treated with courtesy and met with no difficulty.

From Cuxhaven we were taken to Hamburg by rail. It was our first chance to view the German cottages and farms, which were delightful. The Germans make use of every bit of ground and there is something growing everywhere. In north Germany, there is much rainfall, so the fields are rounded at the top with ditches in between to allow the water to drain off. A curious contrast with the fields in Kansas. In Hamburg I sat in our hotel window by the hour and watched the people go by. The crowds are so different from those in America. The pace is slower and the dress so queer. No one bumps you or pushes you off the walk. And the street cars move as slow as they do in Independence. Only the automobiles on the street are in a hurry since there is no speed limit. The little European cars dart around like monkeys on a racetrack. The pedestrian had better jump, or else! Horns are not permitted. And the great number of bicycles and motorcycles don't make the traffic problem any simpler. The traffic officers are imposing, as they stand in their white coats and gloves, silently directing traffic with no whistles.

We called upon the parents of a German boy who was at KU and we were treated royally. They drove us all around the city in their Mercedes sports car, gave us a fine dinner and topped it off with champagne. We left their house very happy and knowing how wonderful German hospitality could be.

We left Hamburg on our bicycles and in the evening, we reached the first youth hostel about four hours later. We ate breakfast there, rode through quaint villages with their narrow streets and ancient houses, stopping as we chose. Later we stayed at another youth hostel and our last. They are nice enough and reasonable but so crowded with Hitler Youth, that we did not find an association of our own age. The Hitler Youth are composed of uniformed boys and girls from six to sixteen, who spend the day in drill and sport.

The rest of the trip we stayed in moderate priced hotels, washing out of basins, and paying good money for a bath now and then.

In a 1959 Wichita newspaper interview, Dad said, "On one of our bicycle trips, during which we would stay in hostels, a teenage youth pulled out a map and pointed to Austria. 'Yesterday that was ours, tomorrow America and someday the world.' Eventually, we stopped staying in hostels because we realized we were not wanted. Even at the inns, we were only tolerated. The Nazi propaganda machine, working through the newspapers, radio, and magazines, strongly criticized America. The true world situation was hidden from the public, with pictures limited and biased."

This assessment was somewhat in contrast to what they both wrote in their letters home. The letters don't convey any alarm, nor discomfort, during this part of their trip. Lois' mother was worried, as expressed in Mom's letters and they may have been careful with the content of their letters, if read by the German authorities.

The countryside of northern Germany is interesting. The farmers were thrashing their grain and there were about five women to every man in the fields. The women wore huge bonnets and full skirts, and as they went home, sat on top of the hay while the men walked beside the horses and oxen.

On our last leg of our bicycle trip to Berlin, we met two interesting German boys who rode into

Berlin with us. We reached Berlin at a late hour Saturday night, which meant that the American Express and Auslandstelle offices would not be open to give us advice. We found the youth hostel to be full and the German boys were most helpful in finally finding us a little hotel after about three hours of aimless wandering through busy Berlin. We could get only one large room with four beds. By that time anything looked good to us, so we all decided to stay. It worked out so well that we stayed there for six days.

From Hamburg we had sent a small bag ahead to Berlin with some clothes but the bag was not sent and we did not locate it until the following Thursday, which meant that for five days we had to wear the same dirty clothes that we had been cycling in. We spent much time on the Den Linden Strasse, wearing raincoats to cover our clothes.

Berlin, Military Parade, August 1938

We visited the Prussian war memorial, in front of which is stationed two Nazi soldiers who stand at full attention for hours at a time. On another day we saw a military band on parade, with fifes and drums and a

*Eyes and Ears*

unit of soldiers, all led by two policemen on fine white horses, with a drum major who worked in the traditional military style.

For a small fee, we were guided through the palace Frederick Wilhelm I and were quite impressed with the severity of the furniture and interior, all done in gold, red, and white. We touched the tables and chairs at which the old King and Prince Bismarck counseled together. We stood before the personal desks of the King and Queen and smiled at the curious novelties that even royalty accumulates. We walked in silence through the King's library with its books just as he left them, and stood in reverence before the bed in which the old monarch died.

I pedaled out to the Reich's Sports Field, the stadium in which the Olympics are held and saw athletic games between the Germans and Americans. I never have seen or dreamed of a more magnificent sports stadium with its clay track and green grass and modern architecture. When the Americans marched on the field carrying the stars and stripes,

Olympic Stadium, Berlin, August 1938

all the spectators stood at Nazi salute while
the band played "The Star Spangled Banner." Truly
a marvelous display of sportsmanship. And when
the American boys made a good jump or ran a good
race, the applause was just as enthusiastic as
for the German boys. The attitude of heckling
that one finds at American sports events was
missing. Lack of rugged individualism, I suppose.

Because of its intended use for Nazi propaganda, Germany's **Olympic Stadium** was built as a vast, imposing building, with hints of the Coliseum in Rome in its design. Soft-pedaling its antisemitic agenda and plans for territorial expansion, the regime exploited the **1936 Summer Olympic Games** to bedazzle many foreign spectators and journalists with an image of a peaceful, tolerant Germany. Most anti-Jewish signs were temporarily removed while the newspapers toned down their harsh rhetoric. Nazi officials ordered that foreign visitors should not be subject to the criminal penalties of anti-homosexuality laws. Germany athletic imagery drew a link between Nazi Germany and ancient Greece, symbolizing the Nazi racial myth that a superior Germany civilization was the rightful heir of an "Aryan" culture of classical antiquity: heroic, blue-eyed blondes with finely chiseled features.

As a token gesture to placate international opinion, Germany allowed their star fencer, Helene Mayer, to represent Germany at the Olympic Games. Her father was Jewish, and she was considered non-Aryan. She won a silver medal and, like all other medalists for Germany, gave the Nazi salute on the podium. No other Jewish athletes competed for Germany in the Summer Games.

These were the Olympic games in which Jesse Owens' medals helped disprove the Nazi theory that nonwhite people were inferior. (However, despite his Olympic victories, Owens still faced racism as an African American back home.)[iii]

We visited the aquarium at the zoo in Berlin and with such an array of sea animals that I had never seen. We didn't visit the zoo as the one in Hamburg, which is much larger, covers acres of ground. All of the animals are displayed in their natural settings with no fences or bars to mar the views, being kept in place by moats which surround their quarters.

We took the train to Tübingen but stopped off in Halle and visited with Hans Martin, the German boy who was at the Phi Psi house last year. He is a member of the SS Elite Guard. (Like our ROTC.) We had a fine time and started for Tübingen at midnight. Traveling at night on a third-class coach is not the most comfortable, but we arrived in Tübingen feeling quite well. The scenery coming into Southern Germany is much different than the North with its many small mountains covered with miles and miles of grape vines.

In Tübingen we stayed in a reasonable hotel until we could find rooms, which we have. We have two large rooms, a bedroom and a sitting room adjoining, plus three meals a day all for 200 marks a month (less than 50 dollars). We have to wash out of a basin and pay extra for the baths, but who in Germany doesn't? Other Americans are amazed at our good fortune. It is occupied and we move in on the first of October.

We bought a good German camera yesterday and hope to have a picture album from now on. I haven't mentioned the German food but let me assure you, the Germans are not starving. The only objection I have to the meals is that the servings are so enormous. Don't think I'll ever be a beer drinker, even though the beer is very smooth and good. If you order water with a meal you have a sad experience, so we have learned to eat our meals dry. Potatoes are the main food and plenty of them. Also, we will get tired of veal before the year is up. Vegetables are in abundance and the marketplace here in Tübingen is most colorful and interesting. It is a lovely little town.

Love to all, and write to us about things back home.

Bill (and Lois)

*Eyes and Ears*

August 24, 1938
Tübingen, Germany

Dear Mother and Dad,

Well, we are at last in our lovely little town of Tübingen. It really is the grandest surprise of our lives. Everyone told us it would be grand, but it is so pretty and old-world with rambling streets and a castle on a hill. It is larger than we thought and has a population of around 28,000. The town is built upon the sides of two very large hills and in two small valleys. The streets are very narrow and run in all directions. Everything looks extremely old yet painted and clean. We just love it.

Tübingen on the Neckar River, August 1938

We went to an open-air dancing place the night we left. We took the 1:15 AM train Saturday night and arrived in Tübingen at 12:00 Sunday noon. Everything seems cheaper here in southern Germany.

We went walking after dinner at our hotel and it was so cold, and we had no warm clothing, so we had to go to bed at 4:00 to get warm. Monday, we moved to a cheaper hotel. We got our luggage and some warm clothes. Most of them are so wrinkled and my iron won't heat on this current.

Monday afternoon we walked up to the Schloss Hohentübingen castle. It was built in about 1502. It is a huge affair with tunnel-like passages. Some of the rooms have been remodeled and are used by the University. One huge room is the town meeting place for the National Socialist.

We went to a beer haus and I had lemonade again.

We were given the name of an American couple here in school, Helen and Norman MacLeod. They have been here a year. We met them and went to their rooms and had a nice visit. He is getting his doctor's degree from the theological school. He came over a year ago and when he found out it was so cheap, he sent for her. They were married in England. They are from New England and are very different from us, but lots of fun.

Next week I will be 24 and my first birthday away from home.

                              August 25

Yesterday we went to tea with the MacLeods and Robert Perry at a nice old maid's house. Robert is a minister from Newark, New Jersey and is leaving next week. It was nice and we enjoyed it. But the MacLeods say she runs after Americans too much and the teas finally become tiresome. Last night we had supper with the MacLeods. They are in a home and have kitchen privileges. We brought the desert, lovely big grapes, and bananas. We have Sunkist oranges almost every day.

Yesterday after lunch we rode our bicycles to the edge of town and then walked up a small mountain which was covered with pine trees. The fragrance was very delightful.

I went to a very modern shop to have my hair washed. It is so cold here I was afraid of washing it myself and letting it dry slowly in the cold air. I had to lean over instead of back and the man who washed it failed to be interested in washing my scalp. Then he set a nice wave and when he was through, put combs all through the waves and made them stand up rigid like.

We have found one desirable place to live so far. German is spoken altogether. The rooms will not be available until the first of October. It has steam heat but no running water. It just does not exist in many places here.

We are now trying to figure out some sort of trip for the next month. It is so cold that Helen and Norman suggested we go to Italy, which sounds like a grand idea.

Love,
Lois

September 2, 1938
Genoa, Italy

We spent four hours in Zurich. We passed the Rhine waterfalls. Spectacular! They are the largest in middle Europe. While they are not high, they are lovely because the water flows so swiftly, and they churn like big, swishy swirls.

Zurich is the largest city in Switzerland. It has many beautiful buildings and wide streets. The shop windows were displayed beautifully. It was nice to see American products again. Bill bought a package of Phillip Morris and we got a *Saturday Evening Post* (30 cents). I was glad for the chance to buy Swiss chocolate. I don't know how they do it, but it is so much better than ours.

Because Zurich is expensive, we knew we wouldn't be back and went in search of an authentic Swiss dinner. In a cafe we were greeted by a cheery, "Good morning" and "What will you have, sir?" Everyone can just seem to see an American coming. We had a ½ chicken and it was grand.

We left on the 4:00 train for Italy. We witnessed the Swiss Alps. I don't suppose by train we were able to see the most beautiful parts but, even so, I've never seen anything like it. They were not snow capped at this time of year but, regardless, they were magnificent! They were full of streams and falls and dotted all over were clearings with little farms and pastures. It is like Germany where there are no weeds and scrub brush. Everything is clean and orderly. We hated to leave Switzerland, but the American dollar does not last long there.

We approached Italy by way of the Saint Gotthard Pass. The Gotthard tunnel is 9½ miles long. I bet we went through 25 tunnels while in Switzerland and it made our ears feel funny. After going through customs, we settled in Como for the night. We thought we had settled the price of the room but the next morning when we started to pay, the bill had doubled. Everything is cheap in Italy but just like Germany, these people are out for everything they can get. In Italy there is a hotel tax, of all funny taxes. The hotels are rated ABCD and you pay accordingly.

My mother later said, "We were uneducated about the beauty of Lake Como. I'm so sorry that we missed it!"

    Yesterday we went to Milan and went directly to the famous Milan Cathedral, the second largest in the world. There are hundreds of statues both inside and out, all made of white stone and decorated for the Catholic Congress, which was being held. We went to the roof and there is just so much to see! No matter how much I would say about it, I could never describe it. We spent two hours on the roof. We wanted to see Da Vinci's *Last Supper* but we couldn't find it. After hours going in all directions, we gave up. We went to the station. It was built in 1931 by Mussolini (Il Duce) and it was huge and beautiful. We took a train last evening for Genoa and here we are. It is part of the Italian Riviera but too commercialized by the shipping trade to be of much interest to tourists.

    We are going to Pisa, Rome, Florence, Venice, Salzburg, and Munich. We won't be in Tübingen until the first of October.

Love,
Lois

*Eyes and Ears*

September 9, 1938
Rome, Italy

Dear Mother and Dad,

We have been so much on the go since I wrote in Genoa. Genoa is a nice seacoast town with palm trees. We ate the grandest of peaches in Genoa and had our first Italian wine. We saw the site where the home of Columbus was supposed to be. The big statue of him was grand. The mountains and the sea were lovely. Trains in Italy are terrible. We had to stand for three hours on the train to Pisa, but we felt fine and had a wonderful view.

Pisa is old and so quiet. There were very few tourists about. We went to the Leaning Tower, a most peculiar sensation. The tower leans 13 feet. We went to the very top and had a grand view of the surrounding mountains. I was so mad at Bill because it was raining, and the marble was wet underfoot. He kept leaning way over to see what he could see!

After the tower, we went through the cathedral. The walls had lovely paintings and sculptures by Paisano and his son. Mass was sung by the monks. Along the way back to the hotel, we visited many lovely churches. We saw the street where Galileo was born.

From Pisa we went again on a crowded dirty train to Piombino to take a small steamer to the beautiful Isle of Elbe. We saw the sunset on the steamer, and I have never seen such colors. We met three people from Genoa there and went to their yacht and had a lovely evening with them. Mr. Cheruti is an old man who talked much and joked a lot, and his niece and her husband, Mr. and Mrs. Pardosa. Mr. Cheruti mined gold in California for a few years. He was the head of the Italian War Industries Board in ten states during the war. In the morning we took a horse and buggy to the home where Napoleon lived while he was exiled there in 1814. The house was built for him, but he only lived there nine months.

Then we went to shore again in the afternoon and caught a train to Rome. Rome is so big, and the streets go in all directions. We'd walk and walk and realize that we were walking in circles, so we decided to take an American Express tour of the city. It lasts three days. I don't think we've missed a thing! We walked to the Trevi Fountain where you toss a coin in. It was fun watching the street urchins recover the coins.

Trevi Fountain, Rome, September 1938

The AE tour was on a large bus with

a guide. We saw an old sewer built in 600 BC, the cemetery where Keats and Shelley are buried, Saint Paul's Cathedral and Mussolini's Forum, the school where many of the youth are trained. It is a huge place where all sorts of sporting events take place there.

Entrance to Mussolini Forum, Rome, September 1938

We went to the church of the Franciscan Monks and, of course, we went to the Parthenon, the former Roman temple. The last two kings are buried there as is the painter Raphael. Then we went to the largest church in the world, Saint Peter's. The highlight of the day was the ruins of the Colosseum. It is most amazing.

Our guide took us to the Vatican City. Part of the museum was the former living quarters of the Popes. The Sistine Chapel, painted by Michelangelo, was disappointing as it was so smoked up by the use of candles.

Colosseum, Rome, September 1938

Italy has nothing to do with the Vatican City. It is a free city. They have their own money, stamps, passports. They are free from duty, so it is very inexpensive to live there. However, only the workers who live there are entitled to buy there. I think about 600 people live there. The Catholic Church is very wealthy. The amount of money sent to the Pope from around the world is appalling. Mussolini is smart enough to be friendly with the Pope. It is said that no one will deny that the Vatican has been, and is, supplying most of the money for Italy's interest in the Spanish War.

On Saturday we ended our tour by going to the Forum and Palatine Hill. On the way we saw Il Duce's office and the large public square where he addresses the people. Amidst the old ruin, we saw the site where Julius Caesar was cremated and where Mark Antony said, "Friends, Romans, Countrymen." On Palatine Hill is the site of the ruins of the Emperor's Palace. Then we saw the site where Romulus built Rome.

Bill said I have only touched upon the highlights of Rome.

Italy is more progressive than Germany in some ways, but the people are so dirty. Every place there is a crowd there is an awful odor. Yet they are more creative and joyous. The Germans are so serious minded. They seem to think more of Hitler than the Italians do Mussolini. There is a lot of building going on here. Mussolini seems to be doing a lot for the people, but so is Hitler. It is only when you talk to people that you realize the restrictions of a dictator. The King gets little recognition.

We realize that this is a critical period in European affairs. But none of us believe that Hitler will be foolish enough to go into Czechoslovakia. Everyone who has ever been there, that we have talked to, says that the "Chezi" will fight to the last man. I think that right now Hitler is too anxious to build up Germany and make it more secure that he wouldn't dare run the risk. They really manage beautifully in Germany not to have too much imported but there is very little luxury. For a family of two, you can only have five eggs a week and ½ pound of butter. There is no coffee cream regardless of where you buy coffee. It is against the law to buy an all wool suit. So, there are plenty of restrictions, but everyone is well fed and clothed.

By contrast, Italy imports all sorts of things. Things that would be a luxury in Germany. Yet the children look undernourished and poor. Dirt is the main thing. A toilet must not mean much to them for they go at their convenience and are completely unashamed. Yet there are some very smart shops and well-dressed people. They go to the two extremes here as in the U.S., the rich and the poor. Yet, Germany is more uniform. We think the

Germans are superior but not progressive enough to live under a democracy. They need someone to push them on.

Everyone in both countries seems to be fully in favor of the Jewish situation and seem to have no feeling as to where they go. They all say we have the same problem in New York. I suppose propaganda tells them so.

It is the youth in Germany who are so strong for Hitler. They are given so many pep talks and drilled so much that it is hard to see where there is going to be any individualism. Of course, that will take 15-20 years to show and I doubt if the system can last that long.

They say there is a large, growing party against Mussolini. You never hear of it because it spreads by a sort of whispering campaign. A missionary here told us of it. He works with people all over Italy. We only get snatches of things here and there, but they are interesting.

We leave Monday for Florence.

Love,
Lois

Looking back, one can see how events were playing themselves out building toward World War II. And my parents, two young Americans from the Midwest, were in Germany and Italy at this crossroads in time, with Hitler and Mussolini in power.

**Benito Mussolini** was a ruthless Italian political leader who became the fascist dictator of Italy from 1925 to 1945. Called "Il Duce" (the Leader) by his countrymen, Mussolini allied himself with Adolf Hitler, relying on the German dictator to prop up his leadership during World War II. In March of 1938, Hitler invaded Austria with Mussolini's support. By October, the two countries had officially joined together as the famous "Rome-Berlin Axis." Mussolini wrote an article in 1938 that aligned Italians with the German concept of the Aryan race. Soon after, Mussolini called for the expulsion of foreign Jews from Italy. As a puppet of Hitler, he also sent them to concentration camps to die.

When Allied forces barreled through Italy in June 1945, Mussolini attempted to flee to Spain with his lover, Claretta Petacci, but was discovered and arrested by partisans searching troop transport trucks. There are conflicting stories about how Mussolini died, but autopsy reports state the dictator was shot by soldiers firing several bullets – with four of them near the heart – causing immediate death. The bodies of both Mussolini and Petacci were hung upside down at the Piazzale Loreto in Milan and displayed for crowds to kick and spit on. He had taken Italy into an unnecessary war and caused pain and destruction of the country. One day later, Hitler committed suicide. The following week, Germany surrendered.[iv]

Susan Kandt Peterson

September 17, 1938
Florence, Italy

Dear Mother and Dad,

The days are all crowded, so full of interesting things. Suddenly I realize that it has been a long time since I have written.

We love Florence so much. It is a city but with a quiet, peaceful way about it.

Sunday, 12:00

We just washed my hair in two bowls with four jugs of hot water. At least you don't have to wait for the water to run down the drain. We are in a pensione that is very nice. The lira is less than 5 cents, so it is cheap room and board. One nice thing about Italy is that there is always fresh fruit for dessert.

Florence is the art center of Italy. There are lots of galleries, but the two main ones are gems. We went to the Uffizi Gallery and enjoyed watching the artists copy the masterpieces. We shopped on a covered bridge. The shops are simply tantalizing; linens, etchings, watercolors, pottery, jewelry, statues of marble, and so on. Everything is cheap and you can always barter them down. We walked around a lot with a map from American Express. As we walked, we had some grand gelato (ice cream). We saw the cathedral and the baptistry and took the circle train ride. We went to the Pitti Palace, a perfectly gorgeous place. We saw the movie, *The Good Earth*, in Italian. Oh, yes, we went to see the original Michelangelo original statue of David, a wonderful work.

We loved our trip to Fiesole, a little Etruscan town near here perched high on a hill. There is an old Franciscan monastery there. Fiesole was conquered by the Romans and there is an old Roman theatre there. It is all so calm and peaceful. While there, we saw a play in Italian, and it was difficult for us to understand in the Florentine dialect. But the costumes and acting were very good.

So much to see and do here. We plan to stay here until Wednesday or Thursday and then go to Venice for two or three days. Then we go back to Germany.

Most Italians are pretty much worried about what Hitler might do. They are not at all like the Germans racially and do not want to fight with them in case of war. To the few people we have talked to, they think there would be a revolution if Mussolini made them fight. It looks like Germany would stand alone. I don't think they would engage in a war with cold weather so near at hand.

Love,
Lois

Susan Kandt Peterson

September 28, 1938
Munich, Germany

Dear Mother and Dad,

So much has been happening here that I've almost forgotten when I last wrote to you. We went to Venice from Florence. It is such a lovely city, full of charm and romance. The canals are so numerous, and the water was quite rough in them. The gondolas are tempting but much too expensive. Pigeons perched on my arms in Saint Mark's Square. We also saw Venetian glass blown. Finally, we broke down and bought a small watercolor. We only stayed one night in Venice as we were running out of lira. We left at 6:00 in the morning. We went into Austria to Innsbruck through the famous Brenner Pass. Innsbruck is in a valley completely surrounded by high mountains. We planned to stay only one night but liked it so well, we stayed three. Everything is so picturesque. The houses

Lois, Innsbruck, Austria,
September, 1938

Bill, Innsbruck, Austria,
September, 1938

are so cute and colorful, they hardly look real. We took a streetcar to the village of Igls and from there took the cable railway to the peak of one of the mountains. It was quite a sensation riding suspended in midair. Then we spent 2½ hours climbing to the very top peak of the mountain. There we were refreshed by good, cool milk and cookies.

Sign near Innsbruck, Jews Forbidden, September 1938

While in Venice, Mom said later, "I was able to read enough in the newspapers that something bad might be about to happen. We went to the American Consul. We were told, 'What are you doing here? Don't you know that war is imminent? You need to leave now, get your clothes in Germany and get out!' We did leave but found Innsbruck, Austria so picturesquely beautiful that we stayed for three nights. Luckily, we did, for we arrived in Munich at a time of great historical significance."

Sunday, we came to Munich. It was another beautiful train ride. We walked to see the town hall at Marienplatz. The clock contains carved figures that come out every few hours. Monday morning, we looked up Carolyn Collier, a Kappa here studying opera, and have been busy ever

Königsplatz, Munich, September 1938

since. We went to Nymphenburg Castle and walked over to watch them make the finest porcelain in the world.

In the evening we went to Königsplatz to listen to Hitler's speech. It is a huge square which is the meeting place for everyone.

Tuesday evening we went to the opera and heard Gounod's *Faust*. Today we went to the Hofbrauhaus, the most famous of Munich beer houses.

We had planned to stay here until Saturday, but due to existing circumstances we are leaving early in the morning so we can be close to the border of Switzerland. For all we know, or anyone else knows, we may be seeing you before long. Don't worry about us as we are being very cautious.

Love,
Lois

In 1815 King Ludwig I commissioned the **Königsplatz**, yet it wasn't completed until 1862, nearly fourteen years after Ludwig abdicated the throne. Three classical buildings eventually occupied the area. It had been Ludwig's dream to turn Munich into another Athens.

From 1933-35, however, things changed at the Königsplatz. During Adolf Hitler's reign the square soon became the National Socialists' "Akropolis Germaniae" in what had become known as the "Capital City of the Movement."

Grassy areas were covered with granite and the neo-Classical buildings used for large Nazi rallies. Trees were removed and the buildings took on different functions. One housed the offices of the National Socialist Workers' Party of Germany while another was known as "The Führer's Building." Additional buildings, known as the "Temples of Honor," were eventually blown up after the war to symbolize the fall of the Nazi party.[v]

**Hitler's speech.** Hitler addressed a crowd of 15,000 party faithful in Berlin's Sportpalast on September 26, 1938, demanding that Czechoslovakia cede the Sudetenland or face invasion. His words reached far beyond the borders of the Reich. Before the Führer rose to speak, the German radio announcer named literally dozens of countries – from Lithuania to Uruguay – where the speech was being broadcast live.[vi] (Was there significance in naming the dozens of countries? Intimidation?)

October 3, 1938
Tübingen, Germany

Dear Mother and Dad,

Well, here we are again! We had six letters from you besides many others. We just eat up every letter with a gobble. What may seem unimportant to you is greatly appreciated by us.

My last letter from Munich said we were leaving because of present conditions. Soon after mailing the letter, we read of the four-power conference to be held in Munich the following day. Of course we decided to remain and get in on whatever was possible. We had only hopes of observing very much because of the seriousness of the affair. But at 7:30 AM, Carolyn called and said to go to the station as Mussolini was coming in by train. We rushed so we were there in twenty minutes.

However, we soon learned that it was to be at 10:30 and that

Lois and Carolyn Collier, Munich, September 1938

Hitler had gone to the border to meet Mussolini. We dashed off for coffee in a hurry as the crowd was thickening rapidly. Then for two hours we stood across the street from the station. There was much ado about making preparations. Many huge black, open cars came and went and finally lined up. The S.S. (Elite Guard) marched in and stood by in full attention. For blocks and blocks there were uniformed guards standing on either side of the street, holding back the crowd. They stand close together, one facing the street and one the crowd, alternately. All the school children were there and in good positions. They always have them around because they yell so loud.

Crowd gathering for Hitler and Mussolini, Munich, September 1938

Finally, the moment arrived, and Hitler and Mussolini stepped out and reviewed the guard and then drove away in a very quick parade. We were only able to get glimpses of them. Goering and Count Ciano were there also. It was a funny experience being in a huge Nazi crowd. Nazi flags were passed out and when the cars passed, there were thousands of these banners in the air. Everyone was shouting, "Heil," over and over again. Several people around us spoke English and told us to put our right arms up. We were too interested in all that was taking place to pay any attention. Then we started back to our hotel and noticed the crowd was lingering. We asked a policeman and he said a parade would come down our street with the members at 12:00. It was 11:30 and while Bill wasn't looking, I saw about a dozen cars pass and I was certain I saw Chamberlain and Daladier. But we went upstairs for the parade which didn't take place. I had seen the men only by chance. It was such a tense situation. Everyone was waiting for some news of what the outcome of the conference would be.

We decided to walk to Königsplatz and see what the activity was around there. We were well rewarded for the conference was being held in one of the buildings. We walked around and after waiting until about 3:00, decided to go for some lunch. We were walking down a street guarded by uniformed guards, and suddenly heard cheering at Königsplatz. We were far enough away and were

*Eyes and Ears*

not in the crowd, and we saw the show of our lives. In the first car was Hitler with Goering, followed by Chamberlain who was followed by Daladier. There were many unimportant men along and each man was followed by four or five cars full of men. We were just breathless! Chamberlain was laughing and we felt encouraged.

We met Carolyn and after going to the American Express we went to the Regina-Palast Hotel where Chamberlain was staying.

About 4:15 he came out, stood up in the open car, took off his hat and bowed. We were carried away with a sort of mob hysteria and yelled time and again, "Heil, heil, heil!" And then Daladier came out. Of course, he wasn't the hero that Chamberlain was, but was well received. We were surprised that there was such a big crowd. At 4:30 they resumed the conference and we went over later and waited until about 10:00 and they left for dinner. We gave up and went to bed. But from our room at midnight we heard the crowd cheering and we knew the conference was over.

The American Consulate was not anxious anymore and we could have stayed another day, but we were tired and decided to leave early the next morning. We had seen history in the making, and for probably the first time in history, a peace treaty without war. Everyone we talked to felt Roosevelt played an important part and helped by his messages. Bill snapped pictures all day long, but we don't know yet if we got anything important. On one building we counted 73 Nazi flags. Everyone was so relieved that the outcome was a peaceful one. Hitler is probably more popular than ever. We are more than glad that things turned out so well. We were in constant contact with the American counsel and were not taking any chances.

We had a nice trip from Munich to Stuttgart. We met an American in our compartment who has been here for two years. He is here for care of his eyes but is going blind. He is a Jew and was extremely interesting to talk to. He has a brother living in Munich. We kept him busy answering our questions. We went to the counsel in Stuttgart and made our permanent registration. They are still heaving a big sigh of relief.

We are all settled in our two rooms in Tübingen. They are well heated. The food has been just grand so far. We have tea every afternoon as well as three meals. We call our bedroom "the bridge on high" because it is the connecting link between two buildings.

Love,
Lois

In March of 1938, Germany annexed Austria. It was widely known that Czechoslovakia's Sudetenland, with its substantial German population, would be Hitler's next demand.

The **"Four-Power" Munich Conference** took place between Germany, Britain, France, and Italy on September 29, 1938. In an effort to appease Adolf Hitler, the corresponding **Munich Agreement** was created in which Europe willingly ceded Sudetenland in exchange for a pledge of peace from Hitler. Prime Minister Neville Chamberlain negotiated on behalf of Britain, and Chancellor Adolf Hitler on behalf of Germany. No Czech representative was invited to the conference. Chamberlain returned to London proclaiming that the Munich pact would secure "peace in our time." The Germans invaded Poland less than a year later and World War II began.[vii]

```
                                      October 11, 1938
Dear Foreigners,

   Once again, the Marco Polo instinct in us has
been grudgingly squelched and we are back in
Germany, ready to adopt Der Vaterland as such for
the ensuing school year. Marco had nothing on us
as he traveled by foot, while we enjoyed the luxu-
ry of those dirty, smelly, nauseating, third-class
Italian railway slums. The people themselves would
not be so bad if they would bathe every third
month and hold a match to their breath to burn
away the obnoxious gases that emanate from their
diet of onions, garlic, and spaghetti. Outside of
```

this, the third-class passengers are very friendly. One need not go hungry among them.

When they discover a stranger without food, they dive down into a paper suitcase or straw basket and shove a sandwich or wine flask towards you. The sandwich is a loaf of dark bread cut horizontally through the center with a leg of beef thrown in between. If you accept the proffered food, which you can't reject without causing offense, the proper mode of attack is to prop the loaf (meat and all) firmly in one hand, hold it firmly against the breast and proceed to saw off a slice with an antique pocket knife. I have never seen a third-class passenger succeed in slicing the stuff. After wallowing it over the front of his greasy coat, he usually gives up and tears the bread and meat off in chunks. The effort thus set forth serves as an appetizer, instead of noisily eating soup as the Germans do. But the German soup is a different story and is something to write home about.

When I wrote the last (and first) letter, we were leaving for our month's trip through Italy. It's all over now, and in spite of the dirty and inconveniences, we are sorry that we couldn't visit more of that sunny land. When we reached Rome, we wanted to go south to Naples and into Sicily, but the pocketbook turned us around and steered us safely back into the Vaterland. I say safely, but after we reached Germany our vacation spirit disappeared, and we began to realize just how unsafe things might be. Crossing into Germany through the Brenner Pass, we stayed at Innsbruck, Austria for a few days, keeping one eye on the English newspapers and with the other, drinking in the magnificent

Bill at Hofbrauhaus, Munich, September 1938

beauty of the Austrian Alps. Then onto Munich where the city was in holiday dress, celebrating the annual Oktoberfest, in honor of the new fall beer. I have always said I would never be a beer drinker, but after guzzling that Munich beer a question hangs in the sky.

In spite of the happy throngs at the festival grounds, the city of Munich was becoming tense with the so-called crisis which we, as foreigners, felt was about to break. On Monday night we went to the famous Königsplatz and listened to Hitler's Berlin speech being relayed through Goebbels's public speaking system. The tone of his speech sounded grave and from it we almost decided it was time to get out of Germany. After talking to the American Consul the next morning, we definitely decided it was time to go and chose

Wednesday morning as the day of exit. All day Thursday we spent with other Americans speculating as to what would happen and when. Our best procedure seemed to be to go to Tübingen and wait there until the last minute. Then we would hop on our bicycles and scoot across the Swiss border. (Bicycles are very handy things to have in such an emergency since the trains are usually overflowing.) Tuesday night came the news that the four-power conference had been called. We were delighted that the chosen place was Munich. Of course, we couldn't leave the city under those circumstances, knowing the following day we would see history in the making.

Early next morning we were called out of bed by the telephone. At the other end of the wire was Carolyn Collier, the Kappa student from Missouri, telling us if we would hurry to the railway station, we might have a chance to see Mussolini come in for the conference. We went and we saw. Not only did we see Mussolini but also Hitler as he had met the train at the border. A long red carpet was stretched from the station entrance to the dictator's automobile while Italian and German soldiers flanked the way. When the dictator appeared on the steps, the crowd broke into frenzied cries of "Heil Duce!" "Heil Fuhrer!" while their hands shot forth in the Nazi salute. School children lined the way to encourage cheering. Everyone was provided with small Nazi flags, two of which we kept for souvenirs.

I got one good shot of the dictator looking directly at the camera and will enclose one now or send it later.

Hitler and Mussolini, Four Power Conference, Munich, Setpember 1938

The procession passed by, the crowd broke up and from then on, our day was packed with excitement. We went back to our hotel and saw Chamberlain and Daladier drive by, coming into town from the airport. After a hurried lunch we set out to find where the conference would be held. The National Socialists have built fine administrative buildings in Munich, the main one being called the Fuhrerhaus. Here the four statesmen assembled, in an attempt to iron out the problem that was about to throw the world into another war. The building is surrounded by the Königsplatz and from the balconies were hung flags of the nations involved; Germany, Great Britain, France, and Italy. The platz was surrounded by SS guards so that no one could get within a block of the Fuhrerhaus. People were standing in little groups or walking slowly, conversing in low tones. No one could dismiss the significance of the occasion, for here the fate of the nations was being decided. These people did not want war. No one knows better than a German what suffering the war brought and what untold miseries the next one would bring.

After an hour or so, the conference adjourned for lunch; lunch, not war, had been declared. We stood at the curb waiting for the statesmen to be taken to their respective hotels. Hitler came first, looking neither to the right or left, his coal black mustache a vivid contrast to his grim, pallid face. Our optimism dropped. Then came Mussolini, his healthy, Caesar like countenance displaying no emotion. Following came Chamberlain. Our hopes sprang high. The English minister was smiling briefly, talking with his companions in the rear of the car. He, too, was cheered wildly by the crowd. Then came Daladier, looking as though he accepted being last in line.

We assembled in front of the hotel where Chamberlain was staying, and Daladier was lunching. A large crowd gathered and when the statesmen appeared, they were more than enthusiastically "heiled." Finally, Chamberlain. He stood in his car, lifting his hat and smiling, bowed to the crowd. I don't know when I have ever been more thrilled. Here was the man, with his bushy grey eyebrows and shaggy mustache, his confidence and manner seemed to say, "No war."

Back to the conference room went the statesmen and back to our watching went we. We waited near the Fuhrerhaus until ten o'clock that night and then to bed, feeling as though our stay in Germany would not be interrupted by "The War." We knew that the results of the conference would probably not be released in Germany that night, and the English papers would not arrive until the following noon as they were banned that day. The conference adjourned about midnight and from our beds we heard the loud cheering of the crowds as the statesmen left for good. The next day we got the gist of the four-power agreement from the German papers, feeling thankful that the differences between nations can be settled around the conference table. Perhaps the League of Nations may someday live in the true spirit cherished by its makers.

Arriving in Tübingen we proceeded to arrange ourselves in the rooms hired before our departure. The bedroom looks like it was tossed into the air and wedged between this and the adjoining building.

Lois and Bill's bedroom, Tübingen, September 1938

I think we are the only people in Germany who have heat in their rooms, thanks to our kind landlady who realizes that Americans are more used to heat. The weather now is chilly enough to be uncomfortable but the Germans scoff at the idea of having heat until it is really cold. As one woman put it, "When we get cold, we go to bed." Luckily, the house has a bathtub (50 pfennigs per bath). In this town of 28,000 people, there are supposed to be only twenty bathtubs. Our two huge water bowls are filled every morning by the chambermaid who also builds our fire and keeps the room clean.

In this letter I have not gone into detail about Italy, the Swiss Alps, etc. Lois and I are preparing a detailed account of our entire trip and will carbon copy them rather than write long, separate letters to everyone.

*Eyes and Ears*

School doesn't start until the first of November. We received your letter of September 4th and were plenty happy to get it. Any news is good news, no matter how trifling or detailed. The clippings are interesting. I expect to study Kant in the philosophy department here.

                                    Thursday

The Queen Mary docked yesterday but it evidently didn't bring us any mail. We'd like to know how you all are doing.

Love,
Bill (and Lois)

Wilhelmstrasse 18/2
Tübingen
Germany

Via a later Wichita news article, Dad said, "What we felt on that day, it would be difficult to say. We knew what was happening was big, that it was important. But I doubt if any of that crowd realized the Munich Conference would, in actuality, be the beginning of World War II. Few realized that Czechoslovakia had been sold out. And Britain's dignified leader, Prime Minister Neville Chamberlain, was the hero of the day. It was to be his finest hour and one of his last great moments. So consuming was the mass hypnotism, that at one time we found ourselves standing on a park bench and shouting, 'Chamberlain!' along with the others. Towards the end of the day, we stopped at a coffee house where our attention was drawn to a little old lady who kept staring sadly and helplessly into space. I managed to engage her in conversation. She said, 'I lost my first husband and two sons in the first war. I married again and raised a second family. Now I am afraid.' This was representative of how the older ones felt."

Dad also told us, "We were not supposed to take pictures in Munich on the day of the four-power conference. I was not aware until an SS officer slapped my arm. So, I laid low for a few minutes until we saw a long Mercedes-Benz convertible enter the square. I raised my camera up over my head, upside down, and took a picture. There were swastika flags waving left and right. The photo shows a flag between the faces of Hitler and Mussolini riding in that car."

October 4, 1938<br>Tübingen

Dear Mother and Dad,

It is raining and it rains a good deal. But I will indulge in one of those rare luxuries, a bath. Bill is waiting for the water to heat up for him. It costs 50 pfennigs per bath or a quarter for two baths. From now on we will have our weekly bath regularly. But we have become quite expert at the art of sponge bathing.

Sunday night we saw Shirley Temple in an old movie. It was funny to hear her speak German.

It wasn't as funny as seeing *The Good Earth* in Italy, an American made picture set in China and spoken in Italian. That can't be played here because Paul Muni is a Jew.

We received our first group of prints from our trip yesterday, and they are quite good. One of Hitler and Mussolini turned out quite well. If it is pretty tomorrow, we are going on an all-day hike. A geologist and his wife asked us to go, also two other American couples. One of them is Helen and Norman MacLeod. And Francis and Fred Helliger live about a block from here. They are both in theological school. This school is world famous for that field. We have met boys from Romania, Peru, Palestine, and other interesting places. We like the boy from Palestine because he is different. He is studying medicine.

Love,
Lois

October 7, 1938<br>Tübingen, Germany

Dear Mother and Dad,

Yesterday we went on an all-day hike to the highest mountain around here but it is not very high. We went with the MacLeods and Herr and Frau Reith. They are a young German couple who are loads of fun. He is an archaeologist and geologist. Now he is writing a book. If he were more in sympathy with the leaders, he would be a professor, but he refuses to alter any of his thoughts. He hopes his book will bring him enough recognition to get him a job in America soon. She is just beginning to speak English, so we are going to exchange lessons. I am sure we can help each other out a lot. After four hours of walking uphill in the mud, we were on the top of the mountain. There was a big youth hostel and we ate lunch there. We could see in the distance castles, dozens of towns, and beautiful fields and woods. By the time we arrived there, I was not feeling well, and Frau Ruth's feet hurt so we rode to Reutlingen with a man who had a car. We enjoyed being sissies for the afternoon. We walked around while we waited for the others. It is very old and until 1803, a free city. It has the third protestant church in Germany, with remains of its old walls and towers. We all took the train home.

Herman and Norman MacLeod, Frau Reith, Lois, Herr Reith, October 1938

Poor Bill needs a haircut but hates to go to a barbershop for fear they will clip up two inches above his ears. Most of the haircuts here are horrible. He can't go much longer, though. Bill's razor works better here than at home. He has a resistance cord to cut down voltage. My iron needs more voltage than the resistance cord will give it. We are going out to buy a small pan so we can heat water on top of our stove. It will help the air, too, from drying out so much as well as take the chill off of our water that we wash with.

These people certainly don't know how to wash. It is one thing that is expensive. They get their clothes clean but will wear them out in no time. They have absolutely no equipment, even a hand turned wringer is almost unheard of. It was $2.00 (9 marks) for seven shirts, Bill's underwear, and two pairs of pj's. A woman instead of a laundry, at that. I get hot water to wash out small things and hang them in the sun to dry.

I have four nice geraniums on the window ledge, nice healthy ones. As cold as it is, the flowers are still lovely, especially the dahlias.

Tomorrow we will celebrate with another bath. It is a great life!

Love,
Lois

Susan Kandt Peterson

October 8, 1938
Tübingen

Dear Mother and Dad,

We have been studying German for three hours now. It is such a difficult language for a beginner to learn but I am anxious to be able to speak it if I can. The other Americans are not very interested in it and speak a terrible German after having been here a year.

We are so pleased with our pensione. Fraulein Keck, who owns it, is very nice. She is probably between 35 and 40. Her fiancé died before they were married so she runs this place. Only six people live here now but a dozen or more eat their noon meal here. We have breakfast, dinner, tea, and supper. We have a difficult time with Fraulein Keck because we generally eat only one helping of everything. She thinks that we don't like her food. It is impossible to make her understand that we just don't eat like the Germans. We can have guests for tea for an extra cost.

We have the last five issues of *Time* magazine and find them so interesting. The MacLeods take it. It is banned from Germany but by private subscriptions it always comes in. How is Charles McCarthy anyway? Someone in *Time* said, speaking of Roosevelt's purge, that it is Roosevelt's ambition to be an Edgar Bergen and have all of Congress be Charlie McCarthy.

Imported swing music is not allowed here. We miss the good Sunday night programs. The Germans have heard vaguely of the Big Apple and are curious. So, when we do hear music it is almost always classical. Most of the people here have such an appreciation for good music.

If it is pretty tomorrow, we will probably go for a long jaunt in the afternoon. That is what everyone does on Sunday afternoon. If you don't go somewhere, they don't understand. I must darn some of Bill's socks.

Love,
Lois

**The Edgar Bergen and Charlie McCarthy Show** was a radio comedy variety show that aired from 1936 to 1955. The show featured ventriloquist Edgar Bergen, and his beloved puppet, the amazing Charlie McCarthy. It is this show which made the duo overnight superstars.[viii]

October 11, 1938
Tübingen

Dear Mother and Dad,

Tübingen is much larger than it first appeared to be. At the far edge of town is quite a large new addition. Close by are the barracks where many of the soldiers live. We think that some of the boys are here for their two-year military training. To promote national unity, they send boys from the north to the southern posts, and visa-versa.

Upon reaching eighteen, boys were required to enlist immediately in the armed forces, or into the **Reich Labor Service**, for which their activities in the Hitler Youth prepared them. Propaganda material called for even more fanatic devotion to Nazi ideology.[ix]

Our dinner Sunday was very queer. All we had was soup, macaroni, and meat sauce. But everyone in Germany had it and then gave 50 pfennigs to the poor, sponsored by the government. If you ate at a restaurant, you paid one mark for it and the establishment kept 50 pfennigs and the next day a collector called for the other 50 pfennigs. It is a good idea if it is carried out right.

Sunday evening the other couple who live here in the pension asked us to their room for wine. In the fall, everyone drinks new wine which has not fermented yet. It is like white grape juice and is quite good. He teaches pathology in the medical school and she is serving her internship and will, by November, be a doctor. He is undoubtedly the tallest man I have ever seen. Bill and I feel like midgets standing next to him. Besides being so tall, he is huge. But to top it off, he has a lisp. His wife is pretty and very nice. I will enjoy visiting with her when I learn more German.

Yesterday was another beautiful one and we rented a rowboat for an hour and had a very good time drifting and rowing. Bill did all of the rowing.

Love,
Lois


**Winter Relief of the German People**, commonly known by WHW, was an annual drive by the National Socialist People's Welfare to help finance charitable work. Its slogan was "None shall starve or freeze." It ran from 1933–1945 during the months of October through March and was designed to provide food, clothing, coal, and other items to less fortunate Germans during the inclement months. Certain weekends were assigned to all of the different Nazi associations, each with their own special badges, to pass their aid out in exchange for a pfennig or two. The Can Rattlers, as they became known, were relentless in their pursuit of making sure every good German citizen gave their share to the WHW. In fact, those who forgot to give had their names put in the paper to remind them of their neglect. Neighbors and even family members were encouraged to whisper the names of shirkers to their block leaders so that they could persuade them to do their duty.

One greatly encouraged practice was the once-a-month one-pot meal, whereby citizens reduced all the food in this meal to a single course. The money, thus saved, was to be donated to the program. During autumn and winter months from 1933 on, the "One-Pot Sunday" or "Stew Sunday" was officially scheduled by the WHW. Restaurants were required to offer an *eintopf* meal at one of several price points.[x]

October 17, 1938<br>Tübingen

Dear Mother and Dad,

By now you have probably become reconciled again to the fact that I am here for some months yet. For several days we did not know if we would be staying. All of the boats were crowded to capacity and all we could have done was get to a neutral country and wait for a boat. Of course, we are all so happy that we did not have to leave as none of these people wanted to fight. The American Consul said if we had to leave without our clothes, he was sure we could get them, but it would probably be a matter of some months. Had not the conference been called we would have gone into Switzerland with our clothes. It would have been fine there as it is always neutral, but all of that is over now and we can just sit still and thank our lucky stars that we are not witnessing another war.

We have been having the finest weather. We spend several hours every afternoon out walking or on our bicycles. Yesterday we went to a town called Rottenburg on our bikes. It is only 12 kilometers away and a lovely ride through four villages. You have to get out on a Sunday afternoon to realize how many babies there are in Germany. There are so few cars that people walk on the highways. I have never seen so many baby buggies.

After we were home and had eaten supper, we went to an organ recital given by a man from Stuttgart. It was rather short but well played. We went with the Helligers and the couple who live in our pensione. The man is the giant I told you about.

Helen's November *McCall's* came, and I read it from cover to cover. All of the advertising is for Thanksgiving dinners. We will have a Thanksgiving dinner here with all of the other Americans. Last year they had turkey and mince pie. You know they don't even know what a pie is in Germany. Of all the pastries they have, they don't make pies. Frau Keck said she heard in the bakery the other day that butter and eggs were getting scarce again. You can only get ¼ of a pound at a time for two people and five eggs a week. We are fortunate to be living in a pensione because Fraulein can always get greater quantities.

Susan Kandt Peterson

    Yesterday was some sort of church feast day for all of the Germans in this district which is the Swabian district. In this section of Germany, they do not have many festivals and expensive celebrations because the Swabians are a conservative, saving group who work hard and take life seriously. This is quite different from the Barish people around Munich who always seem to be having some sort of festival. Each section has its own dialect and it is so pronounced that they cannot understand each other. On the train coming from Munich there was a man who spoke nothing but Swabish German and he could not understand another man and woman who spoke Barish to him, yet they live less than a hundred miles apart. The educated people speak their dialect and the good high German as well. They tease me when they hear me say, "Uh huh," and tell me I am learning Swabish because they also use that same expression. I wonder if that is where ours came from.

    It is almost tea time now. Bill and I love the dark bread and butter and jam. That is what we have almost every afternoon.

Love,
Lois

*Eyes and Ears*

October 20, 1938
Tübingen, Germany

Dear Mother and Dad,

I just finished dressing for tea. Fraulein Keck was very nice and invited Helen and Norman for tea today. So, I should show my appreciation by changing my clothes. I did my washing for the week. I get hot water only for the suds and have to rinse in cold water. It takes more cold water to get the suds out. I can't wash anything big.

Bill has been to the Reading Room reading the London *Times*. They take all of the European papers but no American papers. It is quite difficult to get much American news, even in an English paper. I am reading the October *American* magazine that someone brought in from Switzerland.

One afternoon we went rowing again on the Neckar. This time I rowed some and had a grand time. It made my arms rather sore but that is what I need. Of course, we walk everyday even if it is just around town.

Have I told you about the raw meat they eat here? When we were in Halle with Hans, he ordered a sandwich plate. The largest sandwiches were open face, which all German sandwiches are. It was spread on top with raw, ground veal. We ate it first and with great relish. Another was uncooked ham. It is a delicacy here and we always hurt Fraulein Keck's feelings when we refuse to eat it.

The desk I am writing on belonged to Fraulein Keck's great, great grandfather and is over 300 years old. One spot is pretty badly burned. She said he did it by letting his candle burn down too low.

Love,
Lois

Mom told us, "Fraulein Keck spoke no English, and I spoke very little German. But we communicated beautifully. I would go to her apartment for tea on the fourth floor where she had a canary in a cage and a small dachshund. The canary, with Keck's urging, would sing and sing while the little dog howled and howled. It was very funny to watch, and we laughed! Keck was once engaged to a young man from the Hohner music company family, but he died. Every year she would go to his gravesite and lay flowers."

It is now after tea and I feel like a stuffed toad. Frau Keck really did herself proud. We had all sorts of fancy little sandwiches and rich cakes galore. I feel as if I never want to eat again but supper (we have our main dinner meal at noon) is only 45 minutes away.

*Eyes and Ears*

Saturday afternoon we are going on a hike and shall take the train to a small town nearby and then hike someplace that is supposed to be very beautiful. It is a trip organized by the Auslandstelle for all of the foreign students.

We are still having beautiful weather. Today I have on my brown suit with a white silk blouse and the grape rhinestone clip. My suit is so comfortable and nice, but I have been saving it for more special occasions.

Love again,
Lois

October 26, 1938
Tübingen, Germany

Dear Mother and Dad,

We enjoyed our hike Saturday ever so much. I bought a pair of heavy, double soled hiking shoes and found out I tired less easily. We represented many nations: Egypt, England, Rumania, Peru, America, Germany, and the others I can't recall now. We walked

Hike with other foreign students, October 1938

through a perfectly beautiful wooded section, saw an old Roman aqueduct that used to lead from a spring to Rottenburg. When we finished walking, we went to a hotel and had coffee and meringues filled with whipped cream. We were so surprised to see such a large hotel in such a small, dinky little town. But it is a kind of health spring and people stay there and bathe and drink the foul smelling sulphur water.

The market in Tübingen is so colorful and picturesque that it will always be fascinating to me. I got the cutest bunch of flowers for 20 pfennigs. I must have gotten at least 3 dozen. You can get large, potted mums for about 17 cents, or 80 pfennigs.

Yesterday when I went with Helen to shop, I was surprised at the way you buy things. You can't buy vanilla, you must buy vanilla sugar. None of their spices are put up in small tins but you buy it in bulk. Real honey is so expensive that you buy artificial honey or else artificial with 10 percent real honey. They use so much jam for breakfast that the government sets the prices. Most of it is synthetic but really quite good. You don't buy it in jars but bring your own little container with you.

Last week, the boys who were here doing their military service finished their two years. They had a big celebration and left. Now the new boys are here. They are getting into shape, that is to drill in uniforms. Their band is much snappier than the last. We can hear them march past several times a day. Often, they get up at 3 or 4 in the morning to drill. Most of these boys are eager to continue their education or get started in business, and I am sure they don't really like to do this. They get everything cheaper. Whenever prices are quoted, down to the bottom is the price for the military.

One of the American boys is to receive a large jar of peanut butter. He is leaving in three weeks, so we are all offering to pay the duty and help eat it. They don't ever have it here, or marshmallows or popcorn.

We were lucky to have the American Indians leave us so many vegetables. Here, they don't have any variety in their food. We have shredded lettuce with every meal.

I hope no one scares you on Halloween this year. I guess we won't go ringing doorbells because no one will know what it's all about.

It is hard to realize that Thanksgiving is almost here. We are going to make our own mincemeat this week. We will have a turkey and everything.

Love,
Lois

Susan Kandt Peterson

October 28, 1938
Tübingen, Germany

Dear Mother and Dad,

    We were so happy to receive your letter yesterday afternoon. We have been busy doing nothing the last three days. Bill has much translating to do as there is the usual red tape to go through when enrolling.

    It is so cold here, but the flowers continue to be as beautiful and plentiful as ever. This afternoon I did fancy work while Bill read out loud *Julius Caesar*, Shakespeare. We found it so interesting since we had just been to Rome and saw the places where all of the action took place.

    Yesterday we walked out to call on a professor that Bill wanted to confer with, but he was not at home. We walked on up the hill to the south of town, called Osterberg. It is perhaps the prettiest hill that I have ever seen. It is such a bright green and rolls on and on. On top is a clump of trees and an old, red brick sight-seeing tower that fits perfectly into the picture. You can see the town as a unit and realize how complex it is, for it is divided into so many small parts.

    You have no idea how well dressed I feel over here. I wear my old, grey suit nearly every day with a change of sweater and even then, I feel well dressed. How I hate to have to return and feel plump again! But I am happy to report that most of my frocks can be worn without my girdle. I only hope I can continue to lose but with this potato diet, it is hard to see how it would be possible. My, how they love their starch!

Have any of your letters been opened? Since we are students, I am sure that none of them will be unless they are looking for money. So, don't worry about what you write.

We are doing our banking with DeBerry in Amsterdam, Holland as you get the cheapest exchange there. It sure seems funny to be living in one country and do your banking in another.

Lots of love,
Lois

>November 1, 1938
>Tübingen, Germany

Dear Mother and Dad,

Bill is all registered for school, but it didn't start today after all. What a contrast the beginning of school here is as compared to KU. For a week or more ahead of time, KU is noisy and bustling, students crowding the hall, asking hundreds of questions. Here you walk into a college building (which is new and state of the art) and if you are lucky you see several persons quietly moving about. At KU, for identification cards one carries one about the size of a driver's license. Here, one must tote around a small pamphlet. At KU we enrolled on a small white card, while here it requires a small book with possibly 30 pages or more. So far, I have not been able to tell if the Germans are over or under efficient. I tend to think the latter.

Sunday, we saw Tübingen Nazi flags bedecked for the first time. There had been a sort of driving contest and many people were here from Stuttgart. In the evening, at the market, the winners were announced.

Yes, we are warm enough. These little coal stoves are much better than central heating over here because you can heat the room accordingly. Our bedroom has central heat and is rather chilly. It doesn't matter though because we don't dress in there and go to bed with our socks on until the bed is warm and then take them off. They don't heat their kitchen at all, relying on the stove to heat the room. Poor Helen has to wash her dishes every night in a cold room. The halls and bathrooms are cold, too.

Love,
Lois

Mom later wrote, "We found living conditions were harsh; poorly heated houses, food only adequate."

>November 5, 1938
>Tübingen, Germany

Dear Mother and Dad,

 I have been reading the last two issues of *Time* magazine and am pretty much disgusted with the attitude of the American press in regard to the Munich Conference. I can't see how America is in a position to criticize England for going to war with Germany or to talk so slurringly [sic] of Chamberlain. We Americans are so far away from Europe that it is rather easy to assume such a feeling. Isn't it better to give in to a settlement agreement than to lose thousands and thousands of lives fighting over a small territory? Every Englishman we have talked to says that they were scared stiff because in no way were they prepared for immediate war. It probably would have meant the fatal bombing of London, their institutions, and traditions, which are the very basis of their existence. There simply had to be a way out. And even if it would result in only prolonging a war, it would be far better because then the other countries will be in a state of preparedness. But of course, we hope that everyone will keep his promises and the ultimate result will be peaceful. Another thing is that the English and French are willing to concede the fact that the Treaty of Versailles was much too severe and as a result of it, National Socialism grew up.

In talking to the Germans about conditions following the war, it is almost heartbreaking at times. Just yesterday, Fraulein Keck was telling us how horrible it was. She said that they didn't even have shoes. Many people wrapped old clothes around their feet to keep them warm. They never had any heat in their rooms and practically no food. When a worker got his pay, he had to go out and spend it within an hour because inflation worked so fast. One boy said his father sold a cow one day and by the very next day his money wasn't worth enough to buy a loaf of bread. People can only exist like that for so long at a time. Then they either die or revolt. Naturally, these people are willing to have faith in anything that could help them. Today they are still poor but everyone has shelter, clothes, and plenty to eat. I know that many of the things their leaders do are hard for them to understand, just as it is for us. But they can't forget their former misery and are willing to obey every order. They say they only wish that those English and Americans who speak so harshly of Germany could have lived here in post-war days and then see what they have to say. They often say, what if Germany did start and lose the war, that they are people just like us and if our President declared war, what could we as a people do? It is sometimes hard to see their viewpoint, but we try to see it through the eyes of the German and not the American. We also try never to criticize but ask plenty of questions.

**The Treaty of Versailles** was designed mostly to punish Germany for starting World War I, and it reflected the bitter and vengeful feelings that Britain and France felt toward their enemy. The treaty took away the German empire by seizing its colonies and limiting the German Army to a 100,000-man security force. There would be no German navy or air force. The Rhineland had to be demilitarized and, worst of all, Germany was required to pay a $33 billion reparations bill to the Allies for starting the war. The cost of this bill wrecked the German economy in the 1920s and then, coupled with the Great Depression in America, led to the horrific economic and political conditions that heralded Adolf Hitler's rise.[xi]

Last Wednesday we went to a party given by the Foreign Exchange group. We certainly enjoy the students from other countries and in typical American fashion, put them through a third-degree battery of questions.

Yesterday morning I slipped as I stepped out of bed and fell flat. Never have I fallen so hard! My left cheek is slightly swollen and bruised. My neck is quite stiff and most of my muscles are sore. It is too bad I have always been such an awkward child. I guess that bodily grace is one thing that can't be developed through the years or even in Europe.

We are all getting excited about our Thanksgiving meal. We will have it at one of the hotels. We are going to make the salad because they have no idea how to make an American salad. What are your plans?

We had our weekly bath this morning and we just simply sit and revel in our cleanliness.

I am going over to read the London *Times* to see if I can find out anything about the elections. The "Mars Panic" H.G. Wells radio program received much European publicity. The German papers carried huge headlines, filling up the entire front page. And the London *Times* carried a huge column. Was it a panic or not?

Love,
Lois

**Orson Welles** caused a nationwide panic with his radio broadcast of *War of the Worlds*, a dramatization of a Martian invasion of Earth. Millions of Americans tuned in every Sunday night during the 1930's prime time of radio. Welles' broadcast was so realistic that perhaps as many as a million radio listeners believed a real Martian invasion was underway. Panic broke out across the country.[xii]

*Eyes and Ears*

November 8, 1938
Tübingen, Germany

Dear Mother and Dad,

It is now three o'clock and Bill just left for his afternoon classes. The hours are crazy, start at eight in the morning and go straight through the morning, then the afternoon classes start at three and last until eight.

Bill, Tübingen University, circa 1938

Saturday afternoon we walked to the little village of Bebenhausen. The walk was just beautiful through a forest of tall trees. The leaves were a red gold and as it got darker and darker the leaves took on more and more red. The German forests are simply thrilling. The people really enjoy them, too, for they are full of little foot paths. When we arrived at Bebenhausen, we were refreshed by new cider, bread, butter, and honey. My, how good it tasted!

Yesterday was Fraulein Keck's birthday and how interesting. They make so much of it here. By noon her room was so full of flowers that it rivaled any flower shop and all afternoon they continued to pour in, besides so many presents.

She baked two big cakes and had all sorts of special things to eat. We gave her a set of cute blue pottery.

Most of our ideas concerning Christmas come from Germany. Santa Claus comes from the Catholics and the Protestants have the story that the Christ child bestows the presents. The Christmas tree came from here. They start their Christmas celebrations four weeks before and I guess that there is no place that celebrates it more elaborately. Yesterday we found out that the idea of the wedding cake comes from England. You can easily see how the Americans would accumulate all of these customs.

One of the hardest things for us to understand here is the use of one of their words, "volk," meaning people. It is one of the words brought closely to their minds by the present government. The volk includes all the German people living within their boundary or territory. There is a close unity of the volk for they all are of the same blood, language, etc. Furthermore, they have been closely united for hundreds of years, knitting them so closely together that it is impossible to separate them or penetrate them. Because they are a volk, they feel as they do about many things, such as a Jew can never be a volk. All members of the volk naturally should be united and not living under another power. They say the American has no volk, which is true. But they say, after a hundred years when all immigration has stopped, then we will be completely suited as the German people are and will have a volk. They all talk about it much, but it is so vague that we haven't a clear idea yet. The Germans living in foreign countries are not considered part of the volk but are ausland (foreign) Dutch.

The concept of **Volk** (people, nation, or race) has been an underlying idea in German history since the early nineteenth century. Inherent in the name is a feeling of superiority of German culture and the idea of a universal mission for the German people.[xiii]

National Socialism represented much more than a political movement. Nazi leaders who came to power in 1933 wanted to gain political authority, revise the Versailles Treaty, and regain and expand upon those lands lost after a humiliating defeat in World War I. But beyond those goals, they also wanted to change the cultural landscape. They wanted to return the country to traditional "German" and "Nordic" values, remove or limit Jewish, "foreign," and "degenerate" influences, and shape a racial community (called *Volksgemeinschaft*) which aligned with Nazi ideals. They stressed family, race, and *Volk* as the highest representation of German values. They rejected materialism, cosmopolitanism, and "bourgeois intellectualism," and instead promoted the "German" virtues of loyalty, struggle, self-sacrifice, and discipline. Nazi cultural values also placed great importance on Germans' harmony with their native soil and with nature, emphasizing the elevation of the *Volk* and nation above its individual members.[xiv]

Bill mentioned to the other couple living here that I studied French so immediately they brought me a French play to read. They are both doctors and fluent in many languages. So I am struggling through this because they will no doubt ask questions. Bill failed to mention that I also forgot most of what I learned.

The German doctor loves to read our magazines but he gets so mad at what they have to say about Germany. It is really too bad that the American press never has a good word to say about this country. Most of the articles in *Reader's Digest* have been written by exiles. Whatever may be wrong with Germany, and whatever may be said against it, there is still much good to be said for the German people, their simple way of living and believing. It is too bad that American readers can't get a little of the good. We always let the doctor have any magazines he wants but we always warn him in advance. He realizes that America would never be in sympathy with Germany in case of war and he realizes the possibilities of the greatness of the American army.

Last night we played bridge with Norman and Helen. For the first time, Bill really enjoyed it. He made a grand slam.

I had my hair washed yesterday. I don't know what I will do when it gets too long.

Permanents are not expensive, but they are not so good, either.

Lots of love,
Lois

November 12, 1938
Tübingen, Germany

Dear Mother and Dad,

Yesterday was a happy day for the Americans because we were able to get the election results. I read as much of the Paris paper as I could, and the German. We are going back today to see if the London *Times* is not busy being read. All of the news items carry headlines to the effect that the Republicans are steadily gaining power and that the New Deal is defeated. One of the most difficult questions to try and answer is, what is the New Deal? The German papers gave Kansas as one of the 17 states with a new Republican governor. It did our hearts good to know that maybe there will be an end to our present government set-up. At least 1940 looks brighter.

During the Great Depression, President Franklin D. Roosevelt sought to restore prosperity to Americans through a series of programs called the **New Deal**. This series of programs and projects, instituted by The Works Progress Administration (WPA) and the Civilian Conservation Corps (CCC), dispensed emergency and short-term governmental aid and provided temporary jobs by employing people on construction projects and youth work in the national forests. Before 1935, the New Deal initially focused on revitalizing the country's stricken business and agricultural communities. But then it grew to encompass more far-reaching programs such as Social Security. These measures, enacted in 1935 and 1939, provided old-age and widows' benefits, unemployment compensation, and disability insurance. The New Deal also set maximum work hours and minimum wages in certain industries.[xv]

>     By now I am so disgusted! At three o'clock
> we asked to take our bath and were told that it
> was too late, we would have to wait until Monday
> morning! Someone wisely remarked, after travel-
> ing through England, that they wished the English
> would forget a bit of their traditions and pay
> a bit more attention to bathing. Perhaps the
> Americans do stress the habit too much, but these
> people don't even have the habit.
>
>     There are plenty of oranges and lemons to be
> had but they are expensive, so we rarely buy
> them. We figure we can live without them for a
> year. We get lots of stewed fruit here. We would
> rather see more of Europe and save on everything
> here in Tübingen. It looks like we will have a
> grand trip during the month of March.

The water tastes very fresh, free of chemicals. I believe it comes from the mountains in the Black Forest.

I hope you have a good time in Kansas City over Thanksgiving. There are no turkeys to be had so we will be having goose. It should be a perfectly wonderful dinner as it will cost between 4 and 5 marks per plate.

If you are ever in the mood, you might send over a can or two of unpopped popcorn. They don't have it here (or any corn) and we have tried to explain it to them.

The dishes in this country are just too wonderful. Of course, they are my weakness. I just go mad when I get in one of the stores, but I always think of how horrible it would be to have to get them home, so I only look. The dolls are so cute. I will bring Judith both a boy and a girl dressed in native costumes, to be put away for a few years. You are funny, Mother, when you call her a little lady when she is still a baby.

Lots of love,
Lois

Judith was the first grandchild in the family, born to Lois' brother, Charles (Chuck) and his wife Claybell (Clady).

Susan Kandt Peterson

November 19, 1938
Tübingen, Germany

Dear Mother and Dad,

One of the American boys was successful in getting his PhD this week. He sailed on the *Europa* yesterday to arrive home on Thanksgiving Day. Last year he fell in love with the American girl who was here, and they will be married in June. Another one of the American boys here has sent for his love and hopes she will be here by Christmas so they can be married and go to the Bavarian Alps during vacation.

We are going formal to our Thanksgiving dinner so I will wear my new black chiffon. It is really cold here now and I believe that winter has finally arrived.

Every day we go over to read the London *Times*. The London paper throws mud at the Germans for their unfair treatment of the Jews and the German papers throw mud right back. That man, Joseph Goebbels, must stay awake every night thinking up new propaganda. He has absolutely no conscience and is, indeed, a highly dangerous man. His power and his mind and his works reach nearly every person in Germany every day. We have not seen the Jewish boy who called on us last Monday. I really doubt if he is in school anymore. He has a wonderfully intelligent mind but probably won't be able to do anything with it here in Germany.

When Adolf Hitler (1889-1945) became chancellor of Germany in 1933, he named his trusted friend and colleague, **Joseph Goebbels** (1897-1945), to the key post of "Minister for Public Enlightenment and Propaganda." Goebbels was tasked with presenting Hitler to the public in the most favorable light. He also regulated content of all German media and was instrumental in spreading antisemitism. The press and radio were all under state control. Goebbels forced Jewish artists, musicians, actors, directors, and newspaper and magazine editors into unemployment. He staged the public burning of books considered "un-German" and spearheaded the production of Nazi propaganda films and other projects. Goebbels remained in this post and was loyal to Hitler until the end of World War II. On May 1, 1945, the day after Hitler committed suicide, Goebbels and his wife poisoned their six children before killing themselves.[xvi]

```
What are you planning for Judy's first
Christmas? The shops here are full of toys al-
ready and they are all such charming things.

There is no such thing as scientific baby
rearing here, I guess. The American couple who
lived here last year had a baby and Fraulein Keck
has told us how very particular they were with
the baby. They even bathed him at the same time
every evening and fed him a formula. In many
eating places I have seen babies gulp beer from
their parents' steins and chew on salty pretzels.
```

Again, don't be afraid of saying anything or sending any clippings. Our mail is perfectly safe and a letter would only be opened by mistake. All they are interested in is German marks being sent out of the country. Right now, they are too busy with the Jews and the church, anyway.

I have received all of your letters. They were slow in coming during October because all of the boats were held up and thrown off schedule.

My silk hose are holding up and I am becoming an expert darner. Since we left, I have only had to throw away one pair. I have hardly worn any of my new ones. When you can sew up runs and wear them, it makes a big difference in how long they last.

Lots of love,
Lois

November 22, 1938
Tübingen, Germany

Dear Mother and Dad,

Sunday was such a rainy day that we stayed in except for about 45 minutes in the late afternoon. We went window shopping and bought a couple of our favorite pastries since we don't have tea on Sunday. The streets were crowded with families as now the stores are displaying

Christmas merchandise. I believe the Germans must give their children more toys than the Americans do. It disgusts me to see so many soldier dolls, toy tanks, and machine guns. But the little boys love them and stand by the windows for hours looking at them.

I am making the place cards for our Thanksgiving dinner. We are having our dinner at the nicest hotel here. The other hotel quoted us prices saying they would serve ¼ goose per person. Just imagine!

I think those of us living here are going together and buy Anna, the maid, a new dress. She is very poor and works so hard. It is the custom to always give your maid the very nicest gift. But that is about the only time of year they get much of a break. I hope that I can make some Christmas candies. If enough of the people who eat here go home, I know I can because the kitchen won't be used so much. The Germans specialize more in cookies.

The theology student who lives here talks so loud he practically screams. When he sits next to me at the table, I can put my fingers in my ears and still hear every word distinctly. If I ever learn to speak German well enough, I am afraid I will tell him to calm down. But it is a typical German characteristic to like to be powerful, regardless of what the power stands for. I at least keep my mouth shut, not speaking very much German, and can't say what I often think. Perhaps that is a good thing.

I have received all of your letters. None have been opened. They slit them across the top if they do open them.

Love,
Lois

>November 27, 1938
>Tübingen, Germany

Dear Mother and Dad,

I have had so much to do the last few days that I have fallen behind in my letter writing. I now have three hours before we go to the tea dance at 5:00. Sunday is Germany's big dancing day, I guess because it is the only free time they have. Sunday is considered the day of rest and relaxation. It is their largest play day. We certainly didn't get any of our Puritanical beliefs from them. The Lutherans at home would have picked up their strictness from American sources. This dance is being given by the Auslandsstelle. They say the food will be deluxe.

Our Thanksgiving dinner was very nice. In the morning, Helen and I made two huge, mince pies. I could hardly wait to eat a piece but by the time dessert came around, I was too full to eat it. But Bill managed both pieces beautifully. I wore my new, black chiffon and felt very dressed up. We were disappointed when there was no dressing and they substituted applesauce for cranberries. Of course, they can't be expected to understand all of our customs. The goose was wonderfully cooked and the whole dinner was beautifully served. Bill and I had a bottle of the very finest Rhine wine with our meal. We all sat around and talked until 11:00 and then, as sleepy as we were, played bridge. As we went to bed, we thought of how you were probably putting the turkey in the oven and wondered who was winning the football game.

Thanksgiving dinner, Tübingen, November 1938

Yesterday we went to see the Hohenzollern Castle. It took about two hours to walk up to the castle with Helen and Norman. It is a beautiful sight to witness for the castle is perched on top of a very steep hill. It is positioned for old time warfare, as an enemy would not be able to attack with any advantage. There are two chapels because the king was Protestant and the last king, Catholic. In the Catholic chapel is buried the heart of Frederick I. The castle was sparsely furnished but the floors were inlaid wood and beautifully done. There is wonderful ivy covering the castle walls and the inner court is so romantic looking. You almost look around for Romeo and Juliet. The castle has never been lived in as a residence but was used merely for entertaining guests. I was sore when we returned home. I am not a very good walker. Every place you go around here, you have to go up a steep hill, it seems.

Germany has started her Christmas celebrations. For four Sundays before Christmas a candle is lit at the evening meal. Everyone has an advent wreath (kranz) with four candles. Some are pine wreaths and some are wooden with figurines. Only the Catholics believe in Santa Claus. The Protestants believe the Christ child is the bearer of the gifts to the good. They give gifts to children on Saint Nicholas Day on December 7.

Lots of love,
Lois

*Eyes and Ears*

Monday

I am now waiting for my thimble full of water to do a washing. I am sending Bill's shorts to the laundry so they will get a good boiling. We are happy the first of the month is approaching as that will mean clean sheets. As far as I can tell, all over Germany, sheets are changed only on the first of the month. I'm telling you, that first week the sheets seem so cold and unfriendly. You insult them if you offer to pay more and have them changed more often, so we have never suggested it. But we fool them. There are no double beds in Germany, only very wide singles. So, one night we sleep on one side and the next, on the other. That way, we only use sheets for two weeks.

We enjoyed the tea dance very much yesterday. It was in a big party house with Christmas decorations. They use so many candles here, so it was sweet smelling pine and large red candles. They dance perfectly horribly, but it was fun just the same.

We are going to Stuttgart for the coming weekend. The German American Bund Association has invited all of the foreign students to a Christmas celebration on Saturday evening. We know it will be a nice affair as well as enlightening. Stuttgart is the home or center for all foreign Germans. It will be interesting to see what kind of organization they have there. No doubt during the evening we will be told all of the wonders of National Socialism. It will cost us an extra 15 marks to go and stay in a hotel and eat two meals out, but this is the type of thing we are interested in and want to observe. I have never been to any of the museums in Stuttgart so we can take it all in at once. Sunday we will see an opera.

My wash is now hanging on the line. It is over now for another week or ten days.

Again, much love and write,
Lois

**German American Bund.** In the years before the outbreak of World War II, people of German ancestry living abroad were encouraged to form citizens groups to both extol "German virtues," around the world and to lobby for causes helpful to Nazi Party goals. In the United States, the Amerikadeutscher Volksbund, or German American Bund, was formed in 1936 as "an organization of patriotic Americans of German stock." They operated about 20 youth and training camps and eventually grew to a membership numbering in the tens of thousands among 70 regional divisions across the country. On February 20, 1939, the Bund held an "Americanization" rally in New York's Madison Square Garden and denounced Jewish conspiracies and President Roosevelt, among other things. The rally was attended by 20,000 supporters and protested by huge crowds of anti-Nazis held back by 1,500 NYC police officers. As World War II began in 1939, the German American Bund fell apart, many of its assets were seized, and its leader arrested for embezzlement. They were later deported to Germany.[xvii]

December 5, 1938
Tübingen, Germany

Dear Mother and Dad,

Last night when we returned from Stuttgart, we received your letters. Again, I want to tell you that you need have no fear of sending any printed matter, regardless of what it says, and your letters are perfectly safe. Foreigners are welcome to anything from their own country.

We had a perfectly delightful weekend in Stuttgart. The weather was bad, cold and rainy, but it did not dampen our spirits. We went on the 12:30 bus with ten college students. We had eaten but we went with the others to a cafe. Just for fun, we pretended that we didn't know a word of German. The manager and waiters had quite a time of it. Then we went to the hotel and had a very nice room with running water.

After we hung up our evening clothes, we went out to see the town. We found a couple of street bands playing and Bill talked with the coronet player for a bit. We had tea with an English student. He told us all about school at Cambridge, the class system as it exists in England today, their travel, the average English viewpoint of King Edward and Wallis. They thought Edward was the ideal man for king during the twentieth century, and had displayed such fine qualities during the war, with the poor. The people had trusted him fully and they felt he had let them down. It wasn't the fact that Wally was a commoner, but the fact that she was twice divorced and made such an obvious play to be queen. He said nothing would please them more than to have an American as the King's wife.

Born on June 23, 1894, **Edward VIII** the Prince of Wales was a popular member of the royal family and heir to the throne. In 1931, Edward met and fell in love with American socialite Wallis Simpson. After King George V's death, the prince became King Edward VIII. However, because his marriage to Simpson, an American divorcée, was forbidden, Edward abdicated the throne after ruling for less than a year.[xviii]

We were not hungry at suppertime, so we just dressed and went to the party given by the German American Bund which was in a very modern cafe which was beautifully decorated. At first there was a short program and then four hours of dancing. I felt like a college freshman for I danced every dance until 2:30. There were more men than women. We were hungry after dancing but found only one, smoky place open. My feet hurt so we gave up the idea and went to bed.

While at the German American Bund event, at the Stuttgart Technology University student union, Dad tore a poster off of the wall and tucked it under his shirt and sweater. It reads, "Jews Not Wanted." Mom and Dad kept it hidden and brought it home in 1939.

Poster, "Jews Not Wanted," Stuttgart, circa 1938

Sunday morning, we window shopped. We were surprised that so many stylish things existed. Most of the women were well dressed and some even wore makeup. I look so different from everyone, I am constantly being looked at. I have the biggest impulse to stick out my tongue. Bill just waits until they stare good and long and comes forth with a hearty, "Guten tag." After a wonderful noon meal of ½ chicken cooked over wood coals, we walked around and at 4:30 met the MacLeods and Helligers. They didn't go to the party on Saturday because they are going to be preachers and don't go in for any such doings. We went with them to eat and at 6:00 went to the opera, *Die Meistersinger von Nurnbergopera*, a long opera lasting five hours. It is perhaps Wagner's lightest and it didn't seem so long. The scenes and the costumes were beautiful. We thought that, perhaps, we would have to be educated to learn to like opera, but we were surprised to find it altogether delightful. How we wish Kansas City had a good opera. We had to rush to get our bus to Tübingen and were two tired cookies.

Oh, I must relate an amusing opera incident. In between acts the people promenade around the halls. Many of them are dressed in formals. But, to spoil the rather delightful picture, they open up their pocketbooks and take out a sandwich and proceed to eat it while walking around. If you fail to bring a sandwich, in one end of the hall, you can buy them along with drinks and candy. You might expect drinks, for a German rarely drinks plain water, but the rest is, indeed, queer.

Frau Reith, Tübingen, circa 1938

We were able to sleep late this morning for Bill didn't have a class until eleven. This afternoon I went up to Frau Reith's and we had an exchange German, English class. Then we had tea. She is the one who plans to go to the US with her husband. She told

me of going to buy a record for her husband for
Christmas. She chose a number of Bach played by
Fritz Kreisler and an orchestra. The storekeeper
told her she couldn't buy it because it wasn't
Aryan. He wouldn't sell her the record.

**Aryan**. Hitler was obsessed with "racial purity" and argued that the German was superior to all other peoples, although he wrongly described them as the Aryan race. He used the word "Aryan" to describe his idea of a "pure German race," or "Herrenvolk." The Nazis believed that the Aryans had the most "pure blood" of all the people on earth and had a duty to control the world.

The ideal Aryan had pale skin, blond hair, and blue eyes. Hitler believed that Aryan superiority was threatened in particular by the Jews. He also believed in a hierarchy of "races" created with the Aryans at the top and with Jews, Gypsies, and black people at the bottom. Non-Aryans came to be seen as impure and even evil. These "inferior" people were seen as a threat to the purity and strength of the German nation.[xix]

Bill likes school very much. Of course, it is
entirely different from an American University.
He is taking Latin which requires much time for
it must be composed from English to German. He is
also taking one course in philosophy, Roman legal
history, and a course on the theory of the German
state, beginning before the war up to the present
day. He is also in the German-English language
course which is two hours a week. When he has
free time, he drops in to hear other lectures.

I know you must have had a thrill hearing Bendinelli sing. He has such an amazing voice.

You take my letters wrong when you get angry about the things I say. I only tell you things that I think you will be interested in. I only state things as a fact or observation, and not especially as criticism. In every country certain conditions exist which the average citizen objects to, but which he can do nothing about. (Newspapers, as an example.) But we know that America is more free than any other country and luckily so. I often miss being in America, but I am developing such new interests and I know that my whole life will be much richer and fuller for it. Until next summer, I have no desire to return, for I want to stay and see so much more.

Later, Dad said in his newspaper interview, "We were told by a non-Nazi professor to avoid many of the law classes as they were being twisted by the Party. So, we took some of their classes in philosophy and language. One of their courses consisted of the German constitution and was taught by a Nazi professor. Socially, all foreign students were treated as outcasts as having come from the land of opportunity. The Nazi propaganda had a great deal of influence over the student's reactions. They were afraid of being seen with foreigners. Even a German student, whom I had met at KU, refused to recognize me there in public. He called on us one late night and that was all. A few of the students who were not in sympathy with the

Nazis would meet us at the coffee houses and talk, after they had searched the premises for hidden mikes."

Tuesday Morning

We are going to stay here for Christmas. Fraulein Keck has asked us to not accept any other invitations for Christmas Eve. Also, we shall have Christmas dinner here. We will have a German Christmas dinner with a goose. After Christmas we will go to a small village in the Austrian Alps, Schrocken. It is not far from here and looks altogether inviting. It is a small winter resort with a church, a general store, and a large hotel. It is an ideal skiing place. There is some equipment here Bill can use and I know I would probably break my neck, anyway. While there is snow, there is also lots of sunbathing because it isn't terribly cold. The hotel has a high, glassed-in sun porch for that purpose. We will go there unless we decide we would rather have the money for our spring trip.

We certainly enjoy the papers that you send. We were disappointed not to find a *KC Star* Sunday Society section. They are always interesting with their feature article.

Fraulein Keck just brought us two bananas. She is serving them for dessert today. Because we eat so few compared to the Germans, she wanted us to have only the best.

Today is Saint Nicholas Day and a big day for the Catholics. All the children receive gifts today as well as Christmas.

In Stuttgart on Sunday, we saw what remained of the Jewish shops. None of them were big stores and probably couldn't have accumulated much capital. They were boarded up fronts where the glass and signs were destroyed. Nothing like that happened to the shops here in Tübingen. Any number of good Party members have expressed regret over their treatment. To them it is very humiliating. We will be anxious to know what our German Ambassador will tell the President.

In Time magazine we enjoyed seeing the new cars. I wonder why Hudson is no longer making the Terraplane. Also, I wonder what kind of car the Mercury will be.

Thanks for the papers, write soon.
Love,
Lois

On November 9-10, **Kristallnacht (Night of Broken Glass)** took place as an anti-Jewish program in Germany,

Austria, and the Sudetenland. 200 synagogues destroyed, 7,500 Jewish shops looted, and 30,000 male Jews sent to concentration camps. On December 12 a one-billion-mark fine was levied against German Jews for the destruction of property during Kristallnacht.[xx]

Dad and Mom both spoke often of Kristallnacht. Mom told us, "We vividly recall Kristallnacht. As soon as we heard about it – and the news spread quickly – we went to the burned synagogue in Tübingen. One German man quietly asked if we were Americans, then telling us how ashamed he was of his country."

Tübingen, burned Synagogue, Kristallnacht, November 10, 1938

The **Synagogenplatz Memorial** in Tübingen commemorates the synagogue, which was destroyed during the Kristallnacht in November 1938, and honors the fate of the Jews from Tübingen. Many of them felt compelled to emigrate due to the increasing persecution by the National Socialists.

Susan Kandt Peterson

The Jewish residents of Tübingen who remained were deported by the SS to the Riga ghetto and to Theresienstadt.[xxi]

December 9, 1938
Tübingen, Germany

Dear Mother and Dad,

I have only a few minutes to write now for Helen and I are going to spend a couple of hours with Frances Helliger. I have not seen her for so long that I decided it was high time I went out. They live a long way from here, but it is not so cold today. We will ride our bicycles.

Yesterday I bought a darling, celluloid composition doll about 9 inches high. The little girl who calls for our washing is such an attractive, petite child. So I decided it would be fun to dress a doll for her. The only trouble is, I have few scraps. I have managed to make up a few and shall buy a small amount for a nighty and one dress. I shall bring Judy one of these dolls for they are washable and unbreakable.
We bought Fraulein Keck a lovely picture print for Christmas. She is simply wild about it. It is called *Women in Church* and shows three women praying, three generations. It was a little more than we planned to pay but she is so nice to us and treats us like a couple of kids.

Fraulein Keck is always asking what we are going to give each other for Christmas. She is going to be disappointed when nothing big shows up. I want a lot of small, typical German things but nothing big. I am going to give Bill attachments for our camera and, I think, a pipe. One of those long affairs. They are only a couple of marks for a hand carved one.

We were indeed happy to receive the Christmas money. Probably by spring we will have spent it a dozen times in our minds. It now assures us of a nice visit to England as England is sky high to visit. And if we are careful, we will have enough to allow us to visit Washington on our way home. We will have seen the beautiful European capitals and would like to wind up our trip by seeing our own, beautiful capital. So, thanks very much for your generous present.

Bill and I remember about our teeth so now we are buying oranges two or three times a week.

We received the December *Reader's Digest*. Any magazine can come through private subscription. They are only banned from the newsstands.

Lots of love,
Lois

Oranges were important as a source of vitamin C. Vitamin C prevented scurvy, a disease that, among other things, caused gum disease. This explains why my mother talks about oranges, and why she continually reassured her mother that they were buying oranges when they could.

```
                                December 13, 1938
                                Tübingen, Germany
Dear Mother and Dad,

    Bill is attending a murder trial this morning.
He got in by telling them he is an American law
student. They don't print any newspaper accounts
until after the trial. Bill will be able to ob-
serve much of the court system.

    It is a pitiful fact that the German women
look terribly old. Some women 35 years old look
older than you do, Mother. I think the diet
coarsens the skin.

    We have decided not to go to Schreckens in
the Alps after all. It would be fun but we would
rather visit some place of more historic value.
I have wanted to go to Budapest ever since we got
here. We are going to the travel bureau this af-
ternoon to find out what it would cost. Yesterday
Bill heard of an amazingly cheap trip to Egypt.
It sounds terribly far but is only at the other
end of the Mediterranean. By going to Budapest,
```

we would see Vienna, too. You can imagine how hard it is to decide when you have everything to choose from. Probably the travel bureau will give us a dozen new ideas. But wherever we go, we know that we will have a good time.

A big military unit is marching by. They are accompanied by a band. Generally, they sing. I just love some of their marching songs. This one is so peppy you just feel you could get out there and goose-step with them. They goose-step only when on inspection by Hitler. They believe one does not tire so easily when marching to music. A couple of nights ago I was having a hard time going to sleep and it was almost two o'clock. I could hear in the distance a company marching and a shrill command, "Halt!" It is so cold out there. They really train the soldiers to endure hardships all the time. We see a lot of it here since Tübingen has regular barracks and one unit of the two-year military training course.

I have just about finished my doll clothes. I am real proud of them. Everyone has been so generous with scraps. We are invited to a Winterfest on Thursday. So far, we have not been able to find out much about it. But I believe it is to be a formal affair. I shall wear my green velvet, if so, providing I can steam the wrinkles out.

We have no snow yet. So far, this winter has been much milder than a Kansas winter. If I am going to walk far, I can't wear my fur collar coat, for it is much too warm.

We have been planning how we could furnish a small apartment when we get back to Lawrence for Bill to finish law school and save much rent. One with no bedroom, a pull-down bed in the wall.

It is time for lunch and Bill is not home yet. I prefer to go in with him for I don't understand what is said to me and I can always ask him to tell me.

Love to all,
Lois

December 19, 1938

Dear Mother and Dad,

We are having our first severe cold. I am all cuddled up by the fire so that I can write this letter. Poor Fraulein Keck doesn't know what to do because we ask for so much coal. We are used to having more heat and they are not. There is a wave which has swept the entire continent. Many boats were not able to get through the English Channel yesterday. It is a little warmer today. Our bedroom would be a nice place to freeze meat. All of the water is frozen to solid ice. I had a pair of panties soaking in the bowl and they are frozen in the water. While we were brushing our teeth yesterday, the water froze on the brushes. We have no reason for using our bedroom much. The bed seems cold at first, but it doesn't take long to warm up. I don't know when I have slept so well. Even if we can't have our clothes cleaned here, the germs are killed by them being in that cold room.

Just the other day I was saying now nice it was to be away from telephones for a year. Only a few homes have them. But today I am supposed to go to Frau's, and it is too cold to walk clear up there. I have been trying to figure out some way to let her know but I suppose I will have to go. We have been having so much fun together. I have been helping her make German Christmas cookies. Already she speaks much better English. I hope she can say the same about my German. It is just above zero and I hate the thought of going out.

Last Thursday we went to a Winterfest. It was given by a school organization. It was formal and extremely nice. There were about 6 or 7 skits, mostly take-offs on the professors. Then there were several short speeches given by profs. For once, again, we didn't get a history lesson of National Socialism or boisterous, "Heil Hitler." We have never been able to bring ourselves to shout that greeting. We mainly say, "Good day," in German. There was an orchestra and between skits, dancing. Bill and I are dancing more here than we do at home.

Since it is so cold, I doubt that we will go anyplace after Christmas. We have just about given up on going to Budapest. When it is so cold, it wouldn't be fun to go anywhere.

Bill has gone to the post office to see if he can call any of Frau Reith's neighbors. Whether he can or not, I am not going to see her. Surely, she will understand. I will drop her a card which she will get in the morning.

I just wrapped up the doll I dressed for Christmas. The little girl is coming for the washing today. It was fun to sew two dresses and a pair of pajamas and I hope it will add to the child's Christmas.

Tomorrow is the last day of classes. Hans wrote that his mother is sending us a Christmas cake. It will be almost a two-week vacation.

I am going to make Christmas candies tomorrow. I shall make walnut crunch, fudge, and orange divinity. I will give the Reiths a box. Bill is going to help me so there won't be so much beating to do.

I do wish that you wouldn't worry about me so. We are absolutely safe. There is absolutely no danger. Bill is almost always with me and I am never out alone after dark. We are having a wonderful time and both of us are well and happy.

Hope you both are well and had a nice Christmas.

Lots of love,
Lois

>December 22, 1938
>Tübingen, Germany

Dear Mother and Dad,

Oranges have become somewhat scarce, but we have been able to find them. I bought four today.

Christmas vacation began on Tuesday. On that night we had a Christmas dinner with Martha Long, Jeff Durant (He's the English lecturer who teaches here), the student from Peru, and Hardy, a Bavarian medical student here, the Helligers, the MacLeods and a few others. Every year it is a tradition to have this dinner. It is always limited to a few and Bill and I were pleased to have been included. We paid for our dinner. I have always thought it would be elegant to eat a very fancy dinner and have the correct wine served with each course. Hardy selected the wines and they blended well with what we were eating. We had soup served with melba toast and butter, goose stuffed with apples, mashed potatoes and gravy, Brussel sprouts, hot roasted chestnuts and almonds, and applesauce. Jeff's mother sent a genuine English plum pudding and an English

Christmas cake. The pudding was soaked in rum and burned. My, did it look pretty. They always stick a piece of holly with berries in the center and it burns, too. It was served with vanilla sauce. In spite of the appearance of my tummy, it has only limited capacity and I could not finish all of my portions of the pudding. We sat around the table until well past midnight. Bill and I enjoy visiting with the young people from other countries. What pleases us is that they always think America is such a good place. Of course, no Englishman would go very far in praise of any other country, although admits that England must have friendships with other states. We had that dinner with four different courses for $1.50.

We have had some snow now and it is much warmer. We have learned how to operate the stove so we can keep the whole room warm.

Fraulein Keck has decided to have her big dinner on Christmas Eve instead of Christmas. We were happy with her decision as we can now cook dinner with the MacLeods and the Helligers. Since Christmas Eve is the main event anyway, we will be here with the Fraulein for that.

Yesterday Hardy was here for the afternoon and had tea with us. He's a swell fellow. He's so much more like an American than a German. His grandmother came from Boston.

I doubt that you will receive our little package for Christmas. We mailed them on the 5th or 6th. So far, we have no word of the popcorn arriving. Helen's mother sent peanut butter the last week of November and so far, it is not here.

We have decided not to make much of a trip now. If it does not get any colder, we will go to Freiburg for a few days after Christmas. We would enjoy seeing the Black Forest snow covered.

                                            Friday afternoon

Again, it is very cold. Last night it got down to ten degrees below. Poor Fred and Francis Helliger were simply frozen by the time they arrived. We played Fan-Tan and Hearts and had lots of fun. Francis reminded me of Mother for she shook all over when she laughed. We took our Christmas baths this morning.

We will be thinking of you on Christmas day.

Lots of love,
Lois

Susan Kandt Peterson

December 27, 1938
Tübingen, Germany

Dear Mother and Dad,

Our thoughts have been with you very much the last few days, wondering what you were doing, what gifts you received and how little Judith enjoyed her first Christmas.

At 5:00 Christmas Eve we went to a short church service in the old Stiftskirche. It is perhaps the most prominent building in town for it stands in the very center. It was built as a Catholic church but then the Reformation came and Tübingen became Protestant and the church was taken over by a new group. The service consisted mostly of music. As we sat there in that old, beautiful building, filled with hundreds of people, listening to the Christmas story read in German, one could not help but wonder how this could be the Germany one hears so much about, the Germany that has caused so much concern to other nations. Surely, this was not the church that was being purged.

As we left the church and walked up a small hill about a block away, we had a most thrilling experience. Everything was covered in a blanket of snow. People were hurrying around, all bundled up. The big fir tree by the church was illuminated with many little lights and from out of nowhere we heard a brass band playing

*Silent Night*. It was so lovely that immediately you were swelled up with the true Christmas spirit. The music came from the church tower and flowed over the entire town. It made you wish for Peace on Earth.

All of the stores had closed at four in the afternoon, giving everyone an opportunity to enjoy this event. They will be closed until tomorrow, so that everyone in the whole country has a few days rest and time to take a new lease on life. How different from the American rush for the big day after Christmas sales.

Mom later wrote, "Church attendance and all religions were discouraged, so few attended. So what happened on Christmas Eve was remarkable. The celebration of Christmas starts on December 24th. Trees were bought on this day. Men were seen carrying trees on their shoulders, for few families had cars. To our surprise, the church was filled that night. No dictator or government, regardless how hard they try, can repress a religious faith, for what we believe belongs to us and that cannot be removed from our hearts."

About seven o'clock Fraulein Keck rapped on our door and took our presents in by the big tree. She told us to come in as soon as we heard the music. She played *Silent Night* sung by a ten-year-old boy who has the most beautiful soprano voice. The tree reached the ceiling and was just simply covered with red candles. It was the first candle tree I had seen and was very pretty but mostly, it was the wonderful pine smell. We opened our gifts and then went in to eat. We had a beautiful salad plate of deviled eggs, tomatoes, cress, and winter radishes with wonderful bread and butter. It was so good and just hit the spot. Then we went back to Keck's room and had Mosel wine and hundreds of small Christmas cookies. Later, we had apricot brandy that just made you smack your lips. About ten, Fraulein Keck asked if Helen and Norman were celebrating with anyone. They were not, so they came down and had a couple of hours with us. Bill took portraits of us which were lots of fun. But as Keck says, it is not a true Christmas without little children around.

Lois, Christmas Eve, Tübingen, December 1938

Fraulein Keck, Christmas Eve, Tübingen, December 1938

*Eyes and Ears*

Norman MacLeod, Christmas Eve, Tübingen, December 1938

Helen MacLeod, Christmas Eve, Tübingen, December 1938

Christmas Eve was Bill's birthday and when we got up in the morning, Keck had fixed a birthday table. Around the edges were candles, lovely orange-yellow ones. And in between the candles were small, yellow mums. In the center was a large poinsettia plant. They are very rare here, as they are in most American flower shops, coming from North Carolina. There was a plate filled with cookies and candy. Also, a small box filled with blank paper for Bill to write ten German words a day. I gave him a pipe, one of those funny, long affairs. He has been thrilled and says it smokes beautifully.

Bill says my presents are knick-knacks, but they are all little German things that I wanted. I got a darling cloth-covered scrapbook, a little wine pitcher that will serve as a vase, and a

Bill with new pipe, Christmas Eve, Tübingen, December 1938

liquor set from Bavaria which has a jug and six little cups. My tea warmer is so cute. It is a little gadget in which you set a small candle and your tea pot rests about two inches from it to keep your tea warm. Perhaps my favorite is the little, wooden candlesticks. And I got a dozen small, wooden cutout figures that they use as Christmas decorations. Fraulein Keck gave me a wooden kranz to use as a Christmas centerpiece. Next year we can have a German Christmas table. Bill mostly got camera equipment. Also, a bottle of catsup, as he eats so much of it at home and it is not common at all here. Keck gave him a lovely little album filled with pictures of Tübingen.

Wednesday

And now for Christmas day. We slept late and had wonderful fruit coffee cake for breakfast. Then we went up and helped prepare the Christmas dinner at the MacLeod's. The Helligers were there, too.

We ate about 2:30. We had a fruit juice cocktail, two baked hens with chestnut dressing, peas, beets fixed with brown lemon sauce and seed onion, and mashed potatoes and gravy. Our salad consisted of red apples and cottage cheese. Bill was delegated to carve, and the chickens were too tender, with everyone offering assistance. We said we must have looked like *You Can't Take It With You*. But we all laughed a lot over it and will long remember it. We sat around the table until late afternoon and then we had our Christmas tree for the group and exchanged gifts. We exchanged some lovely gifts and then Norman gave us a set of celluloid bathtub animals because we are the only people who bathe in a bathtub. (They all go swimming.)

Christmas with the MacLeods and Helligers, Tübingen, December 1938

In the evening we were hungry again, so we had fruit salad with chicken in it, bread, butter, and peanut butter. For dessert we had a birthday cake for Fred and Bill; Fred turning 27 on Christmas day and Bill's birthday on Christmas eve. With the cake we had cocoa with marshmallows.

Thank you so much for the package. The marshmallows are quite soft. We have not popped the popcorn.

Lots of love,
Lois

Later, Mom said, "There were very few eggs because they were being processed and stored for the war years to come. Somehow, some American friends were able to make Bill a birthday cake, the five eggs coming from five different countries, one being China."

January 2, 1939
Tübingen, Germany

On Thursday it was much warmer, and we walked for several hours around the Altstadt, the old part of Tübingen. It was extremely lovely with the snow. All the small children were out playing, and we tried

Tübingen, December 1938

to talk to some of them, but their dialect was too Swabish, so it was impossible to understand them. In the evening we popped the corn you sent and talked with Fraulein Keck.

Friday morning, we got up at 6:00 (yes, it is difficult for me to believe, too) for a day excursion to the Black Forest. The weather was too bad for a trip clear to Freiburg, so we went to Freudenstadt, a resort town in the northern part of the forest. It is only two hours from here by a slow train. It was eight o'clock before it was light. By a quarter till we were there and in the worst storm I have ever seen. We decided to take a bus to a small place in the forest, only 40 minutes away. The ride up was worth the whole trip, for the snow-covered tall pine trees were a sight to behold. We had coffee and then went for a two-hour tramp around the woods. We had on heavy shoes and wool socks. In the woods there was no wind and it was quite warm. The snow was so fine and dry that we could walk on top of it, although it was probably two

Bill, Black Forest, December 1938

feet deep. Every few minutes we would step aside for a skier. Bill and I were completely breathless at the beauty of the forest.

We ate in the big resort hotel and had a grand steak, fried potatoes, and salad. At 1:30 we went back to Freudenstadt. It had stopped snowing but was quite cold. We spent the rest of the day shopping. We thought the second anniversary was wood, so we bought a beautiful, handmade cuckoo clock. It is shaped like the typical German house but has a carved man and woman standing by the house. The cuckoo is a native bird of the forest. The system is so simple. It runs by weights rather than springs. And we bought a lovely, big wooden plate. It is all handmade and painted. It represents a country folk wedding and is out of pear wood. We will never use it as a plate for it is too lovely hanging on the wall. All of these lovely things are works of art, but they are made by farm people who work the fields in summer and when they are snowed in, they make things.

We got back in time for a late supper. We had such a good day.

When we got back, we found in our mail an invitation to go to Hechingen for the weekend. Fred Pickell, the boy who had come to see us the day before (he was on the boat), was visiting this family and they invited us. So, on Saturday we went. The Hessars are a very nice family with a beautiful, big house. He is a judge, so Bill had a chance to talk law with him. Also, we met the other judges and the prosecuting attorney. They have three children. The oldest son is an exchange student in Idaho this year. The other son is serving his military service. The girl is 17 and cute as the dickens. As soon as we arrived we had tea, then we went to a coffee house and had coffee. Every Saturday afternoon, they go there and meet a dozen of their friends. At 7:30 we had supper.

Hechingen, Germany, the Hessar's home, January 1939

Then came New Year's Eve. They really have a celebration. Two of the daughter's friends came in and the prosecuting attorney and his wife. (She's 27 and he's 51. She's probably the most attractive woman I've seen in Germany.) During the evening, other young people came in and out. We had nine seventeen-year-olds. As usual, the famous little Christmas cookies. At 11:30 they sang several Christmas carols and took the small cookie ornaments off of the tree, everyone taking just one. At midnight we toasted the new year with hot, red wine with sugar and lemon in it. Every man kisses his wife and there is much more laughter than there is at home. At about 12:45 we went to the hotel to dance. We only stayed until 2:00 because it was so hot and crowded.

We slept late the following morning and had a light breakfast. After dinner, we went skiing for a couple of hours. They had extra stuff for us to wear. It was a very warm day and the snow was too wet. It was so slow it was hard to hold your balance. We went down only a very small hill. Going down was fun, more fun than a picnic, but coming up again, well, that was different. The first time I fell, I couldn't get up again. I tried and tried so I took off my skis and walked. I continued to fall but always managed to get up. My neck is sore, but it was sure lots of fun and I would like to be able to do lots of it.

Bill, Lois, and Fred Pickell
Hechingen, Germany, January 1939

At four we dressed again and went for coffee at the attorney's house. It certainly is a beautiful place, very new, built by a Jew. His wife had her hair all piled up on top of her head, very stylish. She is coming to see me soon. Hechingen is the town where the Hollenzollern castle is. From our bedroom window, we had a perfect view of the castle.

Hohenzollern Castle, 1939

The weather had turned quite nasty, so we took the 7:50 train home. Fraulein Keck had a goose dinner waiting for us. Her soldier was here, and we all talked until 11:00. Oh, I forgot to say, for two days we spoke nothing but German. I was surprised how much I knew. Probably the Germans didn't know what I was talking about all of the time. Keck's soldier is a boy here doing his military service. He's a family friend and Keck mothers him by sending him clothes, etc. He is a young doctor and too old to be spending his time here. He really dislikes it. He is one of the first ones we have met who isn't proud of being a soldier.

Hans Marin's mother sent us a lovely big Christmas box. It had a huge big stollen, which we would call a coffee cake. Also in the box were three boxes of honey chocolate cookies, four packages of Germany's best chocolate, and a big box of cigarettes. I'm glad the vacation is almost over for we eat too much, especially sweet things.

Mother later told me that Hans Martin, who had been an exchange student at KU and joined the SS upon his return to Germany, died in World War II.

I guess Spring is always the critical time for wars to begin. The armies move then, whatever that means. Nobody here seems to be very upset or worried about the possibility. One thing for sure, though, the German people do not want war but whatever the leaders want is another thing. If Hitler plans to spring anything, it is certainly unknown to the people. They all say there would be no Europe if there were to be another war. But you can rest assured that we are safe and happy. It seems as if Ike has been talking too much anti-Germany and has said a few too many insulting things. The Germans are pretty sore about it. They have been talking about it a lot. I believe the relations between the US and Germany are far worse than Germany's relationship with the other countries. It is really too bad and unnecessary. As far as we can see, there are no signs pointing to another crisis. May they not arise!

Lots of love,
Lois

**Dwight D. Eisenhower**, or "Ike," became a five-star general in the United States Army and served as supreme commander of the Allied Expeditionary Forces in Europe during WWII. He later became the 34th president of the U.S.

Ike's opinion of Hitler was clear: he thought him evil and stupid. In his diary on September 3, 1939 Ike wrote, "Hitler is a power-drunk egocentric. His personal magnetism had converted large populations in Germany to his insane schemes and [they] blindly accepted his leadership. Unless he is successful in overpowering the whole world by brute force the final result will be that Germany will have to be dismembered and destroyed…Hitler's record with the Jews, his rape of Austria, of the Czechs, the Slovaks, and now the Poles is as black as that of any barbarian of the Dark Ages."

They were opposites. Hitler was a tyrant and modern history's biggest warmonger. Eisenhower strongly supported liberal democracy and centrism.[xxii]

```
                                January 7, 1939
                                Tübingen, Germany
Dear Mother and Dad,

   Now that the weather is warm again it is ter-
ribly hard to stay indoors.

   Everyone is back from their ski trips and most
of them are pretty sore and tired. It is quite a
dangerous sport when you go up in the mountains.
Helen had such a sore knee. The snow was so
```

loosely packed that there were many snow slides and quite a few were killed. The place where Martha Long went there was a bad one. Seven were injured and they haven't found the body of the other boy yet. I am so glad we didn't attempt to try it.

We are going to play bridge tonight with Helen and Norman. I am going to make lemonade to quench our thirst after eating the last of the popcorn. We have certainly enjoyed it. Fraulein Keck simply loves it.

The oranges have been delicious, and they are cheaper now. Since the war in Spain, it has been hard for other European countries to get enough citrus. Today I bought blood oranges. They are almost red inside. I have never tasted them, but they are supposed to be good.

A sixteen-year-old girl is moving in here. Her father is head of the army here now and his family has not yet moved. There is a school for girls here where they teach practical housework, etc. She goes to the school, so she is going to live here until her family moves. Her father is living in a hotel now. I hope he will be around some for it would be interesting to talk to him, get yet another angle of National Socialism.

In 1937, grammar school for girls was abolished and they were instead steered into domestic education with numerous schools established which taught girls domestic skills to become mothers. The number of young women admitted into universities saw a sharp decline. In a 1934 speech Joseph Goebbels said, "Women have the task of being beautiful and bringing children to the world, and this is by no means as coarse and old-fashioned as one might think. The female preens herself for her mate and hatches her eggs for him. In exchange, the mate takes care of gathering the food and stands guard and wards off the enemy. Hope for as many children as possible! Your duty is to produce at least four offspring in order to ensure the future of the national stock."

The Nazis offered incentives to German women to bear many children. Mothers with three and more children under the age of ten were given honorary cards allowing them to jump shopping queues and get discounts on their rent payments.

A state-supported program called Lebensborn (meaning "fountain of life") was established in Nazi Germany. Its aim was to raise the birth rate of blond-haired, blue-eyed Aryan children through interbreeding. Racially pure women were chosen to sleep with SS officers, many of whom were already married. Babies were taken from their mothers and sent to SS nurseries to be brought up as loyal servants of the Nazi state. It is estimated that 20,000 babies were born, mostly in Germany and Norway, during the years of the Third Reich.[xxiii]

```
   Anna, our maid, has lost all respect for me.
The water on our stove heats so slowly that I
never have enough. Consequently, I wash out a few
```

things every morning. Anna says I just wash all of the time. I looked at her and laughed and I thought, "Anna, if you only knew my mother!"

I think I'll have my glasses fitted here. They need changing. Frances Helliger tells me one of the most world-famous eye doctors is here in Tübingen. Fran is going to get hers fitted and I'll wait and see how hers turn out. She has to wear them all of the time.

I am enclosing a few pictures which we took on Christmas Eve and Christmas day. If Bill's folks ever stop by, be sure and show them to them.

Hope you both are well.

Lots of love,
Lois

*Eyes and Ears*

January 11, 1939
Tübingen, Germany

Dear Mother and Dad,

The present course of events has changed the routine of our lives in Germany. Because the American Consul in Stuttgart is simply swamped with work now in the immigration department, he has sought Americans to come to his rescue. A representative, Jackie, came and talked to Bill about this last Friday. Then we went to Stuttgart and Bill had a conference with Consul General Hanaker. He said the job would only last a few months. After thinking it over, we decided it would offer more advantages than the university. Today a telegram arrived for Bill to report to duty tomorrow. First, don't worry about Bill becoming interested in the Foreign Service, for we are more convinced now that the US is the only place in which to live. While the pay is low for this work, it is enough for us to live on. So, we will have more money to travel with. We will probably move to Stuttgart this weekend. Bill will commute by bus for three days and he should have a wonderful opportunity to find out some international law, immigration law, everything that goes on in a Consul's office. One thing we will find out plenty about is the Jewish situation for that is what has caused the rush.

Many more Jews tried to flee the country as a result of November's Kristallnacht and the heightened persecution around the country. This greatly intensified the work of the American Consulate.

We regret leaving Tübingen but of course are thrilled about a chance to work in the AC for a while. Hanaker said I would be popular if I played bridge. There are six vice Consuls besides Hanaker. Several of the other American employees have American wives. It will be our first experience living in a city. The Consul employs 45 people, but that is not enough. Of course, they are mostly Germans. In case the job doesn't last more than two or three months, Bill can come to the university again for the second semester. Now it looks like we can do our traveling in May or June. I hope we can do it early enough, so we won't have to be in Paris and London with the hundreds of American tourists. I will give you our new address just as soon as I can. But continue to write here and Fraulein Keck will forward our letters. She is very unhappy about our leaving, says she can't eat. She has been very nice to us and we have enjoyed her a lot.

I have been shortening my polo coat and having a dickens of a time with the lining hanging right. I am glad that it is about done before we go to Stuttgart, for they dress there more than here.

I enjoyed hearing about Judy's Christmas. Just imagine her with a purse!

I am telling you the truth when I tell you that I have had no bladder trouble at all. Bill and I have been in wonderful health. I think everyone has those spells when they have trouble going to sleep. Here, we sleep so well.

Bill is taking his bath now, cleaning up for his new occupation.

Morning, 11:00

I am still steaming from my bath. The German bath is hot with a tub full of water.

Norman and Helen came down last night for a farewell game of bridge. Bill had to go to bed early. He had to get up at 6:00 to catch his bus. I guess the propaganda minister, Mr. Goebbels, is leaving his wife for sure. The Germans all feel so sorry for the wife. They say people on the street go up to her and say, "Do you know where your husband's car is parked these days?" I guess he has been a regular playboy for years. Not many people like him but he does good work. They joke a lot about Goering, his figure, etc., but around here the people really respect and trust him in spite of the joking. Carolyn said he was not so popular around Munich. We are all watching the news to see what Chamberlain and Mussolini will have to say. It would be wonderful if the German-Italian axis were to be weakened. That is something which exists only between leaders, anyway. All the people we talked with in both countries said they just couldn't feel a bond with each other.

Lots of love,
Lois

**Hermann Göring** (also spelled Goering), was a leader of the Nazi Party and one of the primary architects of the Nazi police state in Germany. He used his position to indulge in ostentatious luxury, living in a palace in Berlin and building a hunting lodge where he organized state feasts, showed off his stolen art, and pursued his extravagant tastes.

Goering's transparent enjoyment of the trappings of power, his debauches, and his bribe-taking gradually corroded his judgement. Nevertheless, he remained genuinely popular with the German masses, who mistook his extrovert bluster and vitality for human warmth and regarded him as manly, honest, and more accessible than the Fuhrer. He was condemned to hang as a war criminal by the International Military Tribunal at Nuremberg in 1946 but instead took poison and died the night his execution was ordered.[xxiv]

January 16, 1939
Stuttgart, Germany

Dear Mother and Dad,

Your lovely daughter is now a working girl and having more fun. Since Bill was going to be with the Consul, I decided to offer my services and the experience of working in a really hustling and bustling office. Besides, I felt that as an American, I should be willing to help my country. I started last Friday by getting up at 6:00 to catch the bus. Until today, we commuted from Tübingen. Now we are staying in a cheap gasthof, a sort of hotel. Rooms are as scarce as the dickens to find here. We have looked all afternoon with absolutely no luck. We may have to wait until the first to get one. We left the bulk of our things in Tübingen and will send for them when we are settled.

We work long hours, 8-6:30, but it is so interesting that the day is over in no time. All I do is various forms of filing now but so great is the bulk of correspondence that it keeps 5 or 6 people busy. The office receives between 1,000 to 2,000 letters every day and hundreds of telegrams. They are now answering October's mail. I just love the work and don't find it half as tiring as selling. They were able to get 6 American college students and there are many other Americans here, so we have a jolly time. But we are all too busy to talk much during the day. We have 1½ hours at noon. That is really good, having the time to relax and take our time. Bill's work is much more detailed, reading cases and discovering preference cases and non-quotas. It requires reading a great deal of German. He will soon be doing much harder work, but of course, much more interesting. We are making good money in Germany. Bill gets $70.00 and I get $60.00. And we get an exchange rate of $4.20. With that amount, we will be able to save a nice sum and can really see Germany before we leave. I'll probably get to see Budapest yet.

We rather regret seeing so much of the Jewish situation for it is giving us only one side of the picture, not that we haven't heard the German side enough. Every day the waiting room is filled with about 200 of them and often, the hall and stairways are, too. I am always so happy when I file papers that will get a Jewish visa in a short time. Every individual has such an urgent case and when it says 1942-44, I am quite sad for I know these papers probably won't be touched for years to come. My major in sociology and especially the course I took in immigration and race relations has proved most helpful in understanding the laws, etc. In fact, I feel this is a fitting climax to my college education.

My mother later said, "When we needed to go to the bathroom at the Consulate, we had a long walk. This meant going through the waiting room and hall where the Jews were gathered. It was just pathetic. Some of the men wore armbands and had abrasions and bruises. The women were sometimes crying and repeating, 'They came last night and took my man!' The children just sat, staring, probably wondering what was going on."

We like Stuttgart very much. I think it is about the size of Kansas City but appears to be much smaller. We really have not seen much of it yet.

Bill went to the Ausland Deutsche Institute, today hoping they could help find a room. This place is mentioned in the January *Reader's Digest* as being such a huge organization in the propaganda scheme here. Bill told them he was of German blood and they took his name and they are going to look up his whole family tree for free. Also, they gave us little books with free passes to all of the museums, ½ price for an opera and so on. In this town, which is the home of the Auslanders, it pays to have German blood. We had planned to register with them anyway, just to see what type of literature they would send.

Stuttgart, Germany 1939

**Auslander:** a foreigner; outsider; alien [xxv]

The **Deutsche Ausland-Institute** was founded in 1917 for German nationals throughout the world, whether they were citizens of Germany or a foreign nation. The Deutsches-Institute was intended as a center where people could turn for help and advice on any cultural, scientific, or economic problem confronting them. Until 1933, the purpose of the DAI could scarcely be described as political or bellicose. However, with the advent of the SS, Brownshirts, a complete change took place. Officers of the Ausland Institute were replaced by Nazi leaders and political propaganda for advancing the principles of National Socialism and the Third Reich became the DAI's major activity with the objective of converting all Germans in foreign countries to the Nazi cause.[xxvi]

```
    There is so much about the office I would like
to tell you, but I don't think it would be advis-
able to write too much.

    Now that we are both working, we don't know
whether we will use our Christmas money over here
or not. Until we know, we don't want to send
it to Lawrence or to Holland. We think we can
see everything here without it but might decide
to see the World's Fair and Washington DC next
summer.

    I think it is swell that you are going to
Texas. I will have to get my atlas out and follow
your itinerary.

    I will still write twice a week if it is at
all possible. Write soon.

    Love,
    Lois
```

*Eyes and Ears*

American Consul
Koenigstr. 19 A
Stuttgart

> January 22, 1939
> Stuttgart, Germany

Dear Mother and Dad,

We are over in Tübingen for the weekend as we had many things to do here. Our rooms are paid until the end of the month as we are doing our moving by degrees. Then, too, we have to decide where we are going to live in Stuttgart. Last night we had supper with Helen and Norman. This morning we slept until 9:30 and felt groggy from it. It just shows how completely our routine of life can change in a week's time.

At noon we are going to a luncheon given by the Auslandstelle from Berlin. Bill has gone to have a conference with the man from there, now. I just found a piece of gum (Double Mint) in my summer purse and am having fun. The Europeans refer to it as those western barbaric habits. It is never sold over here.

I don't know if this conference was the one he was referring to, but Dad later said, "A Nazi official endeavored to enlist us to work outside of Germany for the cause, but when met with coldness, the official did not try again."

Every day at the Consul we get news reports from Washington. It is mostly about what Congress is doing. We are having a grand time there. The work is hard with long hours, but it is very absorbing, and the day is over before you know it. I do almost nothing but filing but before anything can be filed, it must be checked, so I can read the cases. The office is in such turmoil that filing consists of four processes. First, check the number against the code file to see if it is correct. Second, look in the old files to see if there is any previous material. Third, check to see if there has been a change of address. Fourth, find it in the new members file. Then you always have to see if any non-quota or preference case has slipped by. Of course, this shouldn't be such a condition, but the work is so tremendous that we have to try to keep up with the day's mail and do back-work at the same time. The reason, however, for most of this is that five of the German employees took bribes from the Jews. They messed things up pretty much in order to cover it up. The German government checked up and caught them. They are now in jail. Luckily, it didn't touch the Consul in any way. The Jews money is worthless to them and they were glad to give thousands of marks away. We are now very busy trying to repair any damage done. It was for this reason that they were so eager to employ Americans. Bill does all different types of work. Yesterday he read and checked the reports coming from Washington regarding the contracts held by

Rabbis with American synagogues. If they hold a contract, they can come in on the non-quota. Of course, these have to be checked to see if any fraud could be involved.

The day before, he looked up material for answers to Congressional letters. We have not seen a single Congressional letter from Kansas. I have only run across two letters from Kansas City. Out in the middle west, we have no problem. In spite of feeling so sorry for them, I hate to think of them coming to America.

Next week I am going to get my haircut and get a new permanent. I will be glad to get it off of my neck. The girls in the office told me of a good place to go. There are two girls from the south here. One is from Texas. She came over last summer with a group from Northwestern. Her father is yelling for her to come home now. She wants to stay until next summer and naturally, travel some, too.

I must get dressed now. This pencil is so worn down and my pen is dry.

Love,
Lois

A strict **quota system**, set by immigration laws in 1921 and 1924, limited the immigration of German and Austrian nationals to the United States. American policy makers wanted to prevent thousands of penniless Jews from southern and eastern Europe from entering the U.S. While antisemitism was certainly a factor, fear of communism and a general fear of poor people in a time of depression were at play. As the number of people fleeing Nazi persecution increased, more countries refused to accept refugees, and by 1939 the number of havens available to Jewish refugees dwindled.

Recognizing that the plight of German Jews had reached a point of crisis, Roosevelt called for an international conference to discuss the refugee problem. Delegates from 32 nations met in Evian-les-Bains, France in July 1938, but most countries, including the United States, refused to expand their laws to admit more immigrants. Even as the conference was going on, the American press criticized the participants at Evian for their inaction. As *Time* magazine wrote: "All nations present expressed sympathy for the refugees, but few offered to allow them within their boundaries."

By 1940, emigration from Nazi Germany became virtually impossible and in October, 1941, it was officially forbidden by the German government. From 1933-1938, about 30,000 German Jews emigrated to the U.S., but the government only gave out 30% of the visas it had available for Germans. Despite stories coming from Europe of a campaign to force Jews out of Germany and the horrors of Kristallnacht, the majority of Americans were fearful that an influx of immigrants would only aggravate the serious unemployment problem brought on by the Depression. The notion that "those refugees will take our jobs," prevailed across much of America. While Jews were struggling to obtain visas from the American Consulate, the State Department ordered its Consulates to stall the process.[xxvii]

This was the list of items required by the US government for all German-Jewish applicants seeking an entry visa to the United States in the 1930s and 1940s:

- Five copies of the visa application
- Two copies of the applicant's birth certificate
- Quota number (establishing the applicant's place on the waiting list)

Two sponsors: Close relatives of the prospective immigrant preferred. The sponsors were required to be US citizens or to have permanent resident status, and they were required to have completed and notarized six copies of an Affidavit of Support and Sponsorship.

Supporting documents:

- Certified copy of most recent federal tax return
- Affidavit from a bank regarding applicant's accounts
- Affidavit from any other responsible person regarding other assets (affidavit from sponsor's employer or statement of commercial rating)

Certificate of Good Conduct from German Police authorities, including two copies of each:

- Police dossier
- Prison record
- Military record
- Other government records about individual

Affidavits of Good Conduct (after September 1940) from several responsible disinterested persons

Physical examination at US consulate

Proof of permission to leave Germany (imposed September 30, 1939)

Proof that prospective immigrant had booked passage to the Western hemisphere (imposed September 1939)

In June of 1939, 900 Jewish passengers on the *M.S. St. Louis* cruised off the coast of Miami. Most were passengers trying to escape Nazi Germany. The United States hadn't been on the ship's original itinerary, and its passengers didn't have permission to disembark in Florida. The ship was sent back to Europe after Cuba, Canada, and then the United States immigration authorities turned it away. Nearly a third of the passengers were later murdered.[xxviii]

```
                    January 26, 1939
                    Stuttgart, Germany

          Dear Mother and Dad,

              Today I am propped
          up in bed as I have
          a bit of a cold and
          decided I should
          rest. I came home
          from work with a sack
          of oranges. Bill is
          working tonight. We
          are getting caught up
```

Lois, Stuttgart, Germany, January 1939

on the back work at a pretty good rate now. In a few weeks, the office should be running smoothly. Helen is quitting the first because it is too hard commuting. I will miss her, but we are so busy that we have little time for visiting.

I have been promoted. I now look things up for the officers. When a case is to be called or letters answered, all of the previous material must be collected. This I do. Today I gathered material for answers to letters to the Department of State in Washington. It burns me up when a Senator writes and suggests breaking the law to get Mr. So and So a visa. Also, I have a raise. Now we are both making $70.00. If we find we are getting too many marks, we can get our pay in dollars. Bill had a chance to get on the permanent payroll which would allow us a rent allowance. But we told Mr. Hanaker that we had plans for our future in America and that we would leave by June. It is too bad we were not with the Consul before Christmas because all packages come in duty free. They order eggs and butter from Denmark every week.

Yesterday I had a permanent. It is so soft and nice. I like it better than American hair permanents I have had. On Thursday evening we went to hear the Don Cossack Russian Chorus. They were so good. I had heard them before at KU. In the papers you sent, in the *Kansas City Star* society, there was so much news. Three Kappas had their engagements announced.

It rains constantly. I am going to buy myself an umbrella. They have darling collapsible ones here that are only about 14 inches long. They have also built some into large purses. I want one of those if they are not too expensive. I shall also invest in a pair of galoshes. I have learned my lesson.

There is a very nice chap here from California. He's a student at Heidelberg this year. Last year he graduated from Stanford. He stays here at the same place. His father has a wholesale lumber business in San Diego. His name is Gordon Frost. I wonder if you have ever had any dealings with him.

Well, the Frau just brought me a bed lamp and I am tempted to settle myself in for about 45 minutes and then to sleep. Nearly every noon we eat in a place where they serve only vegetables and fruits. It is alcohol free and no smoking. The food is well cooked. It is a novelty for Europe. The price of food has gone up noticeably during the last month or six weeks. The housewives are really complaining now. One egg costs 14 pfennigs. They wouldn't be so bad if they were fresh eggs. Oranges are very plentiful now and I am eating lots of them.

Thanks so much for the papers. We always enjoy them so much. Do write soon.

Lots of love,
Lois

> January 29, 1939
> Stuttgart, Germany

Dear Mother and Dad,

This has been such a lazy, old Sunday. It is now 5:30 and we are not yet dressed. We bought eggs and oranges and had a big, big breakfast that the Frau fixed for us. Frosty came in and ate with us. Then we talked until now. It is a dark, grey day. We plan to go out for dinner at about 7:00. We get Saturday afternoons off, too. We had quite a crowd Saturday for dinner and beer. Helen and Norman stayed until the 11:20 bus to Tübingen. Early in the afternoon, Bill and I went to look for a room. We found a nice, big, comfortable room that is only about 10-15 minutes walking distance from the office. Yet it is on a dead-end street so there is no noise. It is quite reasonable, 70 marks a month with heat and light. Bill is going to Tübingen on Wednesday to settle up everything and get the rest of our things. So far, we have not seen much of Stuttgart but in a few weeks, we will have shorter hours so we can get out more.

The work is coming along but there is still so much to be done that it is hard to notice any real progress being made on the surface. I am simply fascinated by office life. It is really hard work but not especially tiring. We get a holiday on Washington's birthday so we think we will have a banquet, perhaps. It is supposed to be against the law for an employee to work on a holiday. Now that we have more money, I am going to buy a Bavarian sweater. I must buy Judith a birthday present. I think I will buy her a red polka dot, oilcloth elephant. But I'll probably change my mind. I bought a darling pair of galoshes with fur around the top. They are so warm. My poor fur collar coat is not worth two cents now. I spend half of my time sewing up the rips and tears.

Lois in her fur collared coat, Stuttgart, February 1939

Bill and Frosty are so happy, for one of the Consuls gave them a couple of packages of American cigarettes. Anything from America comes duty free but the cigarettes are supposed to be only for the officers.

*Eyes and Ears*

The other day I came across, at work, an affidavit signed by Mr. Harzfeld. It was interesting to see how much money he had. He was writing for a friend of his in New York. He apparently has no relatives here. New York's Mr. Lehman is certainly run ragged by his relations here. His family has been very generous.

We are going to take pictures tonight for our application blanks. We have to submit two each. One of Bill isn't so bad, but I don't believe I care to submit "Lois with wine glass."

All of this talk about a war scare in March has rather quieted down. We are in a position where we can more or less be in the know and get out if things get hot. I do wish the war in Spain would end. It's hard to realize unless you are close to it.

Write often to the Consul.

Lots of love,
Lois

On the night of July 17, 1936, the Spanish army, inspired by General Francisco Franco, started the **Spanish Civil War**. Franco's Nationalists rebelled against Spain's democratic Republican government with the central goal of destroying left-wing organizations backed by the educated middle class and urban workers. Fascist Italy and Nazi Germany supported Franco's Nationalists. The Soviet Union and Mexico supported the overthrown Republicans with munitions and money. France, the United Kingdom, and the United States recognized the Republican government, but upheld a policy of non-intervention. Regardless, volunteers of the paramilitary units nicknamed the "International Brigades" poured in from countries including Ireland, France, Poland, Canada, and the United States (who called themselves the "Abraham Lincoln Brigade") to participate in the conflict. Violence and horrific atrocities were committed on both sides, with total estimated casualties between 150,000-2,000,000. The Republicans were crushed and victory declared for Franco on April 1, 1939. His dictatorship brought economic and political isolation to Spain. Franco would go on to lead Spain with an iron grip for 36 years until his death in 1975. It was only then that Spain would take new steps towards democracy.[xxix]

February 3, 1939<br>Stuttgart, Germany

Dear Mother and Dad,

Once again you will be honored with a lovely letter on the typewriter, only this time it will be on a nice big Underwood for I am now at the Consul. We came here tonight to write letters.

We moved last Wednesday to our new room. It is very light and airy for a German room. We have a large window on both the east and south. Naturally, there is no running water, but we are used to that by now. There is a nice, new modern coal stove. Our coffee this morning was terrible. It won't be long before Germany has no real coffee and we are going to see if we can get some instant from Washington through the free port here. Germany needs other things worse than to exchange with the tropical countries. You know, you can't help but feel sorry for these people when they don't have enough of the things we enjoy for comfortable living.

The Consul had the flu en masse this weekend. There was an epidemic of flu here. We heard that it had swept over Europe, starting in Poland. We were in bed most of Sunday feeling pretty punk but nothing terrible. Monday Bill still wasn't able to go to the office. Before the day was over, ten people from the visa department were not here. Only a couple of the people at work were really sick with a high fever. I came back the next day but as it turned out to be the wrong time of the month for me, I felt bum. But we moved that night and stayed in bed the next morning. We are feeling much better now.

We received the newspapers today. Since we have not been home yet, I have not yet opened them, but we will certainly enjoy them in the next couple of days. Thank you for all of the effort you go to send them to us.

Bill went to Tübingen yesterday to tell the police about our change of address. That is one of the German strictest rules, keeping the police informed of your whereabouts at all times. It is a wonderful idea to know where everyone is. I don't suppose it would be practical in America though, because it is far too big. Bill also had our trunk sent over. Norman has given up the idea of getting his doctor's degree here, so they are going home this summer. We may be on the same boat. They are happy about it. Helen was getting pretty fed up with the place after a year and a half. Germany is fun while it lasts but I know I couldn't take more than a year of it. I bet most of the men who sign up with the Foreign Service are sorry for it in five years or sooner.

Hope you are both well and happy.

Lots of love,
Lois

In 1946, Robert M. W. Kempner wrote of the **German Registration System:** "Throughout the centuries, one of the basic concepts of government in Germany has been the very tight control of inhabitants by the State. One of the main administrative institutions, through which the grip of the government upon every single inhabitant was and is exercised, is the registration system which assures a follow-up of each person's family status, movements, activities, and occupation, from the cradle to the grave."[xxx]

*Eyes and Ears*

February 9, 1939
Stuttgart, Germany

Dear Mother and Dad,

Bill is in bed today. He got up too soon from the flu. I am feeling fine now. Don't worry about the peanut butter. Because we are married, the Consul let us order some food from the free port in Hamburg. We ordered lots of fruit juices, peaches, peanut butter, tuna fish, Ivory soap, pickles, chili, baked beans, and Pepsodent toothpaste. The main treat will be having fruit juice for breakfast. Now we can have supper at home, occasionally. We get our butter from Denmark. Saturday afternoon we are invited to tea at the Consul General's house. Mr. Hanaker has invited all of the young Americans. He is so nice. I am anxious to meet his wife.

Monday night some of us went to the Consul's house to do some work. He is a braggy, overbearing sort of person but everyone manages to put up with him. They have three small children. Mrs. L'Hereaux teaches

American Consul friends, Germany, January 1939

the two oldest herself because they get such poor training in public schools. Too much politics and not enough A,B,Cs. They have a regular classroom fixed in the house.

Did I tell you that the Kappas are having an exchange next year? Dorothy Blue, Lawrence, is going to Sweden to school. She will live with a family and their daughter will live in Lawrence with the KU Kappas. Just imagine trying to learn that language! Kappa is also having exchanges with France, Italy, and Germany.

Mother, your new dresses sound lovely. You were so lucky to be there when the salesman was. I hope you are having a good time in Texas.

Now that spring is around the corner, we are getting the urge to travel and take the boat for home. Helen and Norman may leave in April or May. He has a chance at a church. Saturday night we had planned to go to a big Fasching Ball. Fasching is the pre-lent period corresponding to the French Mardi Gras. But now that Bill is not well, we will not plan on it. Every place in Europe has a big celebration lasting for a period of weeks.

Now we have Postum for breakfast. Mrs. L'Hereaux ordered some from New York and they doubled the order. So I bought 4 cans from her.

Lots of love,
Lois

*Eyes and Ears*

February 15, 1939
Stuttgart, Germany

Dear Mother and Dad,

Bill was in bed for three days last week. Now he is fine. I don't know about Europe, but Germany is having a real epidemic. Luckily, it is a mild form of it. One of the big banks here had 68 sick on Friday and 100 on Saturday. Today a big air raid practice was scheduled but it was called off because of the flu, too dangerous to put so many people together in those cellar rooms. We are looking forward to it. I would like to see how they do it.

We have been working as usual. While the work is routine, every case is different, so it is very interesting. One more of the German employees got "thrown in the jug" last week. I don't know whether they have anything on him or not. He was a very nice young fellow. He was a former SS member and when he was here, he just quit. And one just doesn't do that in Germany. One man today got a visa who was so wealthy that even with the same amount he was allowed to take (I think 10%), he was allowed $80,000 dollars equivalent. That doesn't happen very often.

Last Saturday, Consul General Hanaker had all of the Americans for tea. They said it would be American but the only thing recognizable was peanut butter. There was so much anchovy, pate de foie gras, etc. How I hate all of those things. Even the apple pie was different. It's a shame when Americans remain away from home for so long that they don't know what we eat. Mrs. Hanaker hadn't been there for years. She gets seasick and all of her close relations are dead. I was so surprised when I met her. He is so smooth and serious, and she is a Billy Burke type, flighty and fast talking. Not that that is a shame for I am a big fan of Billy Burke. Mrs. Hanaker says such typical things as, "I was awfully dumb in school. Maybe that's why I didn't learn anything." I imagine she was a beautiful girl. We stayed until 9:30 and it really was a grand get-together. We listened to American radio over shortwave.

**Billie Burke** (August 7, 1884 – May 14, 1970) was the actress who played Glinda the Good Witch of the North in MGM's 1939 film *The Wizard of Oz*. Her full name was Mary William Ethelbert Appleton Burke (also Mrs. Florenz Ziegfeld), and she had a long stage and film career. She was the daughter of Billy Burke, a famous clown of his generation, and drew her nickname from him.[xxxi]

Sunday, we slept disgracefully late. It was quite chilly, but we walked for about three hours in the old part of town, took a few pictures and then at six, ate a big steak dinner. We sure are tired of German food. If I didn't have to eat potatoes twice a day, I might lose some weight. Today we found a place that makes quite good ice cream. Nearly all of the ice cream establishments close up in the winter. The Germans won't eat it. Their ice cream is not rich, more like our milk sherbets.

Fraulein Keck was here Sunday evening for three hours. We had a very nice visit with her. We plan to go to Tübingen some weekend very soon. It is fun working for the government because you get to observe all national holidays. Next Wednesday we won't have to work because good ole George was born on that day.

Well, I must wash out some stockings and file my nails. It is already 10:00. Thank you for the sweet-smelling Valentine. Bill didn't buy me a thing, said they had no Valentine's Day in Germany. Well, write soon.

Love and kisses,
Lois

> February 18, 1939
> Stuttgart, Germany

Dear Mother and Dad,

I am now inclined to write a thesis on how not to take a bath in Germany. Just about every week I decide it just isn't worth the effort. To begin with, one should never plan anything for the rest of the day. Secondly, one should choose a day when the nerves are rested and one's patience can be greatly extended. It is also always advisable to have something absorbing to read or do. Then the long hours will not seem to stretch into eternity.

Monday evening we finally got to the supper given by an American girl, Ursula, after a much delayed bath time. Ursula, who has been here for four years. She now works for the Consul. She has an adorable little apartment. We had baked beans with catsup, bread and butter and hot dogs. For dessert, Jell-O with pineapple and marshmallows and two kinds of cakes. And, Maxwell House coffee. All the food was from the States. Just imagine tasting real coffee after all of these months. Many store windows with real coffee beans in the displays, have signs saying, "These beans are for display purposes only." Ursula had her apartment all decorated with Fasching decorations. We all had such a good time that we stayed disgracefully late and arrived home at 1:45.

Sunday afternoon, we went to see the first big Fasching parade. This is a three-day celebration here. It was a very good parade in spite of the fact it was cold and drizzling. It was so similar to a Mardi Gras carnival only, of course, New Orleans is wealthier, and it is more elaborate. There were several good political take-offs which really surprised us. One had the men from Mars coming to New York. Many of the people on the streets were in costume. Of course, tomorrow is the big day. All of the stores are closing at 1:00. There is to be another big parade in the afternoon. If we had time we would have gone to Mainz or Cologne for Fasching. Munich also has a big celebration.

Fasching parade, Stuttgart, February 1939

I am surprised Stuttgart has even this much considering how conservative and saving the people of Wurttemberg are.

**Fasching** dates back many centuries and can almost be considered a fifth season in Germany: spring, summer, fall, winter, and Fasching. Fasching, or "Fastnacht," takes place in January and February and originates from the word "fasting." It marks the week leading up to Ash Wednesday and the 40-day period of Lent that follows, culminating in Easter. For many Germans, Fasching represents a time to "let off steam," and live it up before the austere period of Lent. Fasching incorporates festivals, parades, music, and many "foolish" activities.[xxxii]

Bill is at the Consul tonight. I have washed out very much neglected underwear and unpacked some things. I am doing all I can to hold my fur coat together. There is a very nice couple from Freiburg coming to work. We met them this weekend. They are from the University of Wisconsin. He and Bill thought they had met somewhere before. He asked where we were from and said he was in Independence, Kansas once for a National Debate Tournament in 1934. Just imagine meeting him here. He is taking a permanent job here and she says her family is just going to pop! She is so pretty, the Barbara Stanwyck type, only much lovelier. She is going to work, too.

Bill and I are quitting either on the first or fifteenth of May. We are going to a cafe now and order hot chocolate and put marshmallows in it. We are certainly looking forward to that.

Love,
Lois


February 27, 1939
Stuttgart, Germany

Dear Mother and Dad,

We are enjoying your letters about what you did in Texas and am so glad you decided to go to Mexico. I would like to go to Mexico City sometime.

The last few days have been so warm and sunshiny. Saturday afternoon we walked for blocks and blocks. We have tickets for the opera next Friday night and are going to hear *Carmen*. It is not expensive, and we are going to try and go once a week. Sunday, we went out to one of the smaller castles here, Villa Berg. There are so many palaces around here for this was the capital of Wurttemberg and all of the members of the royal family had their residences nearby. After, we went to the Zeiss Ikon Photo exhibition. They make wonderful camera equipment here. They had pictures from all over the world by small cameras and then enlarged. Those from the States were very good.

I mailed Judith's birthday present today. I bought her a pair of handmade Yugoslavian house shoes. They are bright red leather with knitting on top. It does not seem possible that she is almost a year old. We will be so glad to know when Bill's sister, Jo, has her baby and is alright. She has been feeling so poorly and I know she will be glad to have it over with. We'll wait to send something when we know if it is a boy or a girl.

Late Wednesday we went to the Deutsches Ausland-Institute and had them look up Bill's family tree. Of course, it will take several months. It is a very large place with lovely offices. One man, I noticed, had a copy of *Life*

on his desk. About all of the pumping they did
was to ask us what we thought about President
Roosevelt and what he said about France being
our war boundary. We told him we knew nothing about it and he said nothing more. It is a
shame that the United States is becoming more
and more unpopular every day here. The Germans
dislike Roosevelt more than the dyed in the wool
Republicans at home. I feel that relations are
more strained between Germany and American than
they are with any other country. When we are as
far away as we are, that is so unnecessary.

Lots of love,
Lois

> March 6, 1939
> Stuttgart, Germany

Dear Mother and Dad,

On Tuesday evening we went out to the Consul's
house. The boys worked on German correspondence.
I visited with Mrs. L'Hereaux. As I said before,
he is an overbearing sort of fellow. He is very
lazy considering how much work there is to do.
His wife is very nice and pretty.

Thursday evening, we ate supper of our groceries that arrived from Hamburg: shredded wheat
with bananas, crackers, peanut butter, and
tomato juice. Bill wanted a beer, so Jackie went

with him. He is trying to drink several a week to gain weight. He is too thin, having lost some when he had the flu. He has found a Munich export that he really likes.

Today I did not work because the old bladder started burning. It has almost stopped now. I am convinced it is from all of the tomato juice I have been drinking. It was the first thing on Dr. Hoffman's list to avoid. If the burning returns, I shall go to the clinic in Tübingen. Of course, it could have been the Coke or the carbonated water. This is a real opportunity to test which foods might cause it. And probably the fact that I stand all day only eggs it on.

*Carmen* was a bit disappointing because the Germans couldn't get the carefree, dashing spirit of the Spaniards. Sunday morning we had our bath and ate a late lunch. Gordon Frost and an Italian friend of his stopped by and we all had dinner together. The Italian chap, Nino, is charming. His father has money in Germany and he is here to spend it. He seems to be doing a pretty good job of it. He is now studying at Heidelberg. I don't believe that anyone can be nicer or more of a gentleman than a really high type Italian. It is too bad they go from one extreme to the other. He is from northern Italy and now he looks down on the southern Italians. That is one of Mussolini's biggest problems, to build up a feeling of unity in the country. He has wonderful schemes for doing this. How Nino laughed at the Rome-Berlin Axis. He would pound himself on the chest and say, "Axis Boy!" and then roll up laughing. The people just don't feel it. He said last summer an Italian school ship was in Hamburg. There were also French and German ones. One day both the latter invited the Italians to visit the ships. He said all of the Italians went to the French ship and the Germans were left alone. They, the Italians, are much more like the French.

We are going to quit work the first of May. We are going to get our next two checks in dollars, which, if cashed out of the country, you realize their full value. We wouldn't have to work here very long to earn back all that we spent this year. So now we are planning a trip! We are going to the Balkan countries besides the trip to Paris, etc. Pretty soon we are going to decide on our sailing date so we can get a good cabin.

Well, I have to hunt down the Frau and ask for some coal. The room is getting chilly. Last night the butter blew off of our windowsill and we won't get any until Tuesday. Funny joke!

Love, Lois

Mom said, "We were so ignorant and didn't know much about the Balkans. Hardly anyone did. The travel agent suggested it and of course, we were so glad we went."

*Eyes and Ears*

March 10, 1939
Stuttgart, Germany

Dear Mother and Dad,

I have practically nothing to write about. I have been in bed for five days but plan to get up this afternoon. My bladder did not clear up as I thought it would. I have been going to a specialist who seems to be mighty fine. He said I had no cysts and needed no dilation, only had severe inflammation by a certain type of bacteria. I take rust colored pills which stain the urine an identical color. It must be a very common problem the world over for he knew immediately what I had, and his method of treatment is very similar to Dr. Hoffman's. He is a very short, fat man but as clean as a pie. I am going to work in the morning.

Bill just got his invitation to go on the Carl Schurz trip from the 17th to the 30th of May. It sounds wonderful. Now we are going to write and see if I can be included. It is too expensive to go and pay your own way for they let you see the upper crust of Germany, staying in the best hotels, eating the best food. Immediately after that trip, we would start our traveling. We have it planned as far as Munich to Budapest and Vienna by boat down the Danube and from there we don't know. I am sure we won't go further south as it will be too hot. Probably will touch a couple of other places around Belgrade. Then we will come back to Tübingen and get our clothes cleaned up and leave for Paris. Then we will go up through Belgium and Holland on the way to Hamburg to get the boat. We shall probably limit our stay in England to one week. We are certainly excited about it.

Well, I am going to meet Bill for lunch before going to the doctor. I am leaving that bed with a joyous shout!

Love and kisses,
Lois

Carl Christian Schurz was a German revolutionary and an American statesman, journalist, and reformer. He emigrated to the United States after the German revolutions of 1848–49. The **National Carl Schurz Association**, or NCSA, was originally established in 1930 as the Carl Schurz Memorial Foundation, named in honor of the ambassador, senator, and Secretary of the Interior on the centenary of his birth. The founders were several German professors and teachers who each wished to promote and improve the teaching of German language and culture, and to foster friendship between the United States and German-speaking countries. Shortly after the Foundation was established, Gustav Oberlaender founded the Oberlaender Trust for the purpose of sponsoring visits by American scholars to German-speaking countries for the purposes of study and research.[xxxiii]

*Eyes and Ears*

March 13, 1939
Stuttgart, Germany

Dear Mother and Dad,

I bought you a cute little tea warmer Saturday. They are so practical and yet so very attractive. I would like to buy more but they are breakable.

The more we talk to people the more our trip expands. Today we included Constantinople and Athens. Never did we dream that we could possibly go to so many places and see so much. The people who have decided to stay permanently are sure jealous.

They plan and dream with us but have to be tied down with work.

Well, I have nothing much to say and my chatter is entirely aimless. I'll write more later.

Lots of love,
Lois

March 21, 1939
Stuttgart. Germany

Dear Mother and Dad,

Spring is here! And, how! It is wonderfully cold and sunny here. It seems as though quite a lot has happened since I last wrote. For one thing, Germany has increased its territory. This was done with practically no excitement. In fact, from our observation, it seemed to be almost a feeling of indifference. I am sure no one was more surprised than the German people. It was rather difficult to get information as we had to rely on the German papers and radio. It happened so quickly that the London papers arrived too late to be of much benefit. We all said we bet the American newspapers had a good time playing with the big story. Our sorrow is that we bought a nice map of Europe the day before, and the very next day it was out of date.

On March 15, 1939, **German troops invaded Czechoslovakia,** taking over Bohemia and establishing a protectorate over Slovakia. Hitler's invasion of Czechoslovakia was the end of attempts to appease Hitler; it proved he had lied to the Munich Conference and showed he wasn't just interested in a "Greater Germany" (the Czechs were not Germans). On March 17, Chamberlain gave a speech stating he could no longer trust Hitler not to invade other countries. On March 31 Chamberlain promised to defend Poland if Germany invaded.[xxxiv]

Saturday afternoon we went all through the new castle here. It is directly across from the old one. The new one was built about 1760, I believe. It is in the very center of town and we pass it daily. One of the wings was taken up with a museum of war relics; armors, guns, shields, swords. They made you think of King Arthur and his knights. Another part of the museum was crystal, china, clothes, furniture, etc. The other part was the residence section. The furniture was lovely and quite regal looking. The throne room all in red velvet impressed me. It was said that they built this castle and forgot to put in a kitchen. So, for a long time they carried food over from the old castle. We enjoyed the darling little sleighs down in the basement. They were for only one person, drawn by a horse and a driver perched up on a funny little high stool. Some, for the children, were in the shapes of animals.

Sunday was Army day, as if every day isn't. We thought there was to be a big parade at 8:30 in the morning so we crawled out of bed. We saw only two troops pass by. One was good. It was a tank with a band. All of the members of the band rode on the tanks, about 2 or 3 to a tank. They were colorfully dressed and it was really effective and novel.

Army Day, Stuttgart, 1939

We finally gave up on the parade and went to a little town 20 minutes from here to see the barracks. They had about 10,000 soldiers in the unit we visited. They have very modern buildings with comfortable living quarters. Their study rooms with guns and maps were interesting. We also ate eintopf (stew) there.

Afterwards, we came back to a coffee house in Ludwigsburg before we went to see the perfectly huge castle there. It is a copy of Versailles in Paris with formal gardens and is supposed to be the biggest castle in all of Europe. I came upon a statue of a child standing by a woman with a perfectly big stomach. I thought, well, this is the first pregnant statue I have seen until I looked around at all of the statues and saw they were so constructed. They were made during a period of great abundance and it was the fashion to have an overhanging stomach. We didn't get through the castle because it was so cold. We will go back soon.

Ludwigsburg Palace, Stuttgart, March 1939

We hope to have our trip plans settled by the end of the

week so we can book passage home. I didn't realize the World's Fair will be bringing so many people to America. They say they expect 50,000 Britons alone. They are having good excursion rates for the Germans. So, we mustn't wait too long if we want a good cabin.

Well, I must stop now. Write soon.

Lots of love,
Lois

March 25, 1939<br>Stuttgart, Germany

Dear Mother and Dad,

It seems as if we are never going to have any lasting spring here. It has been so bad the last two weeks, so cold and damp. We have nothing much planned for the weekend. I just now finished washing my hair. I couldn't get an appointment and I hate to sit and wait my turn. Anyway, they wash only your hair and not your scalp. Tomorrow night we are going to the opera and shall hear Aida! I am going to read the story of it tonight.

Did I tell you that Martha Long is working here now? She is the American from Tübingen. There is another nice girl here from Leipzig. She is from Illinois. Her name is Louise Bittner. She came over on a Dutch freighter last September, the week of the crisis. The eight other passengers cancelled their passage. She was the only woman aboard. She said she had never been treated so lovely in all of her life. They went a full month on the water. At Valentines, the whole crew chipped in and sent her a box of chocolates. She said she has felt as much respect for the Dutch men as she has disrespect for the German men.

The coffee arrived today! I am afraid our poor Postum will be deserted until the coffee is gone. I haven't been able to read any of the *Cosmopolitan* yet but found the papers very interesting. There are so many Kappas being married now.

Fraulein Charlotte Bulley took us out for coffee Tuesday evening. She is quite a wealthy little girl who visits Tübingen. She is a friend of Fraulein Keck. She is probably no more than twenty. She gets so excited and talks so fast that I only understood about a third of her German.

We think we may have a three day vacation at Easter. We are going to Strasbourg for the weekend, whether or not. It is in France, in Alsace near the German border. There is supposed to be a wonderful cathedral there. In filling out our visas, we wanted to write in, for the purpose of trip, To Eat! Everyone says the food is so good in France. Anything would be better than the starch of Germany.

I imagine my package to Judith for her first birthday has arrived in time. If it isn't her first package addressed to herself, or Miss Judith Woods, at least it's her first from Europe.

Lots of love,
Lois

>April 1, 1939
>Stuttgart, Germany

Dear Mother and Dad,

As we are going to Tübingen tomorrow, we will retire early. Spring is here at last and how we have enjoyed the sunshine these last few days. This afternoon we went out to a lovely little palace built by Wilhelm I. It is a copy of a Spanish castle. It is really very lovely inside. Once every summer they hold a Mozart concert in the largest ballroom. The greenhouse really caught our attention, varying from cactus rooms to rooms of azaleas and hedge roses. The orchids are the real specialty now. Germany has the most beautiful flowers I have ever seen.

Coffee is now rationed out just like butter.

The name Penelope is so nice for Jo and Ross' baby. I'm glad she seemed to have the birth easily.

We now have our actual Easter plans. We get off for four days. Thursday night at seven, we are leaving for Paris. Then we are going to plan every minute of our time so that we can see as much as possible. I hope we can go on an American Express Tour for they show you so much in a very short length of time. The rest of our plans are as follows: Bill it to quit the first of May to go to Tübingen to enroll in the university. He will only be about 10 days late.

"Even though I stayed at Tübingen University only four months, I did return to receive my diploma. It was an auditorium ceremony with the dean of the school and many Hitler salutes. The education I received there was disappointing, all propaganda," Dad later wrote.

I am going to stay here until the fifteenth and then on the 17th we go on the Carl Schurz tour through Germany. This trip is free for Bill, but I have to pay to go. It is expensive but it is cheaper than both of us making a similar trip on our own. This trip lasts from the 17th-30th of May. It starts in Berlin and ends in Cologne, near Carl Schurz' birthplace.

Soon after the Carl Schurz trip, we plan to start out on our own trip. You had better get out your Atlas and follow closely. We will go to Vienna, Budapest, Belgrade by boat down the Danube. Then by train to Bucharest, then to Constantinople and on a boat to Athens, and from there to the Isle of Rhodes. Probably from Rhodes to Cairo and back to Rhodes to Trieste and Venice. It takes nine days on the boat from Rhodes to Venice. The boat stops at all of the interesting countries like Albania. How we thrill at the idea of seeing Venice again. It all sounds expensive, but it is really dirt cheap. This can't be done in less than six weeks so we can't sail until about the middle of July. Then we will stop for a week in England. We must see as much as we can now for when we get back, we probably won't cross the Kansas border for years and years.

I will have time to come home for a couple of weeks before school starts. I have been promised a job at the Royal selling hose directly to the sorority houses. Rothschild's has a store in Lawrence now and I am sure it must have hurt Harzfeld's business. We are trying to locate an apartment. We want a single at the Brady, we think. A big room with a pull-down bed, dinette, and a bath.

Ralph Kole's American fiancée arrived today. They wanted to be married today, his parents' anniversary, but it was impossible. It takes weeks here as they have to prove their ancestry. Ralph and Karen got out of that by being Americans. They have no choice when they can be married, just when they get the call. Imagine!

I feel fine now. The doctor gave me my last treatment. Bill is gaining a little weight now.

Good night, dears.

Lots of love,
Lois


April 13, 1939

Dear Mother and Dad,

Our train left Stuttgart at 6:50 in the evening and we rode all night. There is no real comfort in a third-class train, often nothing but wooden benches. However, we had pillows and managed to sleep a little. The customs were a little more strict than usual because the Germans and French hate each other so.

Louise Bittner, the American girl, and a German boy, Siegfried Arndt, were with us. We went for breakfast. How good the coffee is in France, even with all of the chicory.

*Eyes and Ears*

In the morning in Paris, we started from Place de L'Opera on the American Express trip and saw many interesting statues on the way to the Tuileries Gardens by the Louvre. From there we had an impressive view up the Champs Elysees to the Arc de Triomphe. Then we saw the Tower Saint-Jacques and the Palais de Justice. We went inside the Sainte Chapelle. It was built in the 13th century by Saint Louis as a worthy receptacle for the sacred relics brought back from the Crusades. Then we passed the Luxembourg Palace and gardens. Our next stop was at the Parthenon Church of St Genevieve. Then we went through the university and Latin Quarters. From there we went to an island in the middle of the city and visited Notre Dame. It is the oldest cathedral in France. Then we passed the Church of Saint Gervais where in 1918, on Good Friday, a Big Bertha shot came 70 miles from the German line and 72 persons were killed in the church.

In the afternoon we rode down the Grand Boulevards to the Madeleine Church. It was built by Napoleon, as is so much of Paris. Then we went to the Palace de La Concorde to the Alexander III Bridge, which is the finest bridge in Paris. Next we went to Invalides, a huge building built by Louis XIV for the disabled soldier. Back of this is the Tower of Napoleon. It is beautiful and impressive. We actually visited the Arc de Triomphe. It was built by Napoleon to commemorate his victories. It also protects the Tomb of the

Unknown Soldier and its ever-burning flame. After that we went up to Montmartre and visited the Church of the Sacred Heart. On the way down we saw the artist colony. It is where you see the real Paris life.

We were a little bit tired, so we started out looking for a hotel. Little did we know what troubles we would have. Being Easter there, there were thousands of British visiting Paris. At first we thought maybe they didn't think we were married so Bill said to our manager, "Well, we're married if that makes any difference." The manager said, "If that made any difference, I would have no business." Louise wanted to stay where we were because she thought it was nicer to be chaperoned. So that made it doubly hard. After about two hours, though, we were settled and had a nice room with a private bath.

On Saturday we went shopping to see the Paris stores. Bill got a pair of light tan sports shoes. I bought some darling slacks with a coat and halter for wearing on the boat. We bought a couple of etchings. In the big stores the things are nice and very reasonable. It was wonderful to see well-dressed people again. The women are small and have beautiful legs. Bill thought the makeup was atrocious, so artificial. From our hurried observations, we just love the French people. I guess they are rather weak and have a tendency to degenerate fast. Negroes are socially acceptable in France. They go everywhere and are always with a white person. I was so surprised to see so many of them here. If I were a Negro, I would go to Paris.

I can't say enough about French food. It is so tastefully served and dainty that you feel satisfied at the end of the meal. On Saturday we decided to have lobster since we had never tasted it. Little did we two Kansas numbskulls know that you are not supposed to eat lobster and drink wine with it. As wine comes with every meal, we drank it. It didn't hurt my iron stomach but poor Bill! All Saturday night he was ill. Both of us were awake all night. But he was fine by noon, so we went out. We had perfectly wonderful weather. I felt well dressed in my navy blue and yellow coat. I had violets for Easter.

On Easter afternoon we walked the full length of the Champs Elysees. Here we saw the Easter parade. This is a magnificent avenue. We stopped at a small place and had malted milk. Then we went up the Eiffel Tower. It was an experience and the

Lois and Bill, Eiffel Tower, Paris, April 1939

view was lovely. But it was so crowded that it took forever to get to the top. The elevators can take only so many at a time.

In the evening we ate at a Chinese cafe and had chow mein before seeing *You Can't Take It With You*. It was wonderful to see a movie after eight months. We wanted to go to a typical nightclub but Bill wasn't up to it.

Louise Bitner and Lois, Versailles, Paris, April 1939

Monday, we went to Versailles. It is such a perfectly huge place that in the course of a day it is impossible to see much of it. We went through the parts of the palace that were open. We saw the Hall of Mirrors, where the Treaty of Versailles was signed in 1919. Versailles housed 10,000 people at the time of King Louis XIV and Marie Antoinette. The garden and fountains are perfectly beautiful. Our visit was much too short. We took the 10:25 train back to Stuttgart.

Oh, yes. I had some famous French onion soup made with melted cheese and bread toasted cubes and then baked in a casserole.

Bill just handed me a glass of grapefruit juice before going to bed. I will write soon. We leave for Stuttgart in the morning. I hope this letter hasn't bored you, but you know, these letters are my accounts and I know that I would never sit down and write it all out for myself.

Lots of love,
Lois

April 20, 1939<br>Stuttgart, Germany

Dear Mother and Dad,

This has been quite a day here in Germany. Hitler celebrated his 50th birthday and because of such, there was a big national holiday. Really, all of the celebration was carried out very effectively. Each shop devoted one large window for Hitler. Most of them only had a large picture or bust with floral decorations and flags. Some of them very nicely worked out the history of the Reich. Those shops selling materials told the story of synthetic fabrics very well. The streets have been banner bedecked for a couple of days. Then tonight, all of the houses had windowsills filled with 4 or 5 red tumblers with candles in them. You have no idea how lovely it was in these old houses and streets. If it had been celebrating a different occasion, I am sure

Bad Constatt, German Military Review, April 1939

Bill and I would have been carried away with rapture.

This morning we went out to a small suburb called Bad Cannstatt. There we saw a small review of bicycles and horseback troops. The crowd was more interesting than the parade.

Then tonight there was a torchlight parade consisting of mostly the SA and SS men. There were so many of them that I told Bill that surely, they must be going in a circle and repeating themselves. I know that Berlin must have had a tremendous celebration.

A celebration of **Führer Adolf Hitler's 50th birthday** was held on this day in 1939. The day was declared a public holiday, while Berlin held the largest military parade in the entire history of Nazi Germany. Infamous propaganda minister Joseph Goebbels was the main organizer of the ceremony, ensuring Hitler's cult of personality was reinforced through the event.[xxxv]

```
    Our holiday came as a complete surprise.
Sixty Jews had been invited to get their visas
today and we were sure we would be working. It
was about five o'clock yesterday when word came
around that we were to close. I am sure it must
have come from the Embassy in Berlin or even
Washington as Mr. Hanaker had no intention of
closing. It was better for the Jews for they are
not supposed to leave their homes on holidays.
Then, too, it was more tactful, for after all,
Roosevelt has sent a telegram which won't be
answered until next week. If you could read the
German newspapers, you would know the answer
now, however. They hate Roosevelt more than the
Republicans do.
```

Here is a partial text of the lengthy telegram that President Roosevelt sent to Adolf Hitler:

His Excellency

Adolph Hitler,

Chancellor of the German Reich,

Berlin, Germany

...Are you willing to give assurance that your armed forces will not attack or invade the territory or possessions of the following independent nations: Finland, Estonia, Latvia, Lithuania, Sweden, Norway, Denmark, The Netherlands, Belgium, Great Britain and Ireland, France, Portugal, Spain, Switzerland,

Liechtenstein, Luxemburg, Poland, Hungary, Rumania, Bulgaria, Greece, Turkey, Iraq, the Arabias, Syria, Palestine, Egypt and Iran.

Such an assurance clearly must apply not only to the present day but also to a future sufficiently long to give every opportunity to work by peaceful methods for a more permanent peace...[xxxvi]

In Tübingen, last Saturday, we sold our bicycles. We stayed with Keck and had lots of fun.

I got a letter from Bea Stewart. She was so sorry she didn't know that we were in Europe, but she will be back in July or August. Perhaps we can see her then.

Tuesday night we went to a coffee house that always has musical entertainment. There was a group of Hungarian Gypsies playing, mostly violin and cello. They were so good, had so much personality and life. Their costumes were lovely. They played difficult pieces and yet, can't read a note of music. We plan to go to Heidelberg this weekend. It's one place we must see before we leave.

We have booked passage home. We are sailing on the *Hamburg* on July 13th. We will spend a week in England then on July 21, we will sail from Southampton on the SS *New York*, arriving in New York on July 28. Then we want to spend a couple of days at the World's Fair and go to Washington. We have decided to rent one of the single apartments at the Brady. They are very reasonable, $30.00 for the nine winter months and $20.00 for the summer. They will decorate for us and let us choose the paper.

We enjoyed the pictures so much. Judith has changed so I wouldn't recognize her. She is just as cute as a bug's ear. I was so pleased with the picture of Dad, it's so natural.

Only three short months and then we will have a glorious reunion! I can smell that chicken frying now!

Lots of love,
Lois

April 26, 1939
Stuttgart, Germany

Dear Mother and Dad,

We had a very nice weekend in Heidelberg. It is truly as lovely and romantic as it sounds. Saturday was sunny but Sunday it rained all day. We were with Gordon Frost who worked a month at the Consulate. Heidelberg is certainly not true Germany and I know many American tourists get the wrong impression of Germany. The town itself is quite modern. We noticed that even the coffee

Heidelberg, Germany, April 1939

was better there. The hotels all have running water. The old castle is perfectly thrilling. It was partially destroyed by the French hundreds of years ago and has never been restored, just left to age and go to ruins. The bridge is just as nice and equally old. Both are made out of red sandstone which is peculiar to that part of Germany. It is a place that grows on you and it somehow pulls you back. I already have the greatest desire to return.

Saturday night we went to the former Europaischer Hotel for a small party an American girl was giving. It was lots of fun but we stayed up too late.

Now it is almost time for us to quit work. Monday is a big holiday, the German Labor Day. We plan to go to Freiburg this weekend. Right now, we are busy packing up winter things. It doesn't seem possible that in another three weeks we will be traveling for the rest of our time abroad.

Don't be hurt if I should forget a card on Mother's Day. I have thought of it several times but never at the right times. But you know I love you just the same and shall be thinking of you.

I am drinking one of my rare treats, Coke. They cost about the equivalent of 15 cents here. We sit around and think of what American food we shall have first. I am sure it will have nothing to do with potatoes.

Hope to hear from you soon.

Love,
Lois

May 3, 1939
Stuttgart, Germany

Dear Mother and Dad,

I shall write this while I wait for some water to boil and then I must continue with my "undies," as we are sending our trunks to Hamburg this Saturday and have lots to do. I have all of my wash dresses clean and ready to go but I don't think I'll ever get to wear them. We are having perfectly horrible weather. It is raining constantly and cold.

Our weekend was perfect. The weather was not the best, but we had a clear, beautiful day in Lucerne. We left here on Saturday noon and got to Freiburg about 4:30. It's a grand old, charming

Freiburg, Germany, Maypole Ceremony, May 1939

town and just so typical of the Black Forest area. The cathedral is a beautiful work of architecture. The wood carving of The Last Supper is quite good. We enjoyed watching the ceremony of placing the maypole square by the wonderful old stone church.

We left Freiburg at 7:30 and went to spend the night in Basel. There is nothing there to see as it is a large, industrial city. Early the next morning, we took the train to lovely Old Lucerne.

Dating back to the 13th century, the **Maypole celebration** in Germany is held on the first day of May to herald in the beginning of spring. The same celebration takes place in villages and towns throughout southern Germany. The Maypole is a huge tree shorn of all of its leaves except for growth at the top. A crane hoists it up, unlike the days when men had to muscle it in place. The top of the tree is adorned with decorations, symbols to honor town heroes and with ribbons and wreaths. As the townspeople gather, the beer flows freely and wurst

*Eyes and Ears*

is to be eaten. Bandstands blare music and traditional dirndl and lederhosen clad participants sing and dance, whirling and clapping. The culmination of the celebration is the wrapping of the Maypole in blue and white ribbon, Bavaria's traditional colors. Every Maypole is in danger of being stolen by a neighboring village. Successful raids can result in a healthy ransom of beer and food.[xxxvii]

Lucerne, Switzerland is built by a large lake and rising all around are the Alps. It's no wonder it is always crowded with Americans. In our hotel, we had a balcony that overlooked the lake and the mountains. The proprietor knew we had been eating German food and besides, she just loves Americans. She did feed us! Our tummies were stuffed with butter, steak, ice cream, and whipped cream. We were in Lucerne for a little over a day. We left Monday at noon and spent most of the afternoon in Zurich. There we saw a big Labor Day Parade.

Those poor people down in that little country are scared to death. They hate "Mr. Smith," and say he

Lucerne, Switzerland, May 1939

is so very unpredictable. The night after his big speech, they said they didn't sleep all night. They have all of the bridges across the Rhine ready to blow up at any minute. But Switzerland could do nothing alone. However, I think they are safe from invasion. I think it is poor Poland which better watch out.

We are all hoping that this Wagner-Rogers Refugee Child Act won't go through. It is Germany's problem and not ours. Goodness knows we are doing our share. We are the only country which will allow them to immigrate. If everyone could work with them and read the letters, I am sure they would feel sympathetic. I could weep for the poor people, but I don't think they should be allowed to go over to replace American citizen's jobs. Our economic set-up isn't strong enough for that.

Bill and I were invited to the Hanakers for lunch the day of Hitler's speech, so we got to hear it there. We had a grand dinner.

Love,
Lois


My mother told me that on the train trip to Switzerland she put German marks (Reichsmarks) into a condom and inserted the condom vaginally to hide them. The Germans did not want German money leaving the country and penalties were severe for those who did so. The exchange rate of Reichsmarks to Swiss francs was so much better, but she said they were quite nervous as she sat demurely on the train. If she had been caught, it would not have gone well. Whether or not this was the occasion for an adventure to Switzerland, I don't know.

The **1939 Wagner-Rogers Bill** proposed admitting 20,000 German refugee children to the United States outside of normal immigration quotas. The bill never came to a vote despite congressional hearings and public debate.[xxxviii]

**Hitler's response to Roosevelt**. Though prepared for German ears, this speech was broadcast on April 28, 1939, not only on all German radio stations but on hundreds of others throughout the world; in the United States it was carried by the major networks. Never before or afterward was there such a world-wide audience for Hitler as he had that day. It was considered by many to be his finest speech.

After his usual introductory dissertation on the iniquities of the Versailles treaty and the many injustices and long suffering heaped upon the German people because of it, Hitler addressed Great Britain and its pledge of support to Poland with words which shook an uneasy Europe. Hitler claimed that reports of Germany's intention to attack Poland were "mere inventions of the international press." The inventions of the press, he continued, had led Poland to make its agreement with Great Britain. Not one of millions of people listening knew that just three weeks prior he had given written orders to his armed forces to prepare for the destruction of Poland by September 1 "at the latest."

Hitler next turned to President Roosevelt, and here the German dictator reached the summit of his oratory. To a normal ear, to be sure, it reeked of hypocrisy and deception. But to the hand-picked members of his Reichstag, and to millions of Germans, its masterly sarcasm and irony were a delight. He continued his ridicule of the American President and evoked laughter from his paunchy deputies by reciting the names of countries named by Roosevelt's telegram with exaggerated and sarcastic affect.[xxxix]

```
                                    Stuttgart, Germany
                                        May 8, 1939
Dear Mr. Brown,
```

I was very pleased to receive your kind letter inviting me to speak before the Kansas City Rotary Club on a Thursday noon during the month of August or early September. I shall be happy to avail myself of this opportunity.

I cannot now state definitely what the subject matter or the talk will be. I suppose your club will be interested in things political; however, I often feel that a one year's study on this continent does not qualify a person to speak reliably on that subject. In the weeks to come I shall attempt to formulate the subject matter of a topic, political or otherwise, in which I hope your club will not be disappointed.

I thank you for your kind consideration. With best wishes to you and Mr. Woods, I remain

Yours sincerely,
(Signed) Wm Kandt

May 10, 1939
Stuttgart, Germany

Dear Mother and Dad,

We are so busy packing, buying tickets, mending, that I have only time to squeeze in a letter before going to sleep. Our hotel life begins this Sunday. We have all of our tickets but don't plan to pay for them until just before we leave in case the international situation should get tight again. One never knows what to think these days. We plan to go to Berlin on Monday if our railroad tickets get here. They are included in the Carl Schurz trip.

We have had lots of fun buying gifts for the members of our families. It is fun to go shopping around and plan and try to find something to suit each of you. The men are always more of a problem than the women.

It remains rainy and cold. Bill wears his topcoat all of the time and is still chilly. We hope it will be better in north Germany. The rain has soaked all of the flavor out of the vegetables.

Oranges are very scarce again. I wish Germany would make a barter with another country for some. I sold my fur collar coat. I only got 20 marks for it, but it really was in terrible condition. Topsy, a British girl at the office wanted it. She doesn't have much money and didn't care to invest money in a German coat. She said she would have it repaired and then it would last her a year or so until she returned to England. We had Bill's spring suit cleaned lately and it only took two weeks.

Bill was only in Tübingen for a couple of days. I'm glad he quit the first as we never would have gotten everything done.

Helen came over last Friday and spent the night with me and we had lots of fun shopping and talking. Fred Helliger got his doctor's degree and he and Fran plan to sail the first week of June. He is very anxious to get to his father.

Sorry I didn't have any news. But after this week my letters will be jammed with sightseeing.

Love,
Lois

*Eyes and Ears*

May 14, 1939
Tübingen, Germany

Dear Mother and Dad,

Bill came over here this morning to wait until we can go to Berlin. We wanted to go in the morning but as we must travel on a group ticket, we have to wait until Tuesday morning. Berlin is a long way from here, thirteen hours by train. We were so disappointed because Elizabeth, the German girl at Missouri University last year, invited us for dinner and the theatre on Tuesday evening. Germany is so sectioned that it would have been nice to see a Berlin home.

Yesterday was my last working day. We sent our luggage to Hamburg and we felt sort of lost. Last night the office force had a wonderful farewell party for us. It was in a private room at the nicest hotel. We had a good dinner, then we danced to American records on a portable.

A group of the Visa gang, Stuttgart, May 1939

It was really a grand affair. We were certainly noisy. Get twenty-five Americans together and then compare them to twenty-five stiff Germans. Three of the vice Consuls came and said they wish the Consular parties were as much fun. It was a wonderful party and Bill and I really appreciated it.

We invested in color photography this week. It is so cheap here and so expensive at home. We knew it would be a lifelong regret if we missed the opportunity. I can hardly wait to take some of Judy in a brightly colored dress. Norman and Helen have the same exact thing. The projector is strong enough to use for group lectures, if one ever gave an illustrated talk. Now, if the sun would only come out.

The Neckar is flooded. It has rained so much! No wonder the Germans always want to go to war. If I had to live in this weather for many years, I think I would want to take it out on someone. It is still uncomfortably chilly, and I wonder if it will ever get warmer.

As usual, our plans have changed. In short, we won't have time to go to Hamburg but will go to Belgium and cross the channel at Dover. So just cross Venice and Hamburg off of the itinerary.

Love,
Lois

*Eyes and Ears*

May 21, 1939
Reichenberg, Sudetenland

Dear Mother and Dad,

It has been a busy week but a very happy one. We left Tübingen on Tuesday morning and had a long ride to Berlin. It was supposedly a fast train, but the distance is only 700 kilometers, so compared to our trains, it is very slow. It was a beautiful day and there were eight of us on the train, so the time passed quickly. We had a good meal in the diner.

Train trip to Berlin with the MacLeods, May 1939

We arrived in Berlin at 9:30 and decided to walk up and down Unter den Linden Strasse. In doing so, we met several American students and we all went for coffee and spent several hours trying to solve the world diplomatic situation. I, myself, am very much anti-Nazi now, but just wonder if I won't find myself defending Germany in many ways when I get home and am being dubbed pro-Nazi.

Berlin, May 1939

Wednesday was a free day and we spent most of it getting visas for the Balkan states. Wednesday evening the 63 American students making the Carl Schurz trip met for the first time. We had a huge banquet where introductions were made. We were given luggage stickers and told the rules of traveling. We spent Thursday in Berlin. In the morning we rode through the city.

One interesting stop was at the new subway station. It is huge, white tiled with all new shops in it. This also serves as an air raid shelter, the entire thing being bomb proof. It would accommodate thousands. Berlin is well advanced in this precaution. There is a new square in the center of town which has a victory statue in the center. Under this is a situation room accommodating one million people! Berlin is building so extensively that it will be twelve years before the present building plans will be completed. We visited the Olympic stadiums now called the Reich Sports Field.

At noon we went out to Potsdam. It is 15 miles from Berlin and is a lovely little, old town, much nicer than Berlin, which is now made horrid by so many huge, white pillars. One is never given a chance to forget the government, the Axis, or any power in Berlin.

Berlin, street of the Rome-Berlin Axis, May 1939

After seeing the Palace Sans Souci, we returned to Berlin at about 10:00. Friday morning we went to visit a large, government building in the process of being constructed. The materials looked awfully poor, especially the bricks. I have to wonder how long they will hold up. We visited the wonderful gallery and museum, for not long enough, but we did see some very good things. At noon we had a gorgeous luncheon at the Carl Schurz house. There were many notable guests in the diplomatic and educational field. The centerpieces were all flowers in red, white, and blue, appropriate for the occasion. The introductions and goodwill messages were broadcast.

Afterward we rode three KDF buses to Meissen. It is the famous factory porcelain town, where the process was founded. Early the next morning we went into Dresden. It is a wonderful city, industrial, but it is a grand art center. Many of the buildings are in the Italian Baroque style. The art collection is the best in Germany. We were spellbound to see Raphael's Sistine Madonna. After lunch we went to a beautiful area of low mountains where we saw particular old rock formations. It is called the Saxony Switzerland.

In the late afternoon, we drove to the little resort town of Bad Schandau, a lovely town at a very wide part of the Elbe. This little town was thrilled to have as overnight guests 65 Americans, and they took it upon themselves to give us a big affair. We had a huge banquet with excellent wine, an orchestra, and dancing. We thought it ever so nice of them. Before retiring, we had a farewell get-together for the American Consul from Berlin, who came with us today. He bought a round of real Pilsner beer and then the owners of the beer hall gave us a free one. The mayor then bought a third one! We then went to bed before people started becoming too generous.

Oh, I forgot. In Dresden we went to the City Hall and were greeted by the mayor. Just as we thought we were leaving, they ushered us into a big, paneled room and served us vermouth. We left Bad Schandau this morning and came to Reichenburg. It was a beautiful ride, lovely views. We stopped at the old Czech frontier to see the machine gun vests and barbed wire for defensive measures.

Our crowd is grand and good fun. They have given Bill the name Eyes and Ears because of his camera. They are all representative students from our leading schools. We are fortunate in having no overbearing or unlikable sort of person with us. The three men in charge are fine men and everything is arranged for us. We get to see things that an average tourist would not see. We are always greeted by the mayor or some high city official.

Reichenburg is the capital city of Sudetenland. It is not very pretty but they say it is going to undergo an extensive building program. But it is situated in a valley with low mountains nearby. So far, the people in Sudetenland appear happy and content. They are quite different from the Germans, much more friendly. I imagine that they will start in very gradually, making it like the rest of Germany. We just had a goat dinner. It is a delicious, sweet, juicy meat. Bill has gone to hear Konrad Henlein speak.

Just to save you from planning a meal: fried chicken, rolls, peas, fruit salad, and iced tea. No dessert required. How about it?

I am going to go to bed. Six o'clock comes awfully early in the morning.

Love,
Lois

**Konrad Henlein** was a Sudeten-German politician who fled to Germany after provoking the Czech government and advocating for German annexation of the Czechoslovak Sudeten area. On October 1, 1938, after the Four-Power conference at Munich ceded the Sudeten-German areas to Germany, Henlein was appointed commissioner by the German government for the Sudeten-German territory, and later regional party leader of Sudetenland. At the end of World War II, he committed suicide as a Nazi in Allied custody.[xl]

June 3, 1939
Stuttgart, Germany

Dear Mother and Dad,

I am so ashamed for not writing sooner but I have a thousand apologies and a thousand excuses. After leaving Reichenburg, we simply flew through Germany. I took what little time I had to catch up on washing. When the trip ended, we went to Holland for a few days. Now we are again in Stuttgart. As a farewell gesture, the Carl Schurz trip took it upon themselves to give us all a cold. We are resting in Stuttgart and I am sitting in the sun. At last it is hot here.

As we are not leaving on our Balkan trip until Wednesday, we both will be feeling fine.

Now for the rest of our Carl Schurz trip. Our next stop was Bad Teplitz-Schonau, part of Sudetenland. A beautiful area, green rolling hills with spots of forests and every so often a castle surrounded by a village. We indulged in a lukewarm bath at the baths, but the place was run down. And yet our hotel had hot, running water. I am sure the German Reich will clean them up in short time. It was our only bath the entire trip.

The next day we visited the world famous Karlsbad. It is a lovely location but is so commercialized, everything for the tourists. Some say you get the best food in all of Europe there. The bake shops have a specialty, a wafer like cookie about as big as a dinner plate with a sweet, sugary filling in between. They are served hot and fresh.

Lois and Bill in Karlsbad, May 1939

We went on to a little town to stay all night. It's Franzensbad, a resort town so quiet and restful. There was a good orchestra for dancing in the evening and the other guests had a picnic watching us dance. You know, "swing" is not around in this country. You would love this place. The food is so much better in Sudetenland. People were so friendly and happy.

The next day we left Sudetenland by way of Eger. Here we visited an old city hall, a museum, and the castle was most interesting. The whole town is so old and so German. In the afternoon we went to Bayreuth. It is the town of Richard Wagner. The first opera house, all of painted wood, is a sight of beauty. It was too small for any of Wagner's operas, so he built his own. His house and grave are there.

Nuremberg, Germany, May 1939

We went on to Nuremberg for the night. The town gave us a grand banquet. It was one of those affairs where waiters in tails stand just a few feet apart with a wine bottle in each hand. So, every

time you take a sip, the glass is immediately
refilled. In four or five hours time, you have no
idea how much wine you have had. The next day we
spent going through the old city. It was a real
treat. The castle is built high on a hill and
the huge city walls still stand around the town.
Of course, the town has grown out of it now. The
houses are so tall and narrow because long ago
it wasn't safe to build outside of the walls and
ground was scarce.

Then we drove through the Reich Party fields.
They are so far from being completed, and so huge
in size and so far apart, that it's hard to visualize them as they will be. Right now, they are
ugly but they probably will surface the concrete.
They have a small building showing the models.
There is too much to see in Nuremberg in such a
short time. So, we regrettably left.

**Reich Party Fields:** Hitler declared Nuremberg the "City of Nazi Party Rallies" in 1933 and began construction on monumental buildings in the city's southeastern outskirts for the party's mass meetings. Even today, the remains of these huge structures, built on eleven square kilometers of land, bear witness to the megalomania of the National Socialist regime.[xli]

We went on to Wurzburg. Immediately we went
to hear the woman leader of all German women,
Frau Scholtz-Klink. It was part of the day for
the German students national meeting. We were

pretty much mad that we had to sit through such a long speech. She is a wonderful speaker, full of charm, but not quite clever enough. She gave the same talk as she would give to the peasant women. In other words, she talked below her audience. But the poor, dumb coeds and mothers sat and took it all in. In the evening they were having a "sing" in every square in the city. We walked from group to group and listened. We stayed in a tiny village nearby because the hotels were filled with students in Wurzburg.

**Frau Scholtz-Klink** was head of the Women's Bureau in the German Labour Front, with responsibility for persuading women to work for the good of the Nazi government. At the end of the Second World War Scholtz-Klink went into hiding near Tübingen with her husband using the names Heinrich and Maria Stuckenbrock. However, on February 28, 1948, the couple were identified and arrested by the CIC. She was released from prison in 1953. Her book, *The Woman in the Third Reich*, was published in 1978.[xlii]

The next morning, we were to visit an Arbeitdienst camp, but the boys were home for vacation, so we got some extra sleep.

Nazi Germany established the **German Labor Service**, named Reich Labor Service (RAD) or Arbeitdienst to help mitigate the effects of unemployment, militarize the workforce, and indoctrinate it with Nazi ideology. It was divided into separate sections for men and women. Conscripted personnel had to move into labor barracks. Each RAD person was supplied with a spade, a bicycle, and a paramilitary uniform complete with the RAD symbol – an arm badge in the shape of an upward pointing shovel blade – displayed beside the swastika on the left shoulder. In 1935, men aged 19 and 25 had to serve six months before their military service. It became compulsory for women in June of 1939. Men and women had to work up to 76 hours a week.[xliii]

Frankfurt am Main was our next stop. I don't know whether I like Nuremberg or Frankfurt better. It is an old city, too. The big church is very pleasing and here we saw a military wedding. We visited the house of Goethe. I was surprised to know that he was the son of wealth. At noon the I.G. Farben industry entertained us. I suppose it's more like DuPont than any other U.S. company.

In the afternoon we went to Rhein-Main and went through the Graf Zeppelin. Of course, it can't be used now. They are working furiously to perfect some gas to take the place of helium.

**I.G. Farben** (IGF) was a German Limited Company conglomerate of eight leading German chemical manufacturers, including Bayer, Hoechst, and BASF, which merged to create the largest chemical enterprise in the world. Contact between IGF management and the Nazi government became increasingly close, since the products of the conglomerate were an indispensable element in the Nazi's drive to re-arm. The

221

majority of its board members joined the Nazi Party and, by means of economic and political blackmail, took over important chemical factories in the areas annexed to the Reich or occupied by the Germans. One of the more horrifying aspects of IGF's cartel was the invention, production, and distribution of the Zyklon B gas, used in Nazi concentration camps. After the defeat of the Third Reich at the International Military Tribunal held in Nuremberg, the United States conducted trials against the top officials of three major industrial concerns, one of which was I.G. Farben.[xliv]

**The Graf Zeppelin** (officially known as LZ-127) was the most successful zeppelin ever built. Christened 1928 and in service for nine years, the Graf Zeppelin's flew over a million miles on 590 flights, carrying thousands of passengers and hundreds of thousands of pounds of freight and mail with safety and speed. The Graf Zeppelin was recruited as a tool of Nazi propaganda soon after the National Socialist takeover of power in early 1933 and flew over Berlin at the government's celebration of "Tag der Nationalen Arbeit," the Nazi version of May Day.[xlv]

```
    Sunday, we went down the Rhine and saw its
grand scenery and all of the wonderful old cas-
tles. We stayed all night in Bonn, a nice univer-
sity town. Monday, we went to Liblar by Cologne,
Carl Schurz's birthplace. His mother belonged to
the House of Metternich and he was born in the
castle. The family still lives there.

    We ate in a specially erected tent and had
a parade afterward. The town is so tiny it is
```

*Eyes and Ears*

Liblar, Germany, May 1939

hardly a town. Some of us broke away and sat in the grass at the castle. Even royal grass has lots of chiggers! That night we went to Cologne and the trip was over. In a day or two I'll write about Holland.

Love,
Lois

Mom said, "The Carl Schurz trip was very nice but obviously whitewashed to show us only the better things of Germany."

Susan Kandt Peterson

June 7, 1939<br>Tübingen, Germany

Dear Mother and Dad,

We had hoped to be in the Balkans by the first of the week, but first, our tickets were not ready and second, I wasn't able to throw off my cold. It will be nice being here over the weekend.

My mother thought she had strep throat. Jackie told her to go to a local hospital, so on the weekend, she did. Once there, they were told it was closed and to come back on Monday. She was mad and left saying, "Damn Hitler! Damn Nazis!" Jackie said, "You must not mind going to Dachau. You'd better be quiet."

Mom later said, "We knew, of course, about Dachau and other concentration camps, and that the conditions were horrible. We knew that people were being sent there but we didn't know about the death camps at that time."

Now about Holland. Being only five hours to Amsterdam from Cologne, our trip was spur of the moment. The landscape is not particularly attractive, at least the part we saw. There were few windmills and no fences. Instead, they use small ditches filled with water. The cows are really pretty.

Amsterdam is the largest city in Holland. It is so modern and very Americanized. One popular brand of cigarettes is called Kansas. Holland isn't as clean as Germany, but I have decided that the Germans are clean but not sanitary. Our hotel was on a beautiful platz with lovely flowers and a statue of Rembrandt in the middle. The food was delicious but everything was so expensive.

We saw the movie, *The Story of Irene and Vernon Castle*, in English, with Ginger Rogers and Fred Astaire and it was delightful.

We visited the Rijksmuseum and went through the gallery. We saw Rembrandt's *Night Watch*, but didn't know it at the time. An excursion took us to see Edam cheese farms and to a fishing village with dikes and then to Marken Island to see people who still wear their native dress. It is all very colorful. They say a pair of wooden shoes lasts an active person only 3 or 4 weeks. We went with a guide through several houses and they are so neat and clean. The beds are in the walls and closed off by doors. They have an aversion to gas cooking and use funny little oil stoves by fireplaces. The cows are in stables

Marken Island, Holland, June 1939

for 7 months a year, yet there is no odor. We were there only two nights and then returned to Germany. My next letter will be from Vienna or Budapest.

Love,
Lois

> June 13, 1939
> Vienna, Austria

Dear Mother and Dad,

At last we are making our much dreamed of trip. We left Tübingen Friday, got our tickets in Stuttgart and then left for Passau on the Austrian border. It is only six hours away by train. What an interesting and lovely old town Passau is. We had gone to Passau to catch the riverboat to go down the Danube to Vienna, Austria.

The next morning, we left Passau. The Danube is a beautiful river, so slow and easy going. The landscape is much nicer than the Rhine valley. The castles and cloisters were fewer than on the Rhine but larger and more beautiful. The mountains are quite high and covered with evergreens and then the land much flattened out. We passed the most interesting old town, Durnstein, all built on the Danube and enclosed in the city walls. The castle is 800 years old. We were just sick that we could only pass by. We enjoyed suntanning.

At 4:30 our leisure was interrupted by 400 KdF tourists getting on the boat. This is the organization which allows the workers to travel very cheaply. It's a government project. It was quite an experience being thrown in with such a group. They were all happy Austrians off for a holiday and having a good time. Bill and I had supper after our arrival in Vienna.

Mom's diary states that the KdF group caused them to lose their rare, first-class luxury and to have no supper. Part of the German Labour Front (DAF), the **Kraft durch Freude**, or **KdF**, was a populist movement designed to provide ordinary Germans with holiday and leisure opportunities previously only available to the upper and middle classes, including theatre events, athletics, libraries, and day trips. In order to enjoy these activities, workers had to join the KdF (in English "Strength Through Joy") program. KdF was officially set up by the Nazis to promote employee rights and appease workers. In reality, it was a way of managing the population by controlling what people did with their free time. The start of the Second World War put a stop to it.[xlvi]

Little did we know the trouble we were going to have finding a hotel room in Vienna. It was 9:00, Saturday night, the day before the beginning of music week under the direction of Goebbels and the biggest horse race of the year was to be on Sunday. And besides that, Hitler was paying a surprise visit to the city. Finally, calling one hotel after another, we were able to get a nice room. Compared to the rest of Germany, it is very expensive here. Sunday, we slept late and then started walking about. We found the street roped off in front of the Imperial Hotel and were told that Hitler would soon be coming out. We waited for three hours and then decided, what's the use? We enjoyed walking around the town. We saw the Imperial Palace, the town hall with its many towers, the churches, the Parliament building, and museums.

About 6:30 we saw huge groups of SA and SS walking in the distance, so we followed. We were well rewarded. In about thirty minutes along came Hitler and Goebbels on their way to the Burg Theatre. Strangely enough, Hitler was dressed in civilian dress. He had on a gaberdine topcoat and a light, tan homburg hat. The interesting thing about seeing him here was the contrast to seeing him in Munich. There was only a meager group of people and no excitement or "Heils." When the cars approached, of course, the circumstances were entirely different, but even so, the Viennese had such an indifferent attitude. They were walking about paying almost no attention.

We fell in love with Vienna. These people are so nice and friendly and easy going. You can well see the Sudetenland section being part of the Reich, but certainly not these people. And they do love their cafe life! In the afternoon, the sidewalk tables are filled with people who sit and drink their coffee with whipped cream. Everyone was asking if we had been to the theatre so last night we took in the opera. Venice is known as the city of music, but the musicians must have left with the former government, for never have we seen anything so poorly done.

We are still trying to get visas for the Balkans. We hope to leave for Budapest this afternoon. Our route has changed. We will go through Bulgaria on our way to Bucharest. We will probably stop in Romania overnight as the visa would be too expensive. The US is so strict about visas for the Balkans and they, in turn, make it equally hard for us.

I went to Dr. Stock in Tübingen about my glasses. People all over the world come to him. He just laughed at the fact that I wore glasses. He said there wasn't a thing in the world the matter with my eyes and that the correction was so minimal, it really wasn't doing me any good. He said the trouble with Americans is that they went to opticians who wanted to make money. He said I frowned from reading only from habit and that the eyes get tired when the body gets tired. He laughed at Bill's glasses, too. He did tell us what kind of sunglasses to buy, though, not more than 50%, by Carl Zeiss. We bought them and

Lois in Salzburg sweater, June 1939

they were rather expensive. They are regular ground glass but with no correction.

Yesterday I bought a lovely Salzburg sweater. I have wanted one for ever so long. I am so thrilled with it.

Will write from Budapest.

Love,
Lois

June 18, 1939
Belgrade, Yugoslavia

Dear Mother and Dad,

Budapest is the prettiest city we have seen. The Danube is so wide and curving and the hills rise so gracefully. The bridges are wonderful. We found a grand place to eat and enjoyed the food ever so much. The Hungarians have an eye for business and everything is so artfully done. It is hard to keep from buying too much. We walked a lot, seeing so much, including the palace.

*Eyes and Ears*

We ate in a funny, little stand-up place called American Express. It is a very leisurely city, one you could enjoy for a lazy month or six weeks. On Margarete Island in the Piccadilly we heard wonderful Hungarian music. They play the violin so beautifully. The head of the orchestra came over and serenaded us with his violin. I didn't know what to do as I was the only woman being serenaded and everyone was staring so.

Here we are down in old Belgrade. The town really has history behind it but is not rich enough in culture to make it a tourist center. We walked around all day and felt we had covered it fairly well. There is a beautiful park and zoo built around an old Turkish castle. The boy king lives here and will be crowned in about two years when he is 18. Yugoslavia is a very poor country. Most of the people are literally in rags and half are illiterate. A mixture of people here, all very interesting. It appears dirty and unsanitary. There seems to be a wealthy element that enjoys silver foxes and big American cars.

Bill in Belgrade, Yugoslavia, June 1939

The mixture of Turkish blood gives people an entirely different look.

    Last night on the train we met a young lawyer. He was most friendly and gave us his viewpoint on many subjects. He said his government in Yugoslavia was very friendly with Germany but not the people, that they would be lifelong enemies. He thought the government was forced to be friendly because they were a poor, helpless nation. The people, he said, were willing to go in and help Czechoslovakia but knew that Yugoslavia couldn't do much. He says the people here will absolutely not fight alongside the Germans but think a war is to come. This, he said, is a farming country, has no big industry and therefore, no money. He said Hungary is purely industrial and communistic whereas Yugoslavia is democratic. The hotel here has a somewhat different attitude. They say that the workers of Germany are dissatisfied, which I agree, and are communistic. And in case of war, there will be a revolution. Also, that there was much communism throughout the Balkan states. They seem to be of the opinion that no war will come. They say Hungary is most favorable toward Germany, and the further east you go, the more they are against it. In Budapest, Hungary we found almost no sentiment toward Germany. The waiters and others told us the workers were strongly opposed to Germany. The government is only partially so. In the last election, there were 40 elected who were pro compared to over 150 against. They say a war must stop this thing.

   Belgrade is not as pretty as Budapest. However, at night, it is beautiful when approached by train. Our hotel is the best in town, the Bristol Hotel with modernistic chrome furniture. It has a big American bar and dance orchestra in the dining room. Everything is cheap in the Balkans. The food is good but more like Germany, but the coffee is very black. Very few Americans come here. Today being Sunday, many people in the park and in town, were dressed up in their native costume. I became nervy and took their pictures.

   We are leaving at 4:55 in the morning for Sofia, Bulgaria. Then Wednesday morning we will go to Bucharest. Both of these trips take a full day. Then we go on a boat to Istanbul on Thursday evening. I will write again.

Lots of love,
Lois

Susan Kandt Peterson

June 20, 1939
Sofia, Bulgaria

Dear Mother and Dad,

Yesterday we had a very long ride, but we covered such beautiful territory that it really seemed quite short. We were rather glad to leave Belgrade for its dirt and extreme mixture of people. Being a frontier town, it really has all types. We had beautiful scenery with some mountains and colorful peasants working in the fields. The country, from the train, looks a bit like the western US, rough, hilly and with plenty of men riding horseback. How different it is from Western Europe where culture has reached such a peak.

We had dinner in the diner, which was fancy but very expensive. As we had our own train compartment to ourselves, we were able to stretch out and take a nap.

About 4:30 we crossed the border. Then we met a young German fellow. It was our first such meeting of one outside of the country where we felt free to argue. But he was the type where there is no arguing with him. This kind always begins to tell you that Germany, at least, hasn't had or doesn't have the cruel treatment of the American Indians, the 10 million unemployed, the Negro problem, the coming Jewish problem and so on. Every one of them gives you the same set of arguments as set by the propaganda department. And they justify all of German's actions by the Versailles Treaty. He said he thought we were getting out of Europe about the right time. When asked why, he replied, "Those damned Poles are fools!" He actually believed that if Hitler made demands of Poland, and Poland refused, then Germany went in and found Polish resistance, that it would be Poland who started the war, not Germany. He says they are not civilized. I got so mad at him that I finally just walked away. Bill was furious! But at the railroad station, he was nice to help us find our hotel.

Dad had said that their only real social life with Germans was with Fraulein Keck and the Reith's. He told a reporter, "Germans were advised to stay away from English-speaking people. German students were afraid of being seen with a foreigner. Many of the older people were nice to us. When they felt they could confide in you, they would criticize the Party. One family we visited had a picture with two sides. On one side was the Fuehrer's picture, on the other, a nature scene. It was imperative that all homes have a picture of Hitler. Many Germans felt the nation would expand its borders through war, making the elderly fearful and the youth inflamed with conquest."

Sofia came as a wonderful surprise. It is clean and modern. Everyone is well dressed. We went for a walk before dinner and found a wide street where people were promenading at twilight.

It was nicer than Belgrade and you could easily eat safely at any cafe. In fact, at noon we came the closest to an American lunch than any we had in Europe. We had toasted egg sandwiches with fairly good ice cream sodas. There is a Russian and Turkish influence in the architecture. The cathedral is grand. On the outside it looks purely Russian. Inside the walls are beautifully frescoed with marble encasements. We came upon a marvelous market, the best we have seen with novelties like hairpins, ribbons, fruits, vegetables, and pottery. We called on the American Consul and he said they are quite conservative people, whereas the Yugoslavians were not. Tonight we are going to see a movie with Irene Dunn and Charles Boyer in *Love Affair*.

I think the British are more worried than any other Europeans. The opinion is right that someone should guide America. There is no reason on earth for us to get mixed up in European politics. I'll never forgive Mr. Roosevelt for his telegram. What blunder!

Tomorrow we go on another full day of traveling. We shall have only a half day in Bucharest. I hope the lining stays in my old tweed coat before we are on our way home to America. I have become quite agile in slipping out of it in restaurants. Bill is taking a nap and I am trying my best to wake him up. We haven't gone through the shopping district, yet I'd like to. We can't buy

Coke here in the Balkans so drink one for me. My ham sandwich has made me thirsty. I will drink a sweet wine for you.

Lots of love,
Lois

PS: Never have we tasted strawberries like they have here, and how big they are!

June 25, 1939

Dear Mother and Dad,

To be continuous, I must start with our visit to Bucharest, Romania but I am so bubbling with interest about Turkey that I can scarcely wait. We thought Germany a strict country, but Romania just puts it to shame. The whole thing is so ridiculous. The border was much worse than any we have crossed, with perhaps the exception of Holland. It was a long, tiring process. Every Balkan country has money which is good only within that country. In Romania, you must show money receipts when leaving. They come only from the National Bank. We were determined to have money receipts so we wouldn't get in trouble. We spent most of our time going through red tape. The country is full of fraud. You can tip and get nearly anything you want. So, with all of their strictness, soldiers standing around with mean looking guns, it is all pretty funny.

The countryside is much like Kansas with big wheat fields and a few oil wells. Bucharest has more modern buildings than any city in the world. It is rather pleasing but lacking the charm of Sofia or Budapest. The people are friendly and they simply double up laughing when you ask them about politics between them and Germany. They are exceedingly anti-German. Of course, they talk war, too, but let Russia and Germany fight it out. They are united with only one political party.

For the first time we had a private bath in our hotel. Also, for the first time since we left home, we tasted corn. We ordered a ragout. It tasted exactly like hot tamales but was served as a stew with the corn mixture on the side. It is an inexpensive country.

Our boat coming to Istanbul was the most beautiful thing I have ever seen. It was a very new boat. Instead of a cabin we had a large room with chrome and apricot colored beds, a writing desk, chair, and a lavatory. The lounges were works of art, the bar all in red leather and chrome and deck space galore. Unfortunately, we were only on the boat for one night.

Istanbul, Turkey is a fascinating place. It is perfectly beautiful yet the dirtiest place I've ever been. But the people up from Cairo, Egypt think it is very clean. There are three bodies of water and rolling green hills all around. You have a feeling you are not in Europe, but Asia is about 1/8 mile across the water. Istanbul reeks with history, fighting, wealth, poverty, romance, and garlic. Because we don't know the history, it makes it harder. We kept on the go for our five days here. We would love to come back and see more. We are staying in the oldest part of the city. Also here is the brother of the ex-king of Albania, his princess, and five small daughters. The oldest looks no older than seven. The children look like a biological impossibility. The prince and princess are fat and dull looking but the children are adorable.

Monday, June 26

My, what a thrilling day! But I must begin from the start of our visit to Istanbul. We aren't versed in Istanbul history but try and absorb it all. Our first afternoon, we walked around acclimating ourselves to the city. We went to a beautiful park situated on a point. From here we could look across to Pera. Down below was the old sea wall. The history seems to fill the air. So many cultures have lived here.

At five o'clock we met Mr. and Mrs. Jim Cleveland, he is a professor at Amherst, who are the friends of the MacLeods and whom we had met in Tübingen. And, Mr. Baker, secretary of the very large YMCA here. We all took a ferry and went up the Golden Horn, a lovely body of water. After climbing a hill, we had a wonderful view of the skyline of the city, perhaps the prettiest in the world. Right now, the wailing Turkish music is coming over the radio. How queer it is!

Our next day was a tiring one but one well spent. We took a streetcar to the far end of Pera, a new part of the city but still very old. The stores are very shabby looking and the products are very expensive. Seeing the people and the narrow, rocky streets was the most interesting. The stones cut right through the soles of your shoes. The fez is now forbidden, and the veil is not recognized and is discouraged, so we have seen not a single one. The dress is European. Traffic is a real problem here, but the streets are impossible to change. You see such grand, American cars for taxis all through the Balkans and here, too. They are huge cars and very new. We have ridden in a Packard and two Chryslers.

Some Americans tell us the biggest change they have noticed with the comparatively new government is the expression on the faces of the people. They say that they formerly looked so scared and sad, but today they look almost happy and even laugh some. In the palace, there were emeralds that look as big as your fist. Also, rubies and literally millions of pearls. These sultans were wealthy men. The living quarters were different for they had mostly lounges, pillows, and beautiful rugs. The harem was of special interest to us, although not much to see. We also visited the historical mosque of Saint Sophia. It is the best example of Byzantine architecture in the world. The mosaics were all covered over in a religious controversy but now they are being uncovered and are lovely, about 500-600 BC. An American is in charge of the work.

Sunday, we went to church with Mr. Baker. It is one for English speaking people and is perfectly adorable. It is part of the Dutch Embassy. A Scottish minister preached one of the best sermons I have ever heard. We met many of the American colony which is quite large here; the college faculty group, Standard Oil, and the diplomatic group. Mr. Baker took us via ferry to Robert's College, an American school. It had one of the best views I had ever seen. Several wealthy Americans have invested in the school, so the campus is lovely. We went for tea at a charming, little old American lady's house, Mrs. Manning. Her husband was a professor. She is very smart and says the funniest things in a funny voice. But her big interest in society is the Prevention of Cruelty to Animals (SPCA). She is getting interest from the Turks and building an organization.

Today has been equally busy. We took a train this morning to the walls. We saw where Constantinople started his wall in the 4th century. But the gigantic walls standing today are from the 5th or 6th century. After going through the Princess Mosque, by luck we found a taxi and went along the wall, which is about three miles to the Yedikule side on the Marmara Sea. We visited the remains of the castle. You can just picture the struggles which went on opposite sides of that ancient structure. From here we walked to the church of John the Baptist. It is now in ruins but is very interesting. One must use his imagination.

One afternoon, with Mr. Baker, we started a visit to some huge old cisterns. You go down deep steps and see the most amazing sight: cool, clear water several feet deep covering a square space about 250 feet. This is supported by huge marble columns. No one knows much about them but suppose they were for Saint Sophia, the big mosque. There are several secret passages leading to them. A nice little man rows you around through the pillars. Then we visited the Hippodrome which dates back to Constantine when Constantinople was the capital of the Roman Empire. We were duly impressed. Then we visited the colorful old Blue Mosque of Sultan Ahmed. It is painted in bright blue on a white background.

We had the time of our lives going through the old bazaars. They are the center of all shopping and continue for blocks. We were more interested in the old Turkish things, so Mr. Baker took us directly to the old brass, copper, and silver section. We nearly went mad! My splurge and pride and joy is the Turkish coffee set. I bought an old silver grinder, a coffee maker, a pair of silver cup holders, and cups. My coffee boiler dates back to the Janissaries so it's hundreds of years old. It will be more fun serving Turkish coffee at home.

Everyone thinks it is hot here, but they haven't been to Kansas.

June 27, 1939
Tuesday

We are now waiting for Mr. Baker to come have dinner with us. He has been so nice, and his wife and daughter are Americans now. We went today to Suleymaniye Mosque which is Bill's favorite. We got lost looking for another tiny mosque, but it was not bad, only smelly on the waterfront. This afternoon we went to an old church dating to the 4th century. The mosaics look like paintings instead of little pieces of glass. You sweat a lot but otherwise don't notice the heat much.

The Turks are nice people. I like them. The men are most strange. They don't watch women walk down streets. They have a good government and a good unity. They are very friendly toward Americans. Never have we seen such hate toward Germany. They won't say anything about it that is good. There is no great class distinction here, just good democracy. The people are now being educated and even adults are trying to learn how to read and write. We hate to leave here but our boat leaves for Athens in the morning. I will write again from there. Just think, we land in New York a month from tomorrow!

Lots of love,
Lois

On their trip, my parents experienced a **modern, post-World War I Turkey**, 26 years after the Republic of Turkey was established by Mustafa Kemal. Kemal was the republic's first president, abolishing 623 years of the Sultanate of the Ottoman Empire. His sweeping reforms modernized Turkey toward secular Westernization. These reforms included everything from revisions to the country's language and alphabet, education, religion, penal codes and courts, dress (included outlawing the wearing of a fez), and the granting of equality between the sexes (including granting full political rights to women), and many others.[xlvii]

*Eyes and Ears*

June 30, 1939
Athens

Dear Mother and Dad,

I will write this while Bill is out fixing up an extension on our visas. Our trip from Istanbul was very pleasant. We enjoyed the rest and sunshine on the boat, an old Rumanian ship. We were never completely out of sight of land. And when we passed by the Dardanelles, and the small, barren mountains were very close. It was beautiful during sunset. The heat made it hard to sleep in our little cabin. We arrived at Piraeus yesterday morning and then had a 20-minute taxi ride into Athens. We could see hills with all of the majestic, old Greek remains standing, the Athens of the era BC.

July, 2

We have been rather busy seeing Athens. When we were not eating real, American ice cream, made by a fellow just returned, we were reading our guidebook and walking around. The stores here have such funny hours, from 8-12 and 4-8. They think it gets awfully hot here, so nobody goes out in the afternoon.

It is such a beautiful city. Three times we took a tram to the Acropolis and then walked up to see the majestic remains of the former

Acropolis in Athens, Greece,
June 1939

city and temple. We climbed all over the ruins here. It is so well done that it is difficult to believe that it dates from about 500 BC to probably 800 AD. You can just spend hours on top of that hill getting inspiration. Last night we went to see it by moonlight. Until after midnight we stayed. (Even in such lovely spots bugs can bite and I was polka dotted.)

We've also visited the pile of rocks overlooking the city where Paul came and preached to the Athenians about the unknown god. On this same rock the first murder trials were held. And we visited the platform cut out of stone where the first orations were delivered. Bill was so thrilled with both of these places. The Greeks have contributed a lot to our culture. We spent three busy hours going through the National Museum. We were impressed by the Egyptians mummies. Several were over 4000 years old and well preserved. But I must say they had a peculiar odor. We have enjoyed seeing the Greek things so very much.

The modern Greek today is a very business-like person, well dressed. There are fine looking stores and reasonably clean. They are not so dark and black-haired here. The American influence is great for you know how many Greeks make their money in the US and then return. There are all sorts of soda fountains. They have the best ice cream in Europe. We haven't talked to many people for the language most used, besides Greek, is French.

We leave tomorrow for Rhodes. There we have only a short time before leaving on our seven-day jaunt.

Well, it won't be very long before we sail past the Statue of Liberty. We are so excited about returning! This year has been so absolutely wonderful. But we realize there is only one place for us to live. God save us from the discomforts of European living. Then, too, we will be glad to get away from the crisis area. For we all realize that unless a miracle happens, we will find our situation more than a tense moment. We will even breathe easier when the boat sails out of Southampton.

I won't have time to write many more letters. This is all for now.

Lots of love,
Lois


> July 9, 1939
> SS Palestinia

Dear Mother and Dad,

We are sailing peacefully along the beautiful Adriatic Sea now. Bill is asleep in the sun and I just came in from two hours of tanning and reading Woollcott's *While Rome Burns*. I am so dark you won't be claiming me as your child. However, the first day on the boat, I was sleepy after lunch and fell asleep. When I awoke, the water was very rough, and I spent the day curled up on a deck chair with no dinner.

Now that it's over, I can tell you about our thrilling experience when we flew to Rhodes from Athens, our first airplane trip! We hadn't planned it, but to make boat connections, it was the only way. The plane was a big one, Italian. The take-off was sort of like big stair steps and the wings went from side to side. But after ten minutes we were at 2000 feet and going as smooth as a whistle. Really, it was a lovely way to see the many islands in the blue water. When we landed, you could scarcely tell when we hit land. I wouldn't want to fly again unless it is for a short stretch and the weather was perfect.

My parents later learned that the same, previous flight had crashed.

The ironic part of our flying to catch the boat was that the boat schedule had been changed and we were told nothing about it by the company in Athens. We had purchased the tickets in Germany and the schedule changed on the 1st of July. So, when we got to Rhodes, we found out there was no boat. You have never seen two people more mad than Lois and Bill! We finally made them realize that they were to do something about it. The only alternative was to wait in Rhodes until Friday, the 7th, and catch the Italian *SS Palestinia* from Cyprus. This we did at their expense. They put us up in an elegant big resort hotel with food service included. We were the only two guests. They said we could use their laundry facilities but that they wouldn't do our laundry because we had polyester and they didn't know how to handle it. Our luggage was left in Athens where we had planned to pick it up. Now we arrive in Trieste tomorrow afternoon and our luggage is supposed to be there. We will stay there overnight and then go to Stuttgart on the 11th.

Isle of Rhodes, June 1939

While at Rhodes we took a car and saw the island. It is very interesting and old and full of Greek history. All that remains of the Colossus of Rhodes, the Greek sun-god Helios, is the base. It once stood over 100 feet high. The place is under military control. The Italians got it from the Turks in 1912. They have rebuilt the old walls and castles. It is a beautiful and romantic spot. There are millions of beautiful flowers. It is like a fairyland.

Lots of love,
Lois

Dad later said, "Upon our arrival on the Isle of Rhodes, we were met by two Italian plainclothes detectives who asked us what we were doing there. On a trip, we said, planning to leave the next day. But we learned that Rhodes had been taken over by Mussolini as a submarine base and no more passenger ships were stopping at the island. We were interrogated for several hours in police headquarters before convincing them that we were tourists and the fault of our visit remained with the steamship line which had sold us our tickets. As a result, the steamship company was obligated to provide lodging for us."

```
                                        July 10, 1939
                                        Trieste, Italy
Dear Mother and Dad,

    We arrived here this afternoon. We enjoyed an
hour horse and buggy ride through Trieste. It
has belonged to Italy only since the war. It was
formerly Austrian. Everyone speaks German and it
hardly seems like an Italian city. Of interest
is the old castle or fortress on the hill with
the church beside it. The trees are new and by
each is a small white marble plaque in memory of
an Italian soldier who fell in the Spanish war.
After our ride we went for our luggage which had
arrived from Athens.

    We went to a brand-new restaurant for supper
and had spaghetti. It is now only 9:15 but I am
```

going fast asleep. We have to get up early for a train to Stuttgart. It is a very long ride but the scenery will be beautiful, lofty mountains.

July 12, 1939
Stuttgart

We slept until 9:30 and then went to the Consulate to collect our mail. In the afternoon we went to Tübingen for a final visit with Fraulein Keck and to say our goodbyes. We had a very nice tea. Then back to Stuttgart for a last supper at the Mensa and a beer with the old Consulate crowd.

Love,
Lois

July 20, 1939
London

Dear Mother and Dad,

I will write one last letter from Europe. I left Stuttgart on the 13th and went to Heidelberg to spend the day with Bea Stewart. Bill took an evening train as he had things to attend to in Stuttgart. Just as I walked up to the hotel in Heidelberg, I saw lots of people and men in uniforms. Mr. Goebbels came out and got in a car about 6-8 feet away. As Bea and I were the only two near the car, he looked directly at us. Bea and I had a nice day. I had fun shopping with her for things that the tourists never see.

Bill and I left on the 1:15 train to Cologne on a third-class sleeper. Before London, we had two hours in Brussels, Belgium for lunch. The Channel was very smooth, and we had a nice train to London. We found our hotel in London to be a big, modern one and quite reasonable, the Strand Palace Hotel. There are no private baths but as many as you want, otherwise. The five-course breakfast is so large that we eat only one other meal. It seems so strange to hear English spoken again.

We have spent most of our time in the famous English Common Law Courts. We were fortunate to come while they were in session. We heard numerous cases: divorce, a libel case, and one where three men were charged with manslaughter from abortion. The judge on the bench was a marvel with his oral discourse. The courts are chucked full of tradition. When the judge enters, he is dressed in a red, grey, and black robe followed by the sheriff decked out in velvet and furs, followed by a third man. All three carried beautiful, fresh, flower colonial bouquets. We were left spellbound for over three hours. We also waited in line and went to Parliament, the House of Commons and heard a very dull debate. It was important because it dealt with the problem of insurance and government payment for loss during the war, particularly the little man whose entire savings may be lost.

In the British Museum, we were interested in the historical manuscripts such as the Magna Carta. We have seen Westminster Abbey and Saint Paul's Cathedral. (Bill and I heaved a sigh of relief, "Well, that's the last church for a while!" I wonder how many we have seen.) Naturally, we took in Buckingham Palace with the guards. There was a march led by a Scottish soldier with bagpipes and we followed for blocks. We saw Kew Gardens and the manner in which people are allowed to enjoy themselves there, is lovely. We went to Hyde Park. We took a bus ride through London to Chelsea. Then we went to Lincoln's Inn, the oldest and most famous of the lawyer's inns. In addition, we saw a musical revue, *Me and My Girl*. Today we are going to see the Tower of London, the National Gallery, and the Marble Arch. Tonight we are going to the play by Noel Coward, *Design for Living*.

We leave London in the morning. I am not leaving with mixed emotions, for while this glorious year has ended, I am far too happy to be returning to my own, grand, free country.

Now I must go get my hair washed. It is so damp here, if I washed it myself, it would never dry. We will be with Margaret and John Clement in New York at 554 W. 114th. We plan to not stay more than four or five days, and just two or three in Washington. Will send an airmail with our last and final plans.

Lots of love,
Lois

> July 21-28, 1939
> SS New York

Via Lois' diary:

We sailed from Southampton today! A rainy day but a happy one for us. We were with Helen and Norman most of the time. We were often seasick, propped up in bed or in deck chairs. The last day out was very nice.

We let out a cry at the sight of good ole America!

Going home gang, SS *New York*, July 1939

Susan Kandt Peterson

August 3, 1939
New York City

Our week in New York was very nice. John and Margaret met us at the boat and we stayed in their apartment. We spent three days at the World's Fair. We thought it ever so good. It was our first such fair.

Lois at World's Fair, New York City, August 1939

We saw Katherine Cornell in *No Time for Comedy* and went to a Phillip Morris national broadcast. We went to the Music Hall for a movie and state show. Bill went on top of the RCA. We heard Goldman's band play at the Mall in Central Park and heard the radicals at Columbia Circle. Oh, and we ate in our first automat. We have now gone through the NY tourist mill and enjoyed it. Today we left for Washington DC on the 10:30 train.

Home, here we come!

Love,
Lois

No letters were sent after the one from August 3rd, but personal photos show pictures of the White House, the Capital, the Lincoln Memorial, Arlington Cemetery, the Washington Mall, the Supreme Court building, the Tomb of the Unknown Soldier, and Mt Vernon.

It was only one month later that World War II began. On September 1, 1939, Hitler invaded Poland. On September 3, Britain and France declared war on Germany. My parents had left with but weeks to spare.

Dad and Mom rented a one-bedroom apartment at the Brady in Lawrence, Kansas where Dad completed his law degree. Pearl Harbor was yet to come.

Bill and Lois at their Brady apartment, circa 1939

America was a divided country prior to Pearl Harbor. Isolationists wanted no participation in the war raging in Europe. There were also Nazi sympathizers, Charles Lindbergh being one of the most vocal. The German American Bund staged a demonstration at Madison Square Garden on February 20, 1939 where 20,000 pro-Nazi supporters chanted, "Heil Hitler," and booed President Roosevelt. Roosevelt had isolationist resistance from necessary branches of government, which effectively prevented him moving forward. The Lend-Lease Act finally passed in March of 1941, allowing the U.S. to lend or lease military equipment and aid nations who were deemed important to the security and defense of America. This act brought America, by supplying military aid to Britain, one step closer to war.[xlviii]

On June 22, 1940 France fell to Germany, who had already bulldozed through Austria, Poland, Denmark, Norway, Belgium, and the Netherlands. Germany began the "London Blitz" on September 7, 1940. Americans listened as young CBS journalist Edward R. Murrow and his crew relayed the news during heavy bombing straight from London. His short BBC broadcasts were often filled with the background noise of those bombs being dropped. The all-out assault on Britain began to change American's attitudes; Murrow's broadcasts likely influenced that change.

The thick June 3, 1940 issue of *Life* magazine, with the Statue of Liberty gracing its cover, is the only magazine my parents kept among their letters and documents from that time. Among the mostly black and white ads – Hire's Root Beer, Bromo-Seltzer, Kellogg's PEP Cereal, Kelvinator refrigerator (fully equipped for $139.95), the newest Chrysler, Chevrolet and De Soto cars, Pabst Blue Ribbon Beer, and Palmolive Soap "for a lovely schoolgirl complexion" – were pages and pages of war photos and devastation at the hands of the mighty German army.

In one article, titled "German Conquest Threatens the World," a small, highlighted paragraph states:

> *Hour by hour, in these dark days, the events in Europe shape the course of America's destiny. In this issue Life looks first at the marvelous German army in its swift, relentless invasion of the West. Then it proceeds to examine the beautiful, proud lands that lie in the conqueror's path; France and England, as they were and as they may never be again. How Americans live and think for years to come will depend on whether the Nazi war machine wins its terrible goal or not.*

*Life* included pictures of refugees filling the roads from Belgium with bags, carts, wagons, and bicycles. "Along the road, they were bombed, and machine gunned systematically by German planes."

Lovely color photos of Paris – the iconic places that draw visitors – fill more pages in the magazine. What would Paris become? Photos of England, too – the countryside, the small villages, the cathedrals, and the pubs. What would England become?

Henry R. Luce, the publisher of *Life*, traveled for a month to Italy, France, England, Holland, and Belgium. On May 22, 1940 he broadcast an address over the NBC Blue Network to American listeners titled "America and Armageddon." Here is an excerpt from part of his broadcast, printed in *Life*:

> *America is now confronted by a greater challenge to its survival as a land of liberty than any it has had to face in*

*80 years. When I sailed for Europe in April, the American people were not willing to face the challenge. I believe they are willing to face it now.*

*The events of the past few weeks have shocked the American people. These were not things that happened by accident. These were acts of men, long and carefully planned. They were planned with cunning and efficiency and implacable purpose. These events were an inevitable climax of the history of the last few years. Greater climaxes, of good or evil, are yet to come and soon. The final defeat of Great Britain and France would be another climax, the immensity of which now defies the imagination. If Great Britain and France fail, we know that we, and we only, among the great powers are left to defend the democratic faith throughout the world.*

*First, we have to arm ourselves. We must meet force with force, to meet force with superior force. This is a colossal job. Second, we have to make up our minds what we are willing to fight for. That for us, as a free people, is an even harder job.*

*Armaments are expensive. They are a sheer and appalling economic waste. That means that all of us are going to be a lot poorer than we otherwise might have been. But we will not cry about that. Along with all other democracies, we will take our full share of the blame for not having done our share toward creating a better world and for not having erected stronger bulwarks against monstrous aggression.*

*Secondly, the arming of America must in itself be the first practical test of our ability to act as a united people. For many years we have been anything but united. Let us face frankly the handicaps of democracies in their inevitable contest with autocracies. Autocracies foster, above all else, the will to fight, even the love of fighting. And except on rare occasions, democracies just do not foster the will to fight. For many young men and women who have grown up in a period of great revulsion against war, this is a very unpleasant truth. For seven long years, Hitler and his storm-trooping henchmen have been sneering at us because they say we are soft and effeminate and self-indulgent and greedy for comfort and pleasure. There is, I fear, only too much truth in that sneering indictment.*

*What I am willing to fight for is, of course, America. But not America as a geological mass, nor for its mountains and plains and rivers, though I love them and much though they have concerned me. The America I want to fight for is the America of freedom and justice, the America which has stood throughout the world for the hope of progress in the democratic way of life and for faith in the ultimate brotherhood of man. America belongs to us, the lucky 130,000,000 people who are living here today. But America does not belong entirely to us. A little of America belongs to every man and every woman everywhere who has faith in democracy and hope in a world of peace and justice. We, the living who control the destiny of America today, are the heirs of a great inheritance from men who lived and from men who died to make us free. What they meant by America is what I wish to mean by America. And for that America, I am willing to fight. And I am the more willing to fight because if I know anything, I know that that America, the America we love, has small chance of surviving the tyranny and chaos which everywhere advances unless those who love America make it plain that they are willing and ready to fight.*[xlix]

America rallied behind the war effort after the bombing of Pearl Harbor on December 7th of 1941. America declared war on Japan on December 8th and Germany declared war on the US on December 11th.

In 1942, Dad made the decision to enlist. He felt, as so many men did, that he should serve his country. He was of German heritage on both sides of his family, which led to his earlier interest in studying in Germany. While living in Germany as university exchange students, my parents witnessed the restraints being imposed on the German people, and the growing power of Hitler and the Nazi Party. Many German people were afraid. This, he told me, deepened his fierce belief in freedom and democracy, something he had always taken for granted.

Dad enlisted in the US Army in 1942. Mom sold their house in Great Bend, Kansas where Dad had joined a law firm. She moved back to Independence to live with her parents, Ray and Lelia Woods, at 200 E. Walnut. Dad began his army career as infantry and started at Ft. Leavenworth, KS before going to Camp Blanding Joint Training Center in Florida.

Here are excerpts from some of Dad's letters that were written during that time.

*Eyes and Ears*

November and December of 1942
Ft. Leavenworth, Kansas

Darling,

Finally, an hour to myself. The boys I came in with have gone. I have been transferred to this company. I ran across Eugene Ricketts on the classification staff and he said I would be recommended for Intelligence but it's probably not wise to talk about it. I made OCS (Officer Candidate School) requirements easily enough.

Goddamnit! Here comes that bastardly corporal to break up our leisurely time! We've got to assemble in the snow for some reason. Will write tonight if not on fire watch.

Love,
Bill


Darling,

I just finished sixteen hours of K.P. duty and am too tired to think. And the real training has not yet begun! This being a reception center, there is no drill or training for actual military life, only a lot of detail work to be done in order to run hundreds of men through every day. The boys in my group got their orders tonight and are very excited. I didn't get mine yet.

Love,
Bill

## Susan Kandt Peterson

Darling,

This morning I was assigned latrine orderly at the barracks. The job is considered a good one because after inspection, when the work is done, you can be off the rest of the day. However, that seldom happens. I am in the information building which has a large room for letter writing. Right now, I am next to the telephone girls who are putting in long distance calls for the boys. I am tempted to call you but am afraid that I would choke up and get nothing said.

I wonder if you cried after the train pulled out. I would have, had there not been so many people around.

The group that just shipped out was a dull bunch. They were good men but with low mentality, which is not their fault, I suppose. They heard me called "latrine lieutenant," thought I was an officer, and called me lieutenant ever after! This life is getting monotonous. Well, the new group of boys that came in shows prospects of making good soldiers, or else I have become a better instructor.

I wish that I had some idea why I am being held. Another fellow with similar language qualifications who came in when I did is also being held.

I know that you are doing the wise thing with our Great Bend house and with our furniture. I love you so!

I am not discouraged over the refusal to get leave. We'll get together, somehow, soon. The sun came out today and I feel much more cheerful.

Goodnight, Darling,
Bill


Dearest,

I have passed through some days of anxiety and hope waiting for a shipping order and it has, at last, arrived. I have learned that I leave here at 3:00 this afternoon. It was good talking to you on the phone.

I know that it was hard for you to leave the house for the last time. Let's consider that a chapter closed but retain beautiful memories of our happiness there. I will think of our love on Christmas day and will write to you as soon as I am relocated.

Love,
Bill

Susan Kandt Peterson

Camp Blanding, Florida

My Dearest,

I am in Florida now! Christmas Eve on the train was nothing unusual. An officer and a WAAC got tight and had a good time. Our train accommodation was excellent. We had sleepers and dining car meals all of the way. The Negro shanties of Birmingham are interesting but not a pretty sight. We passed over the red soil of Georgia and through pine trees. The South looks poverty stricken although I have never seen much of it.

I still have not heard as to what I will be doing, my assignment, in spite of previous recommendations. I am very disappointed. With the military you never know anything in advance, and I am resigned to just take whatever I can get. I was the only one of our group to be assigned to Headquarters Company and I won't know what that means until later. Headquarters involves either supply or administration. Maybe I will check our equipment or file papers! God, what a thought! But I am sure I will go through basic, which starts tomorrow, before I do anything else.

I think much of our coming anniversary. My wedding day was the happiest day of my life.

Love,
Bill

*Eyes and Ears*

Camp Blanding, Florida
January, 1943

Dear One,

We have completed a solid week of drill. There has been no let-up. By the end of the week, a good portion of the men were limping and many have gone to the hospital. I spend every night bandaging blisters but eventually forget the pain. On the rifle range I did quite well and think I qualify for the rating of expert.

Our battalion is part of the S.O.S. (Service of Supply) whose main function is to keep the main supply lines open — a very important job. We will do a lot of guard duty and are being trained in that respect. We also take care of prisoners of war and escort straggling soldiers back to their regular outfits. We are subject to call for any emergency, however, and are told that we are to be the best all-'round soldiers of the army. We will learn to handle every weapon, except the big field pieces. I can hear the big pieces rumbling in the distance now, as they rehearse for war. We are learning to handle the rifle and shot gun and will soon take up the Thompson sub-machine gun. Today was a light day of drill and movie film on warfare. Tonight we had a dental check-up. Tomorrow it will be our eyes.

We are now doing calisthenics with the rifle and that is a good work-out. I still seem short winded on "double-time."

We have learned how to throw the hand grenade and how to skirmish by hand signal, rather than verbal command. My knees and elbows are skinned.

Thanks for the books. I have plenty of reading material but no time to read it. Don't worry about your allotment, it will come through.

Are you still being as brave as you were on the train when I pulled out of Great Bend? I know you are, and I love you dearly for it.

Love,
Bill


Darling,

I finally got a weekend pass and went to St. Augustine. The old city reminded me of the Isle of Rhodes and other places of Latin influence that we visited. Remember the wall of Istanbul and the fortress of St Angelo in Rome?

Have you figured out the gist of your anniversary telegram? It was worded in business terms for the purpose of avoiding the FCC ruling prohibiting the sending of congratulatory or anniversary messages. It evidently was deceptive enough to get by. I had to find some way to get word to you.

This week we are drilling but using different muscles. I am sore all over. I suppose we will have more bayonet practice tomorrow. It is unpleasant and hard.

A soldier has just come to sit on my bed. He is from the hills near Louisville, Kentucky. He hangs on like a faithful puppy, probably because he has never been away from home before and cannot read or write. He gets very little mail from home and seems lonesome. I think he is going to ask me to write a letter for him, which I will gladly do. In Kentucky, just inside his kitchen door, he says, "The branch runs by from yonder and it goes so steep that only a mule can barely make the climb." He yearns "fer his smokin' pipe and some burley tobaccer hangin' in the sack in the shed."

We attended a U.S.O. dance tonight and I danced one dance with a young chick from Philadelphia who was trying so hard to talk a la Hepburn. Or is that the honest Philadelphia dialect?

I am glad to hear of your success in dieting but please do nothing to harm yourself.

With mad love,
Bill

Susan Kandt Peterson

WESTERN UNION

KAE15 58 NL=PQ CAMPBLANDING FLO JAN 2
MRS WM KANDT=
200 EAST WALNUT

SORRY WAS UNABLE TO PHONE ON FRIDAY AS PLANNED
REGARDING CONTRACT ENTERED INTO JANUARY 1, 1937.
DESIRE EXTENSION OF SAME WITH CLAUSE OF SINCERE
GRATITUDE FOR YOUR DEVOUT COMPANIONSHIP
AND AFFECTION AND TALENTED HANDLING OF THE
PARTNERSHIP   PLEASE SUBMIT PROFIT AND LOSS
STATEMENT. WILL WRITE MORE DETAIL REGARDING
PRESENT PROGAM WHEN PERSPECTIVE COMES MORE
SIMPLY INTO FOCUS. LOVE =

BILL 1, 1937

February, 1943

Dearest One,

    Measles! All bedding in the battalion area has been aired and it is now under control with only a dozen cases so far.

    Our last night on bivouac was extremely

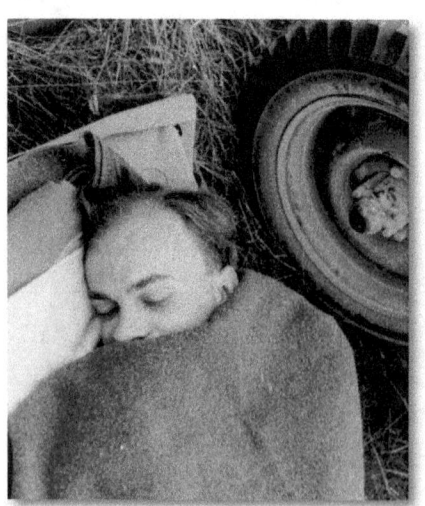

Bill on bivouac, 1943

disagreeable with rain and cold. My bad throat is gone but I have another cold and the inevitable cycle begins all over again.

It was a pleasure having three of your letters waiting at week's end. I am learning how important it is to receive a letter each day and will try to write to you more often.

I know that the army is investigating me but am not considering it hopeful, at this point. It is best to not get one's hopes up. If nothing more, I know that I will be assigned to the intelligence officer of this battalion.

I received a thrill from your mention of our 12 years acquaintance and consider your influence the most important phase of my life. I slept late this morning and had pleasant twilight recollections of our Sundays together. May they reappear soon!

Love,
Bill


Darling,

After digging a hole big enough to stand in without being seen, I dreamed of you. What will our next meeting be like? Will your hair be piled on your head? I know your sweet smile will be the same, and your expression eager and your disposition as composed and lovely as ever. I'm most anxious to see you and to lay plans for the future, whenever that will be.

The Allies are still being defeated at sea by the submarines. I do not hope for the beginning of the end until this menace is overcome. The Japs, too, are far from defeated. So many of the soldiers here expect to be home soon because they do not understand the nature of the struggle or the reasons for being here. I feel for these men because they cannot adjust themselves or find happiness or purpose in what they are doing. I think the army can do something by way of indoctrination to help these men, but perhaps, that will come later. For myself, army life is really the easiest thing I have undertaken, even in spite of my complaining.

Many are the rumors as to the disposition of this outfit. Some of the boys think we are going overseas immediately. Some have us guarding prison camps. The outfit which left before us, was shipped to Hawaii. But I have learned to disregard any form of rumor in the army. And we are far from being overseas material!

Love,
Bill

*Eyes and Ears*

My Dearest One,

On Wednesday the rain came, and we were ordered to stay in the woods. The colonel had a change of heart and let us come in Thursday afternoon. I had 6 letters, 5 of them from you. I thoroughly enjoyed them until I received the angry one, and after reading it several times, I didn't care of I wrote again! I'm surprised that I still love you, but such is the weakness of man, and to prove my love, I will write once a month, at least.

We are getting no salt peter in our food. The boys who think so are the boys who circulate and believe all latrine rumors.

We are getting very crowded in the recruit detachment and are housing more men together than what was intended. It explains why all men in training have some sort of respiratory infection. I lost my lower bunk when I was in the hospital and am now struggling with an upper, which is not fun when we have to meet such rigid inspection requirements.

I have read to the boys your statement about our "camping" trip, and you should have heard the howls that arose; howls of anguish. They think that I have been misinforming you as to the nature of a bivouac in the army.

I will mail you a dozen postcards soon and
hope they will satisfy.

With greatest love which might be greater,
Bill


Darling,

   This afternoon one of the officers gave us a
full session on current events, which was very
successful with the men. I am unable to understand why we have not had more of such training.
It builds morale and unifies the unit by giving
the men an understanding of the purposes and ob-
jectives underlying their army life. Many of the
men have paid no attention in civilian life to
the causes underlying the war, and hence, are not
in sympathy with the necessity for their being in
military training. No man can be a good soldier
unless he understands why he must fight. A military outfit is no better than its leadership.

   Yesterday we put on gas masks and entered a
gas chamber for a little realistic practice of a
gas attack. It was only tear gas, but we got the
idea. The emphasis now on training is for jungle
and combat warfare in the east. We are training
to fight the Japs and had a session on Japanese
fighting tactics observed by Marines in Bataan and
Guadalcanal. The methods employed are not polite.

We will never fully appreciate the experiences of those who died there.

I daydreamed that when we meet you will be waiting for me at a table in a cafe. We had a long kiss and then we sat down and talked about the things we loved, including each other. Perhaps we ordered food, but that was incidental.

The new work at Headquarters begins tomorrow. I will have no more drill but do hope the physical conditioning does not stop as it has been good for me.

Love,
Bill


Dearest,

Today has been exciting. All men with college credits and other qualifications were ordered to appear for a 3-hour written exam for qualification to enter the Army Specialized Training program. It was 9/10 mathematics and physics, but I made the grade. Tomorrow morning, we appear before a board of officers for a personal interview. There is a slight chance that I might be recommended but I consider it doubtful so don't expect too much. I might be squeezed into army administration, censorship, military government, or some such related subject. I don't expect to be on the bus in the final analysis.

The nicest thought is that we will have Sundays together again, one day.

Love,
Bill


Dearest One,

I began work in HQ today and was assigned to the intelligence officer. It is the intelligence unit of this battalion, only. We spent the afternoon in the woods crawling on our bellies and learning how to observe the enemy without being seen. I think later we will learn to observe topography and make maps of the same. We will also spend time studying what we don't know. There is no organization, it's the same as the rest of the battalion. Do I appear to be complaining again?

I am proud that you are displaying a service flag and have invested in war bonds. I have nothing to report on your coming here but keep up hope because I love you so dearly.

Love,
Bill

Darling,

I still love you in spite of all of the girls last night. When it was announced that a battalion dance had been arranged, I went along and enjoyed dancing for the first time in years. They were all young chicks of high school age but were able to follow me. The majority of men are married and are discussing whether or not to tell their wives about it all. The officers and hostesses were pleased, and everyone had a nice evening.

I am very eager to see you, naturally. Tomorrow is my last day of 8 weeks training. I think we should wait two weeks to see if anything happens before you come down.

Have I told you that I love you?

Bill


March, 1943

Darling,

We have learned that considerable weeding-out was done on the applicants for Specialized Training. Because of my grade and educational background, I am sure that I am no longer under consideration. My future in the Service looks bleak.

I try to keep my morale as high as possible, even though it is difficult at times.

We have a lot of fun in the HQ outfit. There are many good men here who also will not get very far. OCS (Officer Candidate School) quotas are closing now.

Love always and always,
Bill


Darling,

I am so anxious for you to come down. I wish my position would become stable enough that we might depend upon seeing each other, often enough, when you are down here. I am still undecided as to the answer, but at present, we couldn't be together much.

I don't expect to be in this work long. The C.O. told me this morning that a general service man like myself should be on the line where I am needed. So, don't be surprised if I become a line soldier again! I hate to give up the nice privileges, but such is the way of the army.

I wonder if the Colonel will approve my OCS application. It's a tough battle, I understand, and requires tact and perseverance. I hope for the best.

I must get to work.

Much love,
Bill


WESTERN UNION

MRS. WM KANDT=
DISREGARD DATES IN LETTER WHICH FOLLOWS AND PLEASE COME TO JACKSONVILLE NOW   HAVE MY FATHER MAKE HOTEL RESERVATIONS BY WIRE THROUGH HIS CONNECTIONS   UPON ARRIVAL JACKSONVILLE TELEPHONE HEADQUARTERS 759 MP BN STATION 48 OR 50 CAMP BLANDING AND LEAVE MESSAGE FOR ME AS TO WHERE YOU ARE STAYING AND I WILL COME TO JACKSONVILE THAT NIGHT   LOVE=

BILL


Dearest,

I know, at least hope, that you will be disappointed not to have a letter from me for a few days. After sending for you, I didn't write because I expected to see you before another letter would have reached you.

I think my wire must have made you feel as if I am about to be shipped or transferred, but no such luck has transpired. I am simply so lonesome for you that I couldn't wait any longer. I will be able to see you on some weeknights and most of the weekends except when I am restricted on detail, provided my line transfer takes place as promised.

Don't expect any big things to happen to me as long as I am with the 795th. I have given up hope. Five men have already left this outfit to study engineering at Georgia Tech.

We will have great fun when you arrive, Darling. I don't mean to sound depressed but know that everything will change when you arrive.

Much love,
Bill


Dearest Loved One,

The interviews on specialized training were held this morning and I was recommended for training in political science and law. I don't know if I am still in or out. In the army, one knows nothing until it happens. Doesn't it sound selfish to want to attend school when our brothers are now in the blood of battle, giving all that others might live.

Love,
Bill

Because of his law degree, German language skills, and extensive travel, Dad was assigned to the Counter Intelligence Corps (CIC). Dad left Camp Blanding in April of 1943 for Chicago, where he completed Counter Intelligence Corps training school. Mom was able to join him there, and they rented a temporary apartment. Then he went to the CIC Staging Area in Baltimore for additional conditioning and combat training for CIC personnel about to be posted to overseas divisions.

*September, 1943*

My Darling,

Since I have not heard from you, I wonder if you have received my new address in Baltimore. Send my mail to:

William C. Kandt
100 W. 23rd St.
Baltimore, Md.

I am wondering if you are still in Chicago and hope that you had no difficulty in getting back to Kansas. I will be anxious and relieved for word from you.

Last Saturday evening, after a very busy week, we were unexpectedly granted passes until Sunday evening. I was caught off guard and didn't know where to go. I decided to go to Philadelphia because of its historical interest. I enjoyed the trip immensely. I arrived in Philly at 2:00 AM Sunday and was looking for a hotel when I met a sailor who took me to Morning Cheer Victory Centre where I had bed and breakfast for 50 cents. The accommodations were very clean and comfortable, and I saved considerable money. The Centre is run by a bunch of church people who volunteer their efforts. I slept until almost noon and when I left, I was accosted by an enthusiastic worker who asked me if I accepted Jesus Christ as my saviour, and who would not release me until I had given an affirmative answer.

Nowhere in a church have I felt an emotional reaction such as I did when I stood in Independence Hall where the policies determining America's Independence were decided upon. I think it must be America's greatest shrine.

Our future from here looks good. We know more about our status than we did in Chicago.

Goodnight, Darling. I miss you so much.

Bill

Dad became an Agent with the CIC in November of 1943.

Several years after the war, the *Wichita Beacon* did an extensive interview with Dad in 1959. He mentions the significance of becoming part of the CIC:

Bill, CIC, 1943

> *I returned to Germany, this time as a soldier. As you can imagine, the climate this time was also abnormal. I was assigned to the CIC, the Counter Intelligence Corps. I was part of an organization whose mission it was, in combat, to counter the enemy's efforts at espionage and sabotage against Allied forces, and whose mission was, after the war was over, to detect and arrest the responsible officials of the Third Reich and of the Nazi party. This was the groundwork for the Nuremberg and later trials.*[1]

He left the U.S. on November 13, 1943 but didn't go directly to Germany. He spent time in Algeria, Tunisia, Italy, and France before ending up in Germany in March of 1945. Dad's post-war handwritten list of his itinerary looked like this:

| | |
|---|---|
| Left US | 13 Nov 1943 |
| Arrived Oran, Algeria | Dec 4 1943 |

| | |
|---|---|
| Left Oran | Dec 29 1943 |
| Arrived Algiers | Dec 29 1943 |
| Left Algiers | Jan 14 1944 |
| Arrived Bizerte, Tunisia | Jan 14 1944 |
| Left Bizerte | Jan 15 1944 |
| Arrived Naples, Italy | Jan 15 1944 |
| Left Naples | June 6 1944 |
| Arrived Rome | June 6 1944 |
| Left Rome | Aug 5 1944 |
| Arrived Naples | Aug 5 1944 |
| Left Naples | Aug 17 1944 |
| Arrived St Tropez, France | Aug 21 1944 |
| Entered Germany from France | March 23 1945 |
| Transferred to 286 Engineer C Brig. | Dec 26 1945 |
| Left Bremerhaven, Germany | Jan 26 1946 |
| Arrived Cont. US | Feb 12 1946 |
| Separation | Mar 25 1946 |

What my father's soldiering and CIC work entailed in North Africa remains a mystery. His activities in Italy, France, and Germany are known to me only through his letters, a book (written by a fellow CIC officer) in which he appears, newspaper interviews, and letters written on his behalf. I have photographs of him, his CIC buddies, captured SS officers, towns with names, and towns without names. His few handwritten notes detailing interviews he held with suspected spies hold no significance, as the suspects were deemed not worthy of further investigation.

*Eyes and Ears*

Few Americans are aware of the CIC and its history. In their declassified account, *The History of the Counter Intelligence Corps*, the National Counter Intelligence Corps Association writes:

> *The demands on the FBI were so great during World War II that an agreement was reached whereby the CIC would handle all security matters pertaining to the U.S. Army exclusively. Thus "America's Secret Army," "Spy Catchers," "Spooks," or "Silent Warriors" was launched, with thousands of operative Special Agents spread worldwide. To accomplish their CIC missions, they often operated in civilian clothes rather than military uniforms and had false undercover identification and concealed weapons when necessary.*[li]

In the only "outsiders" book written about the Counter Intelligence Corps, *America's Secret Army, The Untold Story of the Counter Intelligence Corps*, Ian Sayer and Douglas Botting write:

> *Known as G-men in khaki, the CIC's special agents were the spy catchers of their day – an elite corps which included, at one time, both Henry Kissinger and J.D. Salinger. During the war they acted as gumshoes with bayonets among the first wave assault troops in the invasions of North Africa, Sicily, and Italy; as surveillance operatives in Iceland, Alaska, Panama, the Middle East, and Africa; as security officers on the secret Manhattan atom bomb project and during the preparations for D-Day; and as anti-sabotage experts operating in the Far East and against Otto Skorzeny's special operations commandos during the Battle of the Bulge.*

*The CIC's post-war duties included the dismantling of Japanese Intelligence and the hunting down of Nazi war criminals in Germany. They were pioneers in the covert battle against Soviet espionage, and even ran their own spy networks behind the Iron Curtain. Their adventures and personalities have long needed to be chronicled.*[lii]

Letters during the war were extremely important for those serving in the armed forces and for those waiting at home. Mom and Dad wrote to each other often, with letters often taking weeks to arrive at their destination. Allied soldiers' letters were censored to ensure that military information did not get to the enemy.

Although there are gaps, a good many of Dad's letters survived until April of 1945, when he still had nearly a year left in the military. Dad would have sent Mom's letters home for safekeeping. It is no surprise that they didn't all make it back. The first letter that I have from her was written in November of 1943, and none of her 1945 and 1946 letters are in my possession.

Dad could write nothing about his CIC work, nor where he might be.

*Eyes and Ears*

November, 1943
Independence, Kansas

Dear Bill,

Right now, I find that writing to you is a little hard because I have no idea where you are and if you will ever receive these letters.

Chuck and Clady just left with the children, Judy and Ray, and we had a nice visit. Chuck is going to choose the Navy if his commission doesn't come through. Larry Woods comes home on leave next week. I certainly will be glad to learn where you end up. Not that it matters, for the only important thing is for this war to be over. How glorious it is going to be when all of the boys are home again.

I am writing this from the U.S.O. in between serving snacks. But the crowd is growing and I must stop to wait on the soldiers.

Darling, I am just so happy that I got to see you before you were transferred. I'll always remember the precious moments that we had.

Love,
Lois

Susan Kandt Peterson

December, 1943

Dear Bill,

You boys over there probably do not realize now much you are envied by the boys here in service. Every boy I talk to wants combat or overseas duty.

There is a woman here whose husband died. He was a squadron leader and had been gone less than a month. She is expecting a baby in June. I feel so sorry for her.

The flu epidemic seems almost over. We were lucky not to have it in our family.

Yes, I am asked for dates, but it doesn't take me a minute to say that I don't date. I have only one man in my life and I love him so.

Love & Kisses,
Lois


Dearest Bill,

I have a job, a clerk at the Ration Board. I will start the first of the year from 8-5. I work at the USO until the 29th. Since I won't be with you at Christmas, I am so happy to have something to do to make the time pass quickly.

I love you so much, even though I can't be with you.

Lois


Dearest Bill,

Now that I have one letter from you, I am spoiled and everyday have hopes of receiving another. I am trying to find places for cadets and their wives to stay. It is pretty hard in little ole Independence.

This is our second wedding anniversary away from each other. I wonder where you are and what you will be doing. Just think that you have been my husband for seven years now. I still think that it is the best thing that ever happened to me.

I had better get back to the kitchen at the USO before we have a rush. Do you have a USO over there and is it run by the Salvation Army?

Love,
Lois

In Independence, Mom eventually became a manager of food rationing for half of Montgomery County, a government job. The people in the department each had an area to cover: tires, gasoline, clothing and so on. She primarily worked with restaurants who were also part of the **Rationing Program**. All of her women friends worked for the war effort. Some worked at Boeing, some in factories, some in munitions plants.

While industry and commerce were affected, individuals felt the effects more intensely. People were often required to give up many material goods, but there also was an increase in employment. Individual efforts evolved into clubs and organizations coming to terms with the immediate circumstances. Joining together to support and maintain supply levels for the troops abroad meant making daily adjustments. Their efforts also included scrap drives, taking factory jobs, goods donations, and other similar projects to assist those on the front.[liii]

Dearest Bill,

   I am glad that I am dieting. The radio just announced that the synthetic rubber allotted for girdles has just been taken over by the army. Think of our figures to say nothing about our morale.

   The office has been busy today with applications for tires and gasoline even though our quota isn't large enough to answer all of them.

   Take good care of yourself.

Love,
Lois

*Eyes and Ears*

January, 1944
CIC Det, P.B.S.

Dear Lois,

I am reminding you of my new address with the discontinuance of rank and serial number. I am simply an Agent.

You have no concept of how dark and strange a city can be when completely blacked out. Tonight, we followed a man who was soliciting restaurant business. He took us to his very modest home where his wife served a meal to us at three times its value, which is another means of many families to keep going. You and I did not have to see this side of Italian life and you would have liked it less than the third-class trains we rode on.

We have a deep sympathy for the children who are so undernourished.

Love,
Bill


Dearest Bill,

This is the happiest day that I've had in many. I received your long letter telling me of your good news. It is exciting! I am so happy for your setup.

## Susan Kandt Peterson

I am a jealous wreck having you in Italy. You know how I liked it.

I will worry about you flying but know that you enjoy it. I suppose it is just as safe as boats and trains. Do your duty but don't take unnecessary chances. Just remember that I told you that I am half here when you are gone.

Love,
Lois


Dear Lois,

It seems our correspondence is going to be disturbed again because our location changes constantly. We are now in a bombed out building sleeping on a stone floor with plenty of fresh air.

Last night an Italian soldier brought out an accordion, a Brit turned up with a mandarin, and an American with a guitar. There was singing and a good time. We find the British to be good fellows and a pleasure to work with.

Love from the bottom of my heart,
Bill

*Eyes and Ears*

February, 1944

Dear Lois,

Have you thought of a plan for our next house? Please keep a scrapbook of ideas. We can start with a floorplan similar to Great Bend, as we liked that house so well.

In letters to me, use the title "Mr." as we are no longer hindered by rank. We dress and move about as officers. Our organization and the nature of its activities is no longer secret but do not reveal certain details which you may know.

The CIC is a different organization here than in the States and I am happier than before, both with the manner in which we work and the operation of it all. The men here are excellent fellows with whom association is a benefit and a pleasure.

Fascists are coming to jail fast. It will be a pleasure to handle Nazis in such a similar situation.

I would rather have evenings with you to recapture.

Love,
Bill

Bill, CIC, Naples, 1944

Several excerpts taken from the newspaper article published in the *Wichita Beacon* in 1959 described some of Dad's work in the CIC. Among them:

*Operating in Naples in civilian clothes, Kandt was instrumental in breaking up several German spy rings. One of the methods used was to apprehend a Nazi spy and replace him with one of their own men. Extreme precautions were necessary, and contact was made only after a number of measures were taken.*[liv]


Dear Bill,

I am sure that Italy will not be the same as when we were there, but it must be in better shape than North Africa.

There are certainly a large number in the draft now. Last night over one hundred left here. The whole town went down to the train to see them off. There was a crash today, with a cadet and an instructor killed. I never know any of the fliers. I suppose you boys overseas cannot let such things bother you much. It probably just makes you fightin' mad to see the realities of war. I am sure that over here we cannot picture, in any way, what it must be like.

Do send a picture, if possible. I love you, sweetheart.

Lois


Dear Lois,

I have begun taking Italian lessons. The language is easier than German, but we will see. I am getting more night work now, which cuts in on my time.

I got caught outside tonight, in a blackout, without a flashlight, and almost got lost. I had my trusty .45 on my hip which is much comfort on such occasions. I am going to be a high-ranking officer for a while, for a special reason, of course.

Love,
Bill


Dad "became" a Major for a period of time, investigating a woman thought to be a spy. She would only go out with officers of higher rank.

Dear Bill,

The USO is having a dance tonight and I am going to help serve cake and coffee. Mother and Dad are going to a pancake supper at the Episcopal church.

A boy was in today from desert maneuvers. He saw your address and simply raved about your organization. He said that the CIC worked day and night and had the respect of the whole outfit. I am proud of you, baby.

Love,
Lois


Dearest Lois,

I am enclosing tentative house plans for our post-war home. Dream along with me and we will have something to start on one day.

You would be surprised at the beauty of this modern office I am writing this letter in. I think Fascist funds must have gone into the building. The walls are not trembling tonight. I listen to news from London occasionally and sometimes to German propaganda. The music from various European capitals is fine.

Love,
Bill

Mussolini's fascist government, in Italy, appealed to Adolph Hitler. Germany embraced fascism more than any other country. The Nazi government between 1933 and 1945 was a fascist government. **Fascism** is an ultranationalist, authoritarian political philosophy. It combines elements of nationalism, militarism, economic self-sufficiency and totalitarianism. It opposes communism, socialism, pluralism, individual rights and equality and democratic government. Fascism rejects the practices of representative or liberal democratic government. It holds that these practices interfere with the expression of national will. Violence is accepted, even celebrated.[lv]

March, 1944

My Darling,

I had made a date to write you that long letter tonight as I realize I have not written for several days, but the fate of war has intervened. My heart has resumed its normal beat. I was scared. I think the British were frightened, too, but damn their poise and self-control, they refuse to show it! The aftermath was there to greet us in the morning, naked, ugly, and cruel.

Your good report on CIC maneuvers has pleased the boys. We like to hear of such things.

I love you dearly and hope to dream of you soon.

Susan Kandt Peterson

Always and always,
Bill

April, 1944

Dear Lois,

Tonight, with the other fellows, I am sleeping in a nice apartment, surprisingly, not touched by bombs. It was lived in by an Italian family, but the furnishings are gone. This is the first time I can enjoy Italy and can briefly forget the war. We have an excellent view of [redacted text]. Tonight, huge clouds of fire and smoke are in the air, making the sky grow red.

My work the last few days has been so extremely interesting that I didn't know today was Sunday. When someone mentioned it, I immediately dreamed of you, which I haven't had much time to do lately.

I am always inspired by the endings of your letters when you write of victory. You have a good understanding of what it takes to win. I enjoy it more, however, when you write of your love, which is the best inspiration for me.

I love you,
Bill
Dearest Bill,

*Eyes and Ears*

Today is Sunday and I would rather be playing but there is so much work to do that I came to the office.

You know, it has been seven months now since we gave up our apartment in Chicago. Maybe it won't have to be so many more months before this horrid war is over and you can return home, I can't let myself think about it because it makes me too unhappy.

I love you with all of my heart and I think about you all of the time.

Your Lois


My Darling,

Please send my blue suit, the one I bought in Chicago. I will be needing it when the weather turns warmer. Have 2" taken in from the waist of the trousers.

How situations do change. Tonight I am in a luxurious office, sitting behind a large desk, smoking a cigar. The music from the radio is excellent. I have been reading letters from you and have momentarily forgotten the war except when a German announcer interrupts to tell whether or not enemy planes are over the Reich. Usually, they are.

One afternoon I drove toward the mountains. I parked the jeepadillo by a gentle, grassy slope. I walked up the slope and lay in the grass. In front of me was the sea, above the blue sky and behind, a staggering wall of mountains. On the slopes were arbors, orchards, and gardens. It was a tranquil, Mediterranean scene, such as we have known together. It betrays the handwriting on the wall.

I am happy that your work is interesting and is keeping you busy. I have the opportunity to apply for OCS in J.A.G.D. but would not trade it for CIC.

We will have sweet endings together, Darling. Just wait until then.

Bill


Dear Lois,

Long time no letter from Lois. Long time no letter from Bill. I think we both understand.

Yesterday a Capt. walks up to me, "What time, please?" "0920 hours," I says. "Say," says he, "where can I get a watch like that?" "Right here," says I, and I gives him the watch and he pays me

50 bucks! So, I takes part of the 50 bucks and buys Lois two more pairs of Venetian vases.

I've been working on one thing for over a month and just submitted a 33-page report, which the chief says is the best report he has seen in CIC. So what? Does it make any difference to the Army? Hell, no!

Don't feel concerned that I sold the watch. I finally got a G.I. one which is doing well.

I love you,
Bill

May, 1944

Dear Lois,

Today I had a close-up view of Marlene Dietrich. She didn't seem to recognize me. I suppose that things between us are over.

I can imagine how tired you are working such long hours. You are having administrative headaches, as we are. I have not written to you the last few days because my morale is so low. Sometimes it is difficult to keep sight of the main objective. And I miss you so much sometimes, to the point of forgetting my work. Do not take the remarks about the women too seriously. I have learned that when one has lived and enjoyed the very finest of human relationships, there is no use in trying to duplicate it. Only with you can I experience such deep joy again.

It is difficult to read and write in the dark, especially when the earth is shaking under you.

Love,
Bill

Bill, CIC, Italy 1944

Dearest Bill,

Six months ago, we were standing beside that train in Baltimore where I had come to see you off. You and I were not dramatic, not a single tear. We were both putting on a terrific show.

You were showing me how to take it and I was determined to send you off with a smile. Well, we both got through the act until the final curtain, didn't we? I'm glad we did it that way for I can now picture you standing on the platform and waving a big wave. It is a beautiful picture. I look prettier when I do not cry, and I wanted to look pretty for you those last few minutes even though my heart was crying.

I love you,
Lois


Dear Lois,

A word about Miss B. I am not taking Italian lessons from her any longer. Many of our boys find themselves in peculiar situations with families of girls of the "better class."

Roughly, there are two classes of girls here, those who do it for money (very numerous during the war), and those who do it for marriage. It seems that of the latter class, if a boy once dates one of them (always with some member of the family present), he is considered practically engaged to her and the obligations, therefore, become too uncomfortable for an American who is not accustomed to such things. The family is careful to guard the girl's virginity, for if she loses it to a man who does not marry her, then she will never find a husband among men of that class. Here the man insists on marrying a virgin and then establishes himself with a mistress after the marriage.

I have strayed from my subject. I have enjoyed Miss B's company, and her teaching. She knew from the beginning that I had a wife and that I love only my wife. But, none-the-less. I don't take lessons anymore. My heart belongs entirely to you and neither war nor distraction can alter my love.

Yes, I am still too thin. My clothes hang on me like on most Italians, but I am healthy and feel good.

I can tell you a story about how words influence other people, even though they are not conscious of it. The building I live in is an army billet and every few days a corporal comes around to check names and room numbers to see if the persons are properly billeted here. The corporal came yesterday while I was in my room and we engaged in conversation. He said that the first day I moved in, he made the check but could not find any markings on my bag, so he got the information from a letter on my table. He informed me that he does not make a practice of snooping through other people's mail, but that one sentence of the letter caught his eye: "Do your duty but don't take unnecessary chances." He said that sentence from your letter became a proverb with him which he keeps in mind, particularly since he is often on duty during air raids.

Now, when he makes checks, he does not look for my name. He opens the door, sees your picture fastened on the mirror, knows that I still occupy the room, then says to himself, "Okay, Mrs. Kandt," and closes the door.

I am proud of you in so many ways!

Okay, Mrs. Kandt,
Bill


Dearest Bill,

I am sorry that you had to give up Italian lessons with Miss B. The people have a very narrow-minded viewpoint. I am not the least bit jealous. You need to enjoy what companionship you have, honey, and don't let your conscience hurt you on my account. Ours is a wonderful love!

You know that I am very broadminded about such things. All I ask is that you be careful so that all of our lives we won't have to regret a few hours of bliss for you. I have heard that the rate of disease runs high when a country has been taken over. I certainly would not ask you to be a saint when you are gone for so long. I do believe in a double standard and what goes for you does not go for me. I know that you encourage me to date, but I have no desire to do so. The boys at the USO are fun to talk to and sometimes dance with but that is as far as it goes. They are mostly younger and it's fun to tease them. They are lonely and need conversation with women who support them.

My greatest love is only for you,
Lois


My Dearest Lois,

   This part of the Bella Italia is getting soaked with rain. They are of a short duration and do not flow unceasingly like Italian conversations.

   Sometimes you express fear for my safety. You needn't be worried. From your reports, I believe you are working harder than I am.

   The flowers here are in abundance. The ugly grey walls appear quite different now that the flowers are in bloom. I wish that I could give you an armful of them.

I love and miss you,
Bill

*Eyes and Ears*

Dearest Bill,

I have been worried after reading about Italy in this week's *Time*. If I only knew some of the things you were doing, I would probably be sick with worry. When you were at Camp Blanding, I was worried because I could not recall all of the little things about you. But this time, nothing much has slipped away. I can remember the little things you do and say which makes me feel closer to you. All of this because I love you so much.

I was surprised to learn that you had had your fill of Europe. But I can see how living in a war-torn country could make you feel that way.

Lois

June, 1944

My Darling,

I didn't get very far with the Italian language and am thinking of starting another which I will need soon. It is one you studied for several years.

In the midst of war, I am on vacation. I feel I have earned some time to myself as much as anyone in the army. I am running around in my jeep with the top down and exploring every nook of this vicinity that I had, heretofore, missed. I am quite removed from the war and am not suffering wartime hardships such as your letters indicate you worry about.

Right now, there is laughter and music coming through the window. One small boy is doing a thorough job of swearing in English. He probably doesn't know what he is saying but if he did, he would say it anyway. I am often tempted to shoot the little bastards who enjoy petty thievery because they won't leave the jeeps alone. They tramp on the starter, blow the horn, turn on the lights and would drive them off if we didn't have the steering wheels secured. We Americans hesitate to be firm. We are generous.

So long until next time,

Love,
Bill

On June 5, 1944, Dad saw the city of Rome liberated. The day was referenced in Dad's 1959 newspaper article published in the *Wichita Beacon*:

> *Kandt was loaned to the Fifth Army for the invasion of Rome where he targeted many informers and Gestapo agents for arrest. On one occasion, Kandt and his men learned that the Gestapo had planted a cache of explosives in the city to be used when the Allies took over. A man was planted in the*

*Eyes and Ears*

*Gestapo unit and he learned of the explosives location. The canisters of explosives were dug up before they could be used.*

Dear Lois,

Please note my change of address. Use the title, "Mr."

I have been too busy and too tired to write, and I know that you will understand why.

Coming into this place was like a triumphal march, except the dignity that one would expect was missing, as we were weary and dirty and quite surprised at meeting no opposition. We came in during the daytime, June 5, on the heels of the advance troops, who had arrived the night before. The population lined the streets for miles, cheering and allowing space for only a single line of vehicles.

The Germans had told them that if they came into the streets, they would be shot, so they went to the rooftops and waited throughout the night. It was like a Roman holiday and the women were beautiful and nice. We were impressed with the dignity and nice appearance of the people and the quiet and cleanliness of the town as compared to Naples.

I came in my jeepadillo with my windshield down. I wore goggles for protection from the dust and with the trailer and jeep loaded with many things. We had passed through much devastation. The smell of death was there, and starving people, too. It is hard to face starving people when you are eating a meal, but if you feed them, there will be more than you can handle. It is our difficult duty to take care of ourselves first.

Immediately upon arriving, we had and will have, much interesting work to do. I have not had a bath since leaving Naples, but I did here. We have bathtubs but the water has to be carried. I have much responsibility. I am in charge of the section of the language for which I am qualified and have very little assistance. I am meeting many nice people who speak the same language, and some not-so-nice.

I have seen the old stadium by moonlight. I thought of you when I accidentally bumped into the fountain where you and I bought fruit and bread and ate our lunch. I have run into many other places that you would recognize.

Good night, my Darling. I can see your head resting on your pillow and your lovely face as you sleep quietly on.

Love,
Bill

Dearest Bill,

Did you hear about the girl who requested her boyfriend be more careful, for his good conduct medal scratched her?

So, this is D-day! Most people have taken the news quite calmly here, but with a reserved sort of pride. I am glad that there hasn't been a mad hysteria and celebration, for that should come with victory after we know that no more lives have to be taken.

I'll send a picture soon. Remember that I love you.

Lois

**D-Day**, on June 6, 1944, more than 160,000 Allied troops landed along a 50-mile stretch of heavily fortified French coastline to fight Nazi Germany on the beaches of Normandy, France. The day was a turning point in World War II but wasn't without enormous casualties. It is estimated over 425,000 troops – both Allied and German – were killed, wounded, or went missing.[lvi]

Susan Kandt Peterson

July, 1944

Dearest Bill,

I am awfully blue today. Everyone coming in the office has been so crabby and unpatriotic, not at all willing to make sacrifices for the war. It makes you lose faith. They say not to write anything but cheerful news to the boys overseas, but you have always wanted to look reality squarely in the face.

I am beginning to be concerned about no letters from you. I had only two in seven weeks. There is just a big hollow inside my ribs when I don't hear from you. I am quite miserable without you and having to worry just adds to my missing you. It is hard on my morale. I know that you are busy but please do not make me worry unless it is absolutely necessary.

I love you so,
Lois


August, 1944

Dearest Bill,

After staying glued to the radio for two days, I have found out where the 7th Army is operating. I try not to worry about you and for the most part, I do well, for the news is certainly favorable. I will try to be more patient waiting for your letters. You know that isn't one of my greatest virtues.

Tonight, Mother and I are going to a movie. Your mother really doesn't like to go out anymore. I thought she was going to cry last night when I told her the 7th Army was going to invade France. I talked her out of it, but you should write to her soon. I told her that soon you might be in Paris and that it would be just like when you were in Rome.

Take good care of yourself, honey.
Lois


My Dearest One,

The trip here was pleasant. Along the way we stopped and purchased watermelon from the natives and drove into the shade and ate the melon from our jeep. Our satisfaction was lessened by the dirty, hungry kids who flocked around us. We gave them some and drove away feeling better by our deed than from having eaten the melon.

I left Rome feeling that I had accomplished something there. It is an excellent town to work in but also hard on the nerves due to the volume of work and the limited time to perform it. I liked best the intrigue created by the international elements of such a cosmopolitan place. I had experiences there that I could never duplicate.

I am now back in familiar streets from not-many-days ago. I am back in the army and expect to be somewhat a soldier for a while. The streets are dirty and much overcrowded, and I no longer have a jeep to bounce around in. But I have leisure time, which is something. In Rome last week, I worked two nights without sleep. Now I can eat, sleep, and study language.

I love you so deeply that I find nothing but vast emptiness without you. Like you, I am only half alive waiting for the day of our reunion, about which I do not dwell, for the date is too uncertain. It may be months, it may be years, but it will surely come and for that, I live.

I cannot believe that you have not heard from me in seven weeks. The mail must have been lost or delayed in arriving.

I love you and goodnight,
Bill

The Allied invasion of southern France, which took place late in the summer of 1944, was an operation first code-named "Anvil" and later "Dragoon" and marked the beginning of one of the most successful – but controversial – campaigns of World War II. On August 15, landing troops sailed from

*Eyes and Ears*

Corsica and surprised the German and Vichy French defenders at the French Riviera, at the Cavalaire-sur-Mer, Saint-Tropez, and Saint-Raphaël beaches.[lvii]

Having started with a different CIC Detachment, Dad was transferred to the 307th CIC Detachment sometime in Italy. A letter he wrote to a CIC friend in 1992, said:

> I believe it was Warren "Deacon" Anderson who got me into the 7th Army C.I.C. unit. I was fooling around in the Naples office one day when in walks Deacon wearing a trench coat and looking the worse for wear. He had holed up with a C.I.C. unit on the beach at Anzio and the Germans were giving them a bad time. He got me into Col. Crowell's 7th Army unit in time for Operation Anvil (the invasion of southern France.)
>
> The Navy handled us for the landing during Operation Anvil by spreading a huge rope net over the deck of the ship and having us drive our jeeps with trailers, loaded with all of our stuff we wanted to take along. We then threw our barracks bags and other things into the net as they drew it up over everything and ordered us to hang on. The ship's crane then let us down gently on the deck of an Infantry Landing Craft. We moved closer to shore. The front of the landing

craft was let down and we drove off on the sandy beach of St. Tropez and that was that.

Bill heading toward St Tropez, France, August 1944

The Germans must have known we were coming because they headed for home. Our flyboys caught them on the highways and machine gunned and bombed the hell out of them. Then the Division's huge bulldozers came through to clear a path for the Infantry. They pushed aside dead men, horses, tanks, bicycles, and vehicles of every kind. I drove through the area several weeks later and the sweet smell of death still permeated the atmosphere.

## Eyes and Ears

```
   During the next two years, I had the
most impressionable experiences of my
life.
```

Robert Richards was with the same CIC 307th Detachment as Dad. In his later book, *Alias the Fox, The Wartime Recollections of Robert R. Richards,*[lviii] he further described Operation Anvil:

*On the way to St. Tropez, there was fighting in the streets and even small children were racing around with guns. The streets were littered with dead Germans and horses and with cars that had been destroyed by gunfire.*

*Having engaged a chef who worked on the Normandie, we drove to the Villa Bagatelle, in Marseilles, where Victor de Guinzbourg had secured earlier. The home had fifteen bedrooms, and baths and showers. Admiral Darliand had employed eleven servants. The huge kitchen was fully equipped. It was not difficult for our cook to move right in and make us a delicious dinner that night. The chef we had engaged was a very good cook, and we called him Pop. He would stay with us for a number of months, across France and into Germany.*

*We were kept awake all night by artillery bombing. We heard that the Germans had surrendered and that the Battle of Marseilles had ended.*

*With the German surrender, the city of Marseilles came to life, that is, a more peaceful life. The streets were festooned with dangling trolley wires and broken glass. People all along the way shouted and waved and cried as we passed in our jeeps with our American flags on our arms. They were shouting,*

*"Merci," and reached to shake our hands and kiss us when we stopped.*

*While in the city, we arrested and interrogated a number of spies.*

In August of 1944, Floyd D. Snowden, Major, M.I. Chief of the CIC Home Area Allied Command wrote to recommend that my father – Agt. Kandt – receive a commission in the Army of the United States:

```
Subject: Agent William C. Kandt
To: Commanding Officer, C.I.C. Detachment, 7th
U.S. Army, APO #758, U.S. Army
```

1. I wish to take this opportunity to highly commend Agent William C. Kandt who recently left this detachment. While in the Rome CIC Detachment he was Agent in Charge of the German Section of this organization. He used excellent judgement, skill, and ability, and his knowledge of C.I.C. matters is far above that of the average Agent. His loss to this section was great and I do not hesitate to recommend him highly for any position which he might seek.
2. During his stay with this detachment in Rome, he investigated and developed many highly important espionage cases which concerned German Nationals. He speaks the language fluently and is well qualified in temperament, judgement,

and ability to be an officer in the Army of the United States.

3. I believe that if any opportunity exists that this Agent will make an excellent officer and highly recommend that he be given every opportunity to receive a commission in the Army of the United States.

Floyd C. Snowden
Major, M.I.
Chief CIC, Rome Area Allied Cmd.

September, 1944

Dearest Lois,

Our French cook is an artist with imagination who loves his art. We are eating very well. I am trying to put on weight but will probably be pulled out before that happens. The countryside is a garden with cattle and a variety of vegetables. The population is doing well except for a shortage of grain. The people in the cities are not so fortunate.

I am losing hair fast. My time for baldness is sure to arrive. My life is comparatively dull these days, but it won't last long. I am sad most days and am beginning to be quite weary of overseas life. There is something I miss very much and that something is you. I love you.

Bill

Following St. Tropez and Marseilles, Dad's photo is included in Richard's book, in September of 1944, in Epinal, France. Richards wrote:

> *On October 1, we moved into a new CP headquarters in Epinal, France, I had a nice room with Bill Kandt, an agent from Kansas. Altogether, there were 17 of us in the area. Epinal had been heavily damaged by artillery and we could still hear the guns in the distance. After our arrival, three of our CIC boys were killed by German snipers.*
>
> *On October 13 we arrested a spy in Marseilles. The security nature of this case was so important that his name was not given in any of our records. He was arrested at his home at midnight. He had just finished broadcasting to Germany. He had been doing so since August 15, 1944, the date of the Southern France invasion. We arrested another agent who was a tough character. He was in a cafe in Epinal where he was trying to engage soldiers in conversation. He was wearing an American division patch on his shoulder. A few days later, we caught more Germans in 45th Division uniforms.*

Dad's 1959 *Wichita Beacon* interview correlated with Richard's account, and included some other interesting details:

> *In France we arrested a man who claimed to be a Frenchman who had escaped to Switzerland but was returning to help the Allies in their cause. Our investigation revealed he was a German intelligence officer whose mission was to discover the location of gas pipelines from the coast inland to Patton's Third Army. He confessed his job was to pinpoint the pipeline for parachutists who would drop in and blow up the*

*pumping stations. He thought they might come in anyway as the Nazis were getting desperate. Radar units in the area were alerted and ten days later we picked them up before their mission was accomplished.*

Dearest Bill,

I am listening for the confirmed news that we are in Germany now. This war has been going on for five years now and all of this time we have been waiting for the day. Maybe German supplies will finally give out. I wonder how long it will be before we are in Berlin and wonder if you will go there. This whole thing has been so horrible for a civilized world. We all want you home and I am sure that those of you overseas want it even more.

I love you,
Lois


Dearest Bill,

It has been 24 days since I have heard from you. That's a long time when a war is raging. I am naturally beginning to be a little concerned. There is always, in the back of my mind, that something may have happened to you. I hope that you are well and safe.

I do believe in the point chart for the demobilization of the army. It is only right that men with children should return before those without. You might just put down that you sure did want to have a couple!

Honey, I am wondering if the wonderful new drug, penicillin, might help cure your skin rash.

We had a crash out at the base last night. Two officers were killed. It was the first air crash we have had in a long time.

Living and waiting for your return. I'll keep my chin up.

Lois


Dearest Bill,

After 27 days I received a letter from you and that grin hasn't left my face! Your mother has been worried about you and I said she should be, with all of the French girls kissing you!

The photos you sent helped me visualize you more in your work. It looked like you were sleeping very peacefully. Two days spent in the big chateau must have been very luxurious compared to the days that followed. I hate to think of you sleeping on the ground now that cold weather is coming.

Mother and I went to see *Two Girls and a Soldier*, an amusing show. The newsreel had some good scenes of Marseilles. I always look for you in a crowd. It was easier when you were in Rome but I don't know where you are now.

Good night. Under the chin kiss just for you, honey.

Lois

October, 1944<br>France

Dearest Lois,

Here is another picture. The little guy in the picture is a Nazi who doesn't live here anymore. The other guy is a slothful sleuth wearing a suit that doesn't fit him anymore. As the boys say, "Home was never like this. Can you beat it?" When doing an undercover job on a female subject, "Where can you beat it?" When the chow is good and you have a bed to sleep in, "You never had it so good. You found a home in the Army!"

Does this sound like doubletalk? I feel like a double person tonight. A split personality. I don't know who I am or why I am here, and I can't reach definitive conclusions about anything, except that things don't make sense. After a while, you engage in cynicism and seek only stark realities. Where are the ideals of youth? Was it worthwhile to pretend belief in them and attempt to apply them while devouring energy which may have been put to sterner use? Were we wrong? Were we trying to escape from obvious human cruelties by assuming attitudes of piety as a cover for inner frailties? Was our direction wrong? Were we purposely stubborn, hoping to find an easy path?

That ain't thunder you hear, bud! As one of the boys said, "When I return, will I find anything the same?" A colonel says, "We can't help Europe. Why should we try? Who cares what happens to Europe?" A dogface says, "I want to go home. These people will always fight. They are interested only in our money and supplies. I want to go home." A captain says, "America should not attempt to influence the peace. If we stay over here, they will make suckers of us again."

We are a new generation. We are bitter, we harbor prejudice, we are cynical even with reality, our minds are warped with hate. We have lost faith. We are not capable of creating a lasting peace. Where are those who are? Will they step forward or is it too late?

Be good my darling, and dream of me.
Bill

*Eyes and Ears*

Dearest Bill,

The Bob Hope show is on the radio tonight. Last night, Millie and Jo and I went to a double feature. I don't know what we would do without our two movies a week. I can now sit through a double feature and enjoy it.

Actually, honey, I don't think that any of us are interested in fighting a war for Europe or the Europeans. It is for our own interests that we became involved in battle. Would you want to live here in the States with a Nazi-dominated Europe? We have become such a small world that we could not live our way of life with servitude on the other side of the Atlantic. I think that it is for America that we are fighting. As for their appreciation of our arms and men, I do suppose that it may be taken for granted. Don't let it get you down. Try your best not to be too cynical.

Remember that I love you darling and that I think of you so much.

Lois

Susan Kandt Peterson

Dearest Bill,

I have been reading about the planes dropping winter clothing to the soldiers in France. I do so worry about you being cold and know how much you suffer. I can still see you huddled up in a suit and a robe by a fire at Keck's in Tübingen. You are so thin that you won't have the resistance that you once had.

It has been over twelve days and I finally heard from you. I am deliriously happy!

It is discouraging to think of not seeing you for many months, yet I hadn't really counted on anything. I have always felt that your work and qualifications would keep you over there. I have become much more of a realist due to the war. You have to look at things as they are instead of what they should be. You have long held this philosophy and I am rather new to it.

Give Anderson my best and tell him that I will give him the third degree on your behavior when he gets back. So you had better get together on your stories!

I love you, honey.
Lois

*Eyes and Ears*

France

Dearest Lois,

Your letter of the 7th arrived today and I can't stop looking at the pictures, between bomb bursts. I can't but be surprised at how thin you look. The silly beret looks nice and the suit does, too. The soldier wolf in the background seems to have a gleam in his eye. The boys told me that he is your escort who stepped back while the picture was taken. And why is she standing in front of the Officer's club?

Lois, Independence, Kansas, 1944

The room I am in is paneled. The chandelier is a candelabra with crystal. One of the boys is playing Beethoven on the grand piano. I am working on a large, walnut desk. With the Germans here first, and then us, the place is a bit worse for wear.

It is good that you have finally realized that I will not be home very soon. My qualifications have nothing to do with it, as it is a general situation. However, I am one of the few similarly qualified and will have a great share of the burden.

The lights are out again, so by candlelight, I look at your picture. You look lovely and I love you.

Bill

In his book, Robert Richards wrote:

*On November 2, Bill Kandt and I began preparations to go to Germany via Aachen. On our way we stopped at Rheims where we saw the Cathedral in the moonlight. We stayed that night at the Hotel de Lyon.*

*The next evening, we arrived in Brussels. We found a fine double room at the Hotel Metropole. The next day we explored the town and took pictures. We had car trouble because there was water in our gas tank.*

*On November 6 we went to Spa and visited the CIC of the First Army Headquarters. A Colonel and a Major gave us a hard time and demanded to know if we were officers so they could determine if we should eat with them. I refused to tell them, which was according to our orders. Not knowing for sure what our ranks were, they decided they'd better let us join them.*

*That night we witnessed our first German buzz bombs as they went overhead. They were small planes that carried bombs with no pilots. They were also being used to bomb England.*

*The next day we left for Kornelimunster, Germany, where we met with the CIC of the Seventh Corps. From there we went to the Refugee Cage at Brand where we interviewed CIC agents who were working there. We then drove to Aachen which had really been pounded by repeated bombings. Returning to Brussels that night, as we tried to sleep, more buzz bombs flew about, and we were awakened by sirens. We would hear the bombs coming...a sudden silence...and then a boom. It was not pleasant.*

*But there were also high moments as well. We spent November 8 and 9 shopping in Brussels. It was terrific fun, like being back home, a welcome break for us. We stayed at the Palace Hotel and were invited to dinner by Albert Cnockaert of the Agfa Corp. Bill and I gave Cnockaert and his family a carton of cigarettes, chocolate, and a ten-in-one ration which was very welcome because food is in such short supply. We were told that the people of Brussels went wild after the liberation.*

*On November 11 we celebrated Armistice Day! It was a beautiful day in Brussels. Red, yellow, and black flags were fluttering in the wind. We left that morning and stopped at Waterloo to visit the Panama Building and the huge monument. From there we went to Luxembourg.*

*In Luxembourg, everyone spoke German. We learned that the king and queen had just returned from England, where they had fled for their safety. That evening we left at dark and arrived back at Eupen.*

*Amid our daily work schedule, we planned for a wild boar hunt with Colonel Silbaugh, who was in the Artillery. I knew him from before the war in Ohio. We saw six wild boars but didn't shoot because some of the fellows were in the way.*

*That evening, many thousands of refugees from St. Vie began coming through our lines. Their city had been burned by the Germans, a despicable act.*


Dearest Lois,

Your snapshots are quite nice, but I was startled at how thin you look. Your eyes and nose are the same as when we met about 15 years ago, when we managed our first date in the basement of our old high school. We were sixteen. You were wearing a Pep Club sweater and skirt and glasses and were trying to appear unconcerned and nonchalant, although anyone could plainly see that you knew it was the best break you ever had up to that time! Anyway, it was for me. We were a bit bashful and it required much courage for me to approach you.

Goodnight, my love. Keep the Montgomery County rationing program running smoothly, but don't you dare get thinner.

Much love,
Bill

*Eyes and Ears*

November, 1944

Dearest Bill,

    Last night I went over to see Mary. It was the hardest thing I have ever done. Mary is sure that Bill is dead. I couldn't find any words to comfort her. The whole town seems to be rather blue. So many boys are missing in action or are killed. No doubt some are prisoners. It will be such a relief when it is all over.

I love you so very much, darling.
Lois

Richards wrote the following in his book:

> *In November Bill Kandt and I, at the request of General Patch, went from France up to Belgium and across to Aachen, which had fallen to the American First Army. We interviewed the counter-intelligence agents up there as to what problems they found. We found that after they went into Germany, our agents didn't have any real resistance as far as their work went. However, the American counter-intelligence there were not using the CIC agents in accordance with the directives from Washington and therefore, they didn't have the freedom of action. They were not being asked to do counter-intelligence work.*
>
> *Bill and I were in Aachen for two or three days, then we crossed to Brussels for a day or two before returning to Aachen. We gave a report to the Seventh Army G-2 as to what we found up there and told him of the inefficient way*

Susan Kandt Peterson

*the First Army CIC was operating, which is quite different from the Seventh Army and Third Army areas.*

December, 1944

Dearest Bill,

More sad news about boys not coming home. It is so sad to receive this news right before Christmas.

Mother is mad at me tonight and I don't care. I get so sick of the petty little things that she dwells on. We disagreed over the icing of Dad's birthday cake. The only way I can cook is to have her out of the kitchen. I thought it would be good for Mother and Dad to have me home while you were gone. She also was angry at me because my leg makeup left a ring in the bathtub and asked me not to use it anymore. Because we are not able to buy stockings, I will continue to use it and told her that I would gladly clean the bathtub. I suppose it's hard on all of us. I was used to having my own home with you and my privacy. To be fair, so were they.

I am reading a wonderful historical novel. I wish that we were in our own home, sitting in our big chairs, reading and fighting over the ottoman.

I love you dearly and think about you so very much.

Lois

                                              Somewhere

Dearest Lois,

After shifting about in the great outdoors for a while, it was good to come in and find two nice letters from someone who means everything to me. I wish that I could continue to write to you as I did in October, but it is not always possible.

Bill, CIC, 1944

We are set up well here. We are in a home abandoned by Nazis who suddenly decided they had better not stick around. Food was still on the table. We had fun rummaging around before the household stuff was turned over to the French authorities. We have electricity, steam heat, and hot water. It was nice of the people to leave us coal, potatoes, and other things that we can use.

How do you like the enclosed pictures? One is of Robert (Bob) Richards who took them and several others that I sent to you. Richards was with me on the whirlwind shopping tour in Belgium when we bought the gloves and things which you should have by now.

I love you so much, so deeply and sincerely and it will never be otherwise.

With deep love,
Bill

Richards adds some details of this in his book as well:

> *On the second of December I went to Saverne, France and took over a 15-room house at 55 Detweiler Strasse, where the head of the German railroad had lived. The Germans had left in haste, leaving food still on the table. The other agents joined me the next day.*
>
> *We apprehended and sent to prison all sorts of characters whom we would then give over to the American Military Police or the French Securite Militaire. They were usually shot.*
>
> *Most of the spies we caught were not German but were Swiss, French, or other nationalities. As agents, we were instructed to give only our name, rank, and serial number if*

*ever captured, and nothing else. But apparently, the training agents for the Axis had not included these imperatives. When we interrogated suspected spies, we pretty well exhausted them as to their life history.*

CIC group, Saverne

*On December 15, we suddenly found out that we should leave Alsace immediately. The Bulge was up there, and we were at the Saverne Gap, a very narrow passageway through the mountains between Alsace and France. That evening I got word that the seventh Army would be retreating quickly that night, westward to the city of Luneville, France.*

*When we arrived in Luneville, we took over an apartment we thought was very good. It had been a brothel with about fifteen or twenty rooms. We set up operations there. The signal corps put in telephones for communication with the airfields so we could immediately be contacted. We began making arrests.*

## Susan Kandt Peterson

*On December 18 I learned that the Germans had broken through the American First Army where Bill Kandt and I had been five weeks before. I heard that the Germans were disguising themselves as Americans.*

France

Dearest Lois,

For three or four days I have not written to you, not because I haven't wanted to, but I cannot give you an account of my activities and I must search the air for things to put on paper.

The notification of your *Time Magazine* gift to me has arrived. I am glad that you made that arrangement.

The lights have gone off and I have the old candle burning. I, too, get that vacant feeling, but we both must realize that it will pass off as time passes on, which will bring us nearer to each other.

All the love I can send from this distance, I am yours forever,
Bill

*Eyes and Ears*

Somewhere

Dearest Lois,

I've not been able to write much about my activities, but the enclosed commendation will give you some idea. We are very proud of it because we are such a small group and sometimes, maybe, the army doesn't know that we are around. Our present plans are quite ambitious. We will be very, very busy. Then, perhaps, I will not be so lonesome and won't have much time to dwell on it.

I'm sure that your Christmas was very pleasant, but I know that you are very lonesome, too. I hope your New Year will be a happy one and that you pass our anniversary in pleasant thoughts of the past and of the things that lie before us.

Love,
Bill

The letter Dad referenced was written on December 6, 1944 by A.M. Patch, Lieutenant General, U.S. Army, Commanding to the Commanding Officer of the 307th Counter Intelligence Corps Detachment, APO 758, U.S. Army:

Subject: Commendation

1. The 307th C.I.C. Detachment has shown the highest of professional standards during the planning and operational phases of the DRAGOON

(ANVIL) Operation. For the successful carrying out of all assigned tasks, and for the effective prevention of Seventh Army forces from the insidious attacks of espionage and sabotage agents, I wish to express my appreciation and commendation.

2. Displaying outstanding initiative, resourcefulness and leadership, the members of this detachment have caused the development of a splendid system of road-blocks throughout the Seventh Army area which has led to the apprehension of numerous dangerous enemy agents, thereby defeating enemy plans and efforts to obstruct the progress and injure the troops of the Seventh Army. This splendid achievement reflects great credit not only on the 307th Detachment but also on the entire Counter Intelligence Corps.
(Signed)
A.M. Patch
Lieutenant General, U.S. Army
Commanding

At this same time in December of 1944, the commanding offer of the 307th Counter Intelligence Corps Detachment Headquarters of the Seventh Army, Lieutenant Col. G. Kenneth Crowell, wrote the following to the Commanding General Seventh Army recommending my father for promotion:

*Eyes and Ears*

December 13, 1944

Subject: Recommendation for Battlefield Assignment

To: Commanding General, Seventh Army, APO 758, U.S. Army

Statement on demonstrating outstanding ability to command in actual combat, under fire, citing instances, dates and circumstances: Agt. Kandt's performances both in the Italian campaign and in the present one has been of a high order. The following instances are cited as demonstrative of his ability to command in actual combat, under fire;

As a member of the 6788th CIC Detachment under Major Floyd C. Snowden, Agt. Kandt was selected to enter the city of Rome, Italy, with an S-force, assigned the mission of raiding Gestapo offices and other intelligence targets. Agt. Kandt led a team of two men into the city at 0700 hours 5 June 1944, under artillery fire. Despite the enemy arms fire and sniping, Kandt and his men proceeded with their work, obtaining valuable and timely information which led to the capture of numerous dangerous enemy agents hiding in the city. During their work, Agt. Kandt and Agt. Raymond

P. Daguerre captured two German soldiers who had been hiding in one of the buildings being searched by the S-force. For his leadership and organizing ability in making up raiding parties, consisting of Military Police, CIC agents and Italian plainclothesmen (SIM), and for courage shown in his personal apprehension of dangerous suspects offering armed resistance, Agt. Kandt won the highest commendation of Major Floyd C. Snowden, his Commanding Officer. Major Snowden stated at that time that, in his opinion, Agt. Kandt should be a commissioned officer.

Ray Daguerre and Bill, Rome 1944

Agt. Kandt was a member of the advance party raiding enemy intelligence headquarters and espionage targets in Lyon, France, and entered that town at 0800 hours September 1944 while street fighting and enemy sniping were still in progress. In one instance, while Lt. Abraham W. Brussell of this detachment was examining documents in the office of Captains Paul and Vincent, FFI officers, 2ieme Bureau, Lyon Section, an enemy sniper concealed in an apartment directly across the street opened fire with a machine pistol on Lt. Brussell and his party, wounding both Captain Paul and Captain Vincent. Agt. Kandt, who was standing on the street below, covering the street entrance to the hotel, directed his FFI Militia Team in returning fire upon the sniper, thus protecting Lt. Brussell and his party and preventing the outbreak of uncontrolled and dangerous small arms fire. In organizing and directing the efforts of FFI teams and in obtaining counterintelligence information under the above conditions, Agt. Kandt contributed greatly to the success of the Lyon Advance party.

A fluent German linguist, Agt. Kandt was selected to accompany Robert R. Richards of this Detachment on a trip to the First Army area, 3 November 1944, to obtain information on CIC operations in the Aachen-Eupen area. During this trip, it was necessary to contact Corps and Division personnel to obtain first-hand information on actual DID field operations in Germany. This was accomplished despite constant exposure to enemy shell-fire. Agt. Kandt's thoroughness, his devotion to duty and disregard of personal safety in carrying out his mission was commended by Lt. Richards at that time. As a result of Kandt's efforts, much valuable information was obtained for future operations.

Agt. Kandt has an extensive knowledge of Germany and German intelligence organizations, as well as having had considerable practical experience handling emigration problems in the office of the American Embassy in Stuttgart, Germany, before the war. Because of his fine soldier qualities and his outstanding performance on missions in combat under fire, this officer believes that Agt. Kandt should be a commissioned officer. As such, Agt. Kandt's value to the Counter Intelligence Corps and to the Service would be immeasurably increased, especially to contemplated future operations."

G. Kenneth Crowell,
Lt. Col., Infantry
Commanding

The father that I knew was not a soldier. He was a gentle-speaking man who loved to read, wrote for law journals, laughed easily, participated in theatre, and always had a curiosity to learn new things, auditing university classes. If conversation eventually bored him, we would find him in his study, reading a book, even with dinner guests still sitting at the table.

He was not a man's man. He wasn't a sports enthusiast, nor a hunter. As a father he read us books, took us horseback riding at the VFW, encouraged us in music, fished on the pond in front of our house, made model planes and cars with my brother, drove on family vacations (always stopping to buy soft vanilla ice cream), took us to museums and let us play in the vast courtroom and offices he inhabited as a judge. He humorously awakened us in the morning with, "Rise and greet the glorious morn!"

He puttered in the garden, fiddled with his vintage Packard cars, corrected our grammar, and later taught himself how to play a recorder with soft melodies that floated upstairs as we drifted off to sleep. He might cry in a movie theatre. So, it surprised me to learn that he was ever in the line of fire, incidents of which he never spoke.

Per Robert Richard's book:

> *We found, in Luneville, a small hotel where we could all stay. When the CIC arrived, they had been quite busy on their trip to Luneville. They brought nine espionage agents with them. Once the spies were marched to prison, we had a few hours of sleep before we all had to rise. Agent Scott McCoy returned to Saverne and brought back the people who had been cooking for us. We were concerned that the Germans would capture and torture them seeking our identities.*

## Susan Kandt Peterson

*From our position in Luneville, we were right in the heat of battle. All about us, German planes were filling the skies. We were catching numerous enemy agents, both male and female.*

*On January 15 we had information from a spy that an enemy agent would be dropping in by parachute. We arranged for a plane to be waiting for him and had patrols put on the roads.*

*Three days later the big Russian offensive began. The Russians were fifteen miles from the German border.*

*By January 22 we were able to begin setting up a special radar system around Luneville. It was operated by the signal corps with phones to our office.*

Bill, CIC, Luneville, France, 1945

*Eyes and Ears*

January, 1945
France

Dearest Lois,

I am sorry that my mail has not been reaching you. I am particularly sorry that you worry, for it is unnecessary.

The snow is now falling heavily. As I walk around town, I am much reminded of the year we were over here. I even laugh when I touch the radiators, vainly trying to get warm. I do feel sad when I think that once again, we are apart on our anniversary, which seems to be a bit of a habit. The past eight years have been the proudest of my life, being married to you.

It is nice that you are making blood donations. If you could see how it is being used here, you would be proud.

You should see my office. It is a dumpy place, but we have made it quite comfortable. We gathered up chairs, tables, and lamps and are getting work done. We are sleeping on

Bill, Luneville, France, January 1945

cots but find it fine, especially with mattresses. I have set up two walnut panels from a cabinet, behind my chair, so I can brag about my paneled room.

The Commanding General has ordered that, by act of Congress, I am to be a gentleman and an officer. Which has been done. It is not quite known how Congress can make a gentleman, but it can make an officer, which we don't dispute. I am particularly pleased that I have just plugged along in an independent way and did not resort to politics or "pull." I will continue to be known as "Mr." I think it best that you not let my rank be known, or when I was commissioned. Such information is classified and for all outward purposes, I am a civilian. My present allotments of pay will cease and I am making arrangements for new ones.

It is very late and I must get some sleep for the morrow. I love you and could not love you more.

Bill


Dad was commissioned a 1st Lieutenant.

The article, "G-Men in Khaki" was published in The American magazine in January, 1945 by Gordon Gaskill, an American war correspondent. He wrote:

*Few people, even the Army itself, know much about the Counter Intelligence Corps, for obviously, it must operate behind a smoke screen of secrecy. CIC has two major functions. First, to catch enemy spies, saboteurs, and subversive agents. Second, to prevent our military plans and secrets from leaking out to the enemy.*

*The Corps is a puzzling mixture of G-men (FBI agents) and plain GI. Although its agents scoff at any cloak and dagger mystery about themselves, they have, in fact, done detective work that rivals any Oppenheim novel. They have literally caught hundreds of enemy agents. By recovering lost Allied secret papers and by discovering equally secret enemy ones, they have unquestionably saved thousands of American lives.*

*But they are also soldiers. They have ridden the very first waves of every African or European (and many a Far East) invasion by landing craft, glider, and parachute. They have done front-line intelligence work that has won them many medals and more compliments.*

*Not the least of the CIC romance lies in its own agents, who remain as anonymous as possible, never appear in print, and sometimes fool their friends about their real jobs. Perhaps no other Army unit has men of such consistently high-calibre men of astonishing talent, experience, and education.*

*The Army was combed to find men of exactly the right background. Hundreds of names were examined, only a few thousand were chosen (the exact number is still secret). Mostly they were ex-diplomats, newspaper men, accountants, lawyers, private detectives, FBI agents, foreign representatives for American firms, and some college professors. The Army favored men who had traveled extensively abroad and who could speak at least one foreign language well.*

*Their teachers were America's best-former secret service agents, FBI aces, narcotics investigators, military intelligence experts. They learned all known detective arts, and also such things as jujitsu, enemy spy methods, the powers of interrogation. They became crack pistol shots. They also got rigorous, toughening field training.*

*Today a CIC agent may find himself posing as anything from a deserter to a diplomat, from a clerk to a colonel. One day he may lounge in a smart London bar; the following week he may be assaulting an enemy invasion beach. He may be interviewing a beggar or a general, a duchess or a prostitute; he may be wearing a dinner jacket or torn trousers.*

*Almost without exception, they would laugh at transferring to another branch of the service. For now they are having adventures that a few years ago would have seemed the wildest dreams of some novelist. They are on the inside of great happenings.*[lix]

February, 1945

My Dearest Lois,

So, this is Paris, again! Not the same city that you and I saw with the gloom of impending war but perhaps somewhat gayer and relieved that actual war has passed it by. Night clubs and galleries and museums are closed for the most part, as are restaurants and cafes. So, people just walk around and promenade and mill about. The people are well dressed and most of the beautiful women are with British and American officers.

The longer I am away from you the more I miss you. Reading does no good and writing is torture. Entertainment is frivolous and without purpose. Last night I attended the ballet. It was graceful and colorful and nice. I had to prepare a training lecture or would have stayed in Paris longer.

I will avoid buying a dress uniform unless it is absolutely necessary. Perhaps before then, the war will be over. Could anything be nicer? I can't get the thought off my mind.

Love,
Bill


Dearest Lois,

I have just "come in" after being away for over a week, during which time I could not write to you. I had a very dull time, including shell dodging, but it was not as bad as it may sound. Although, I would agree with the boys who know that artillery shells are a greater strain on the mind than other weapons. The Germans are catching much hell and giving it, too, although it is only a matter of time with them.

This is the first time that I have written optimistically to you on the subject. I make my statements with caution, however, because I know that there is tough going ahead before the end, and probably plenty of it after. Many of the boys get quite excited about rotation and furlough, but when I come back to you, I want to be there for good.

Lois' picture by Bill's desk in France, 1945

I have the photo you sent pinned up on my wall right by my desk so that I can look at it all of the time. The boys have nice things to say about it.

Well, damnit! It's now midnight.

Goodnight, darling.
Bill

From France, Dad entered Germany in March of 1945. In Sayer and Botting's book, they wrote:

> *Until they stepped across the German frontier, the CIC had never set foot on real enemy soil in Europe. Guns had been turned against them in entering North Africa, but North Africa was French, not a true enemy. In Italy they had advanced through co-belligerent territory.*

> *But Germany was decidedly different. Germany was an enemy for whom the Allied soldiers had a profound respect, and a form of regime and vision of society for which they had nothing but loathing and contempt. Germany was taken very seriously. The fear of werewolves and other fanatical resistance organizations was universal. Never would the expatriation of Nazi spies, saboteurs, subversives, propagandists, ideologues, party die-hards, officials, and war criminals be more vital for the future of the civilized world.*

The next letter is the last found among the records he kept.

March, 1945

Dearest Lois,

    Your letter announcing Larry Wood's death just arrived, how he was killed in action. I can understand how it came about. I know his parents have suffered, and believe they will make the proper adjustment. Casualty lists must still increase before this is over. We don't get too sentimental over battle casualties but know that it is hard on you at home. If you were here, you would understand it better. There is nothing to do but remember them as they were and attempt to build a better world to make up for their absence.

    There are various opinions on the CIC article. If reader's have liked it, that is all that matters. It was written for home consumption.

```
Today I went for more coal tar salve for my
rash and was told the army doesn't make it any-
more. Now I don't know what to do and don't want
to go to a hospital because interesting things
are ahead.

You don't know how it thrills me to know that
you are so interested in the house we will one
day have. I am happy about your choice of Early
American.

The sun is being good to us these days. I
would like to get away from the desk and get a
jeep job again.

Love always,
Bill
```

After this March correspondence, world events moved quickly. President Roosevelt died on April 12, 1945. The Dachau concentration camp was liberated by the 7th Army on April 29. On May 1, German radio announced that Hitler was dead. On May 7, Germany signed their unconditional surrender, bringing six years of war in Europe to an end.

Japan's surrender brought the "official" end to WWII, although it didn't take place until September 2 of 1945.

Sayer and Botting's book describe the scene at war's end:

> *There had never been, in the whole history of the world, a place quite like Germany in the first eerie, havoc months and*

*years of peace after the war. Not even Russia could equal Germany in the widespread leveling of its cities, the almost total dismantling of the political and economic fabric of society, and the moral unhinging of the lives of the citizens.*

Robert Richards wrote:

*On May 3, our CIC moved into Augsburg, Germany, and secured a villa. We eventually learned that north Germany, Denmark, Holland, and Norway had surrendered. The 19th German Army surrendered to the Seventh Army, signally the end of fighting for our division. We were busy capturing and interrogating all kinds of characters.*

CIC, Augsburg

*I took over as investigation officer during Bill's Kandt's absence. He had been working at the German 6th Army Group Headquarters. I was in charge of processing over 40 Gestapo agents caught in Salzburg.*

*In early June, Bill Kandt returned from his investigation of the German Army troops. He had located a super-secret radio and teletype transmitter which alternately utilized various ranges of wavelengths. He also captured SS men working for the American Military Government.*

Bill in confiscated SS uniform

## From Dad's 1959 Wichita Beacon interview:

"In the case of another man we interrogated, he claimed to be a German Communist and wanted to help us win the war. We decided to try him out and sent him to locate a large German railroad gun which was playing hobs with our troops in the area. Actually, we didn't expect to see him again but two days later he showed up at the designated point with the desired information. Using these informers was a calculated risk but sometimes it paid off."

*Another hunch paid off for Kandt when he decided to listen to the warnings of two Russian girls the Germans had enslaved to work at a German inn. Kandt was named to set up headquarters at Zell am See, Austria to accept the surrender of German forces moving that way. Offices were set up at the inn and a security check was made of the inn's employees. Kandt was warned by the Russian girls to not overlook the clerk.*

*"He had told us he had been a German officer but was neutral and working in the inn. Investigation proved, however, that he was Nazi intelligence whose previous job had been to report to Berlin on British and American shipping past Gibraltar."*

*Kandt and his first sergeant stormed a mountain lodge at Holtschlag on a tip by the local forester and captured, with two .45 automatics, a Nazi intelligence colonel and his heavily armed staff who had hidden in the lodge to make plans for sabotage. The unit surrendered without a fuss, bewildered as to how anyone knew their location.*

During the 307th CIC's Detachment's stay in Augsburg, the concentration camp at Dachau was liberated. Built in March of 1933, Dachau was the first concentration camp of the hundreds created by the Nazis across Europe during their 12 years in power. By the end of World War II, the death camp system stretched from France to the Netherlands in the west to Estonia, Lithuania, and Poland in the east. The exact number of dead will probably never be known, nor will the total number of people the Nazis held prisoner in camps.[lx]

One section of the Counter Intelligence Corps Detachment was sent to Dachau for counter-intelligence work. The Seventh

Army made a report on the site, which included the CIC Detachment's report. Roberts and a few others went in and witnessed the horrors of the concentration camp. He wrote:

> *Victor de Guinzbourg, Tom Emmett, and I searched the death camp at Dachau the day after it was taken. I saw the death chambers and incinerating furnaces. There were huge piles of naked bodies inside rooms and outside buildings. The furnaces were still smoking. There were also dead SS guards who had been struck down by inmates. Their bodies were lying in the moat which surrounded the prison camp, their heads under water, their feet on the banks. We had a count that 31,000 people from 38 different countries were still alive in the camp.*
>
> *We found groups of prisoners standing around in black and white striped pajamas. They were smiling and took their hats off to us. They had made an American flag from old rags; it resembled the real thing.*
>
> *We made a report of the conditions we found there. One prisoner had kept a diary at great risk. We were to learn that there were at least fifteen concentration camps, some more terrible than Dachau.*

I know that Dad also went to Dachau, though I don't know exactly when.

While American soldiers prepared to return home, the CIC was far from finished. In July of 1945, Roberts wrote, "We learned that the CIC was declared essential in Europe, which meant it might be awhile before we could go home." The men with the CIC who had been active longer than Dad were able to return home sooner, Robert Richards among them. But Dad's work continued, as evidenced in this letter I found, stamped SECRET, among his papers from that December:

```
307th Counter Intelligence Corps Detachment
Headquarters Seventh United States Army
```

December 26, 1945

To Whom It May Concern:

1. I certify that the bearer, MR. WILLIAM C. KANDT, is a Special Agent, Counter Intelligence Corps, proceeding to the United States. I further certify that under the provisions of paragraph 18, Confidential Letter, War Department, The Adjutant General's Office, file AG 322 CIC (31 Oct 44) OB-S-B-M, Subject: "Counter Intelligence Corps," dated 13 November 1944, it is deemed essential that Special Agent Kandt be addressed as "Mister" and that military rank not be revealed.
2. Mr. Kandt has worked in this theater as Special Agent of the Counter Intelligence Corps since 13 November 1943, and for security reasons it is highly important that the above be strictly observed at all times.

3. Mr. Kandt is authorized to carry such secret documents as are necessary to protect his identity.

```
JOHN G. HAMMOND
Major, Infantry, CIC,
Commanding
```

Dad stayed in Europe until February, 1946. There are photos of him in Munich, Baden-Baden, and Austria. Among Dad's WWII photos are several of captured Gestapo (secret state police) and SS officers. The names of most are written on the back by Dad, but I have no information as to who they are nor when they were captured and interrogated.

The work of the CIC was vital in post-war Germany. It continued its presence, doing some of the detachment's most important counter-intelligence work up to that point: dismantling the Nazi presence in Germany.

On March 31, 1946 the *Kansas City Star* printed a large, two-page article talking about the Allied "crack down on a Nazi attempt to regain power and re-establish Nazism in Germany."[lxi] Included in the article was this quote:

> *The movements long range plan, designed to revive the Nazi ideology in Germany, was "the most dangerous threat to our security encountered since the war," Brig. Gen Edwin L. Siebert, U.S. Intelligence Chief, asserted.*

Dad described one of his post-war incidents in the 1959 Wichita Beacon interview:

> *We had a streak of luck after the war when a group of die-hard Nazis attempted to reorganize the Party. Led by a man named Heideman, the 'Die Partei der Anstaedigen'...'Decent People's Party'...was organized under the disguise of a trucking firm. He was drawing the Hitler Youth together in southern Germany and posing quite a threat, as the idea was spreading rapidly. But we managed to infiltrate a German lawyer into their midst, and he got the job as chauffeur to the head man, Heideman. In this capacity, our agent was able to learn of the plans.*
>
> *I suggested waiting until all of the potential uprisers were involved, so enabling us to get them all at once. This plan was followed, and neo-Nazism came to a halt a short time later when counterintelligence moved in."*[lxii]

I found a letter, written to Dad in May of 1946 from a C.I.C. buddy who was, by then, also back at home, which said:

> Say, Operation Nursery certainly got a big play, didn't it! But of course, that only ran true to your contentions from the very beginning. Too bad you, Hochschild, Reis, and Nordhein couldn't have gotten a little something more than self-satisfaction out of it. Even the Seventh Army's name was left out.

Before he returned to the United States on February 12, 1946, Dad was awarded a battlefield commission to go along with his counter-intelligence rank as a result of street fighting against the Gestapo. He was involved in wide-ranging battles and campaigns in Naples-Foggia, Rome-Arno, Southern France, Rhineland, and Central Europe. He earned a European-African-Middle Eastern Theatre campaign ribbon with five bronze stars, an American Theatre campaign ribbon, and a Victory ribbon. My father was far from alone in his dedication to the war effort. He was not wounded, nor did he lose his life, as so many thousands did, including some with the CIC.

Dad was honorably discharged on January 7, 1946 although his formal date of relief from active duty was March 26, 1946. He arrived back in the U.S. on February 12, 1946. After three years of separation, Mom, wearing a new dress, went to Kansas City to meet Dad. They went to the Muehlebach Grill for dinner. She admitted later it was strange being together again. Because she was still living with her parents, they stayed in a residence hotel for ten days so that they might have privacy before returning home.

Mom and Dad moved into a post-war neighborhood in Wichita, with homes built for returning service men and women. My brother was born in 1948 and I followed in 1949.

My parents kept in contact with Fraulein Keck, who sent them beautiful, delicate teacups and saucers. My brother and I received German dolls and a stuffed terrier dog. Dad went to visit her after the war and again in 1956. She had moved about five miles outside of Tübingen, where she lived the rest of her life. When the war ended, Mom and Dad knew that Germany was, once again, financially devastated. They sent Keck large care packages of food and clothing. Much of the clothing was used but they knew that if she couldn't wear them, she would know of those that could.

Dad brought home a German general's pistol with the officer's name on it, a Nazi flag, and two German Luger pistols. Hanging in our home were framed paintings from Germany and other countries, the cuckoo clock and wedding plate from the Black Forest, and a collection of delightful beer mugs. Our Christmas table delighted me with angels adorned on the wooden kranz centerpiece and other Christmas treasures from Germany.

Dad kept in touch with several of his CIC buddies through letters. Robert Richards, Warren "Deacon" Anderson, and Bob Blake came to visit in Wichita. Mom and Dad took trips to their homes, too.

In 1951, Dad became a judge of the Sedgwick County District Court in Wichita, Kansas. In 1956 – ten years after his return from WWII – he was one of eleven lawyers invited to review West Germany's judicial system, in all of the principal German cities, at the invitation and expense of the West German government. He told a news reporter, "While the German court study project is intended for improvement of the court system, it is also being offered as a token of appreciation by the German Federal Republic to demonstrate its gratitude for the vast program of German rehabilitation promoted and supported by the United States."

*Thus, on the third try, I finally found the German people as they really are: warm, friendly, and curious. They seemed*

Judge William C. Kandt, circa 1955

*to be applying their lessons learned, by contrast, of the worth and the dignity of man and the value of human freedom.*

He was gone for six weeks. Here are excerpts from some of the letters and postcards he wrote back to us at home in Wichita, Kansas:

```
                    April 11, 1956
                          New York
Dearest Lois,
```

As I supposed, I have not had much time to myself. Last night after dinner, I took a long walk to Times Square. It is still there. The Island is not very wide and does not seem as large as the first time we visited it. Last night I had dinner with Vic de Guinzbourg from the CIC. He works for the United Nations. He has a nice office overlooking the East River.

Sparks (CIC) showed me around N.Y.U. Law School and I met the faculty. Even people here, including Vic, seem impressed and envious by the German invitation to visit the courts.

I am going to be at the de Guinzbourg's tomorrow night. In the meantime, I shall get the German visa, read the material I am supposed to, rearrange my bag somewhat, buy a pair of $3.00 slippers I saw in a window, and think of you.

Love,
Bill

Victor de Guinzbourg, in Dad's 307th CIC Detachment, was generally acknowledged as one of the most remarkable of the CIC agents. His achievements were legendary. "He was truly a giant among us," said Nelson Dungan, who also served in Seventh Army CIC.[lxiii]

April 17, 1956<br>Bonn

Dearest Lois,

Victor de Guinzbourg and Bill, Epinal France 1944

## Susan Kandt Peterson

You will receive a postcard from Monschau. It is a lovely, untouched medieval village. The Bruckmann's also took us to see the ruins at Zulpich. The ruins were revealed when a bomb blew up a church.

The weather is damp and chilly, just as you will remember it. Except that there is real heat in the radiators, day and night! You would not be disappointed in the pastries, and with real whipped cream.

Yesterday afternoon there was a conference with the Ministry of Labor. Every day, Mercedes autos with chaperones are at our disposal.

This morning we had our first conference with German lawyers and judges, and it was very interesting. The German girl who interprets is splendid. We discussed each other's problems and tomorrow we will discuss what to do about them. However, I do not think the Germans are as interested in reform as we are.

I know that you would be pleased to see the absence of uniforms here and the informality around the government offices. Quite a contrast to the stiffness and the Hitler guards we saw in 1938 and 1939. They are running the offices with the ease, openness, and friendliness similar to Americans. In fact, they say they learned it from us, and they like it. I am surprised at how well we are considered by the German population. American influence is everywhere to be seen. They seem to be looking at us as a sort of ideal to achieve. After our reception at the Foreign Office, I overheard a woman minister say to another, "The Americans are better than us. Why? Why?" They seem to be catching on to the free development of the individual. I hope that they don't lose it.

Love,
Bill


April 18, 1956
Bonn

Dearest Lois,

Today the limousines picked us up and took us to a session of the Bundestag (Congress) in the new Bundeshaus (capitol). Its architecture is modern and, of course, in the best German style. The only uniforms visible were pages dressed in blue tails, bright red vests, brass buttons, with white ties and gloves.

The house has the same informality as our Congress. The Social Democrats were giving the government cabinet members a bad time, English style, questioning them about government actions. Some of them brought Nazi policies and atrocities into open discussions, and it got pretty hot.

They do not seem to be excusing or hiding from the past...yet. The Social Democrats wanted the government to dismiss a naval officer who made a speech which served to praise a former admiral under Hitler. And they also demanded to know why the German Ambassador in Paris had objected to the showing of A Night of Fog, a concentration camp film, at the Cannes film festival. The government said they did not want the truth hushed up but had objected for other reasons.

In the afternoon we were taken to the Ministry of Justice. We held a three-hour conference around a large table with the head minister and about 10 members of his staff. I should not have told them that one section of their constitution sounded a bit authoritarian. Their answer was politely proper, but we did pick up some new ideas and I'm sure they did, too. They seemed to be particularly interested in how we, in Sedgwick County, use $1.00 of each cost deposit to keep a law library, which is one of their most serious problems. They did not want to admit that their cases are too long in the courts, but they finally did.

I was informed that Claus Holthausen is a prominent lawyer in Hamburg.

It is late and I must try and sleep.

Love,
Bill

(Claus Holthausen was the KU exchange student who turned out to be an SS spy. Mom and Dad visited his parents while in Germany, in 1938, blissfully unaware of the situation.)

                                          April 19, 1956
                                                   Bonn

Dearest Lois,

   This afternoon was very interesting. We, at the Foreign Office, heard the German version of the political situation. Then we heard the German version of their remarkable recovery.

Love,
Bill


                                          April 21, 1956
                                            Heidelberg

Dearest Lois,

   I was sorry not to have written to you yesterday, but I just had to get some sleep. We arrived here yesterday afternoon and they have kept us busy every minute! Today they kept us going from 9:30 AM until a few minutes ago, 12:30 PM.

   This afternoon we went to the Law School and the Institute on International Law. Then tonight, the big dinner here at the hotel where we are staying.

I had the opportunity to walk to the CIC quarters and, I must say, I had strange, emotional feelings which I am unable to describe. I got over it shortly and now I am not desirous to visit other places. I think I got it out of my system.

The Germans at the dinner tonight all spoke excellent English. There were some very interesting people, lawyers and judges. The conference was a good one.

I now want to write a few postcards and then to bed.

Love,
Bill

*Eyes and Ears*

April 22, 1956
Heidelberg

Dear Jimmy and Susan,

This is the view I saw today from a spot where your mother and I stood years ago. Perhaps we shall all see it together, sometime.

I love you very much.

Love,
Your lonesome father


April 25, 1956
Stuttgart

Dear Lois,

This is a bit of a break and a chance to write. The rest of the group wanted to see Stuttgart, so I stopped off with them for a few hours. They are out seeing the town so I am in a Bierstube having a beer, soup, and bread for lunch. It is a low-priced sort of place under the Konigstrasse. They rebuilt everything and made a tunnel underneath the Platz, with escalators, which is where I am now. This place has an American atmosphere, practical and fast, no tablecloths and you just stand and eat if you are in a hurry. Or sit and take your time.

## Susan Kandt Peterson

It is amazing and interesting to see the friendliness. I believe that they like us and look to us for ideas and leadership. I am particularly pleased to see that the G.I. made himself popular, rather than the reverse, as in Italy and France. Yesterday it was interesting to see, in the constitutional court, the highest in the land, how the judges were informal and friendly. They didn't insist on shaking hands. They lounged around like we do and seemed to be frank and open. They have all been to the United States and know more of our constitutional law than we do.

Here, in Stuttgart, where the Consulate was and where we worked, it has been rebuilt, but the town seems poorer and slower to recover than other towns. It is rather depressing to me. The lovely old marktplatz and altstadt are gone and very modern buildings are going up. I do not think you would enjoy being here.

The high court judges drove us to Baden-Baden in five Mercedes black cars yesterday and gave us a party in a Kurhaus there.

Train time will be here soon. Tell the kids I saw cranes in the park yesterday. They were sleeping heads-under-wings and on one long leg.

Love,
Bill

*Eyes and Ears*

The **Kurhaus** is a spa resort, casino, and conference complex in Baden-Baden, Germany in the outskirts of the Black Forest.

```
                                    April 26, 1956
                                    Munich
Dearest Lois,

   This morning we visited the American Consulate.
The quality of the staff seems to be better and
I was pleased to learn that they are required to
learn the language where they are stationed.

   Then we were received by the Bavarian Minister
of Justice, and then the Munich Bar Association.
Our conferences were fruitful on both sides. We
then had the noon meal, four courses, of course,
with beer for the first two and wine for the last
two. I have let my belt out two notches already and
the trip is only one third over!

   Bavaria seems better than other places, the
people gay and humorous. Building has progressed
mightily and the people look well and prosperous,
except the lawyers, most of whom are not doing well.

   It is now 11:30 and we must be ready by 8:00 in
the morning.

   Love,
   Bill
                                    April 27, 1956
```

Susan Kandt Peterson

Munich

Dear Lois,

Whoosh! The Munich Bar Association finished us up with a lavish dinner at the Park Hotel.

I gave the response at the dinner tonight. The American Consul General invited the group to the Hofbrauhaus, but I tore away. We leave early tomorrow morning.

Love,
Bill

April 29, 1956
Dusseldorf

Dearest Lois,

Last night after the opera, we were taken to a Bavarian supper, then to a nightclub. American music, American dances, American influence everywhere. And what seems strange to me is that the Germans are accepting of it. On the train today, a German woman of about 53 spent two hours telling me what wonderful men we Americans are to our wives. She said American women don't appreciate what they have and that they should live their lives only for their husbands. This seemed sort of good to me! I thanked her and told her politely that I would be glad to discuss this with my wife. She also told me that American men buy dogs for their children instead of for themselves. This touched her deeply in the heart, she said.

I turned in my sleeper reservation and took an earlier train to avoid the sleeper. I learn more traveling among the Germans, alone.

It was also nice to have a letter from Keck when I arrived here. She seemed pleased and does not object to my staying in a hotel in Tübingen. I am sleeping poorly again, probably from being keyed up most of the time. Tomorrow we start another round of conferences and dinner.

I sure miss you.

Love,
Bill

April 30, 1956
Dusseldorf

Dearest Lois,

This is a swank hotel. All hotels we have been in are new since the war, all bombed and rebuilt.

Every night when the activities are over, the first thing I think about is to write to you. That is because I love you.

Tonight was the prettiest dinner of all, by far the most lavish. I sat between the president of the Bar Association and the Attorney General. My neighbors did not speak English, but we got along well in German. I learned early not to tell them I have been here before, because it ruins their fun. They expect to entertain people who are seeing Germany for the first time. But I usually give myself away by my accent. When they get suspicious, I have to lie a little.

When I got back to my hotel, I opened a window. You wouldn't believe that a hotel in Germany could have so much heat.

The people here look good and busy, but their poor town still has lots of ruins.

I wonder if I told you that I visited with the three little girls we fed in our mess in Heidelberg. Only they aren't so little anymore. They are grown ladies working for the Americans. The youngest one, Maria, who was so fond of me, came to Heidelberg. I was not in the hotel, so she stationed herself on the bridge and took a chance that I would come along. I did, and she recognized me! What a coincidence after 10 years. We went to a cafe and visited for an hour. She cried when I left.

Goodnight. I love you.
Bill

*Eyes and Ears*

May 1, 1956
Dusseldorf

Dearest Lois,

I hope that I am not writing you too many letters. Tell me what you think about when you go to bed each night.

I think it is a good idea to have the TV fixed. Don't worry about the dandelions. The season is short, and I will mow them down.

I went to the dining room tonight, sat quietly, talked in German to the waiter, and was getting along nicely when <u>they</u> came in and found me! I was suddenly turned into an American tourist. Next time I will go to a Bierstube.

Judge Hessar has written me a very nice letter asking me to come to Hechingen. We should have much to talk about regarding the courts.

In Munich I went to the apartment of an American Consulate. They sure are living better than they used to.

I love you and miss you. You, too? I sure am glad that the war is over.

Love,
Bill

Susan Kandt Peterson

May 3, 1956
Kassel

Dearest Lois,

The people who have never been here before want to see everything. I guess I will have to get up early tomorrow and see another castle.

There is a new wrinkle in hotel service. The maid comes in every morning and puts a snow-white mat on the floor by the bed so you won't have to step on the carpet when you get up in the morning. I hope that I won't be too hard to live with.

The woman who sat next to me tonight is the only female member of the Labor Court. She is a squat little widow with three children. She seemed horrified when I made the mistake of telling her that we throw our coffee grounds away instead of using them three times. We never did get back to conversation after that.

On to Hamburg and then Berlin. I hope we don't have to have too many dinners. Then I shall see what I can do on my own.

Love,
Bill

*Eyes and Ears*

May 4, 1956
Kassel

Dear Jimmy and Susan,

This print of the painting, "Saskia," is in your Rembrandt book. I saw the original today. It is beautiful. I had difficulty leaving it. I hope you may see it someday.

I hope you are being nice to Mommy. Remember, she deserves it.

Love,
Daddy


May 5, 1956
Hamburg

Dear Lois,

It has occurred to me that Mother's Day will be this month. I hope you enjoy the gift mailed from Dusseldorf. It has been wonderful living with you, and I have been very fortunate.

No word from Claus.

Love,
Bill

Susan Kandt Peterson

May 6, 1956
Hamburg

Dearest Lois,

I finally called Claus Holthausen today. I realized that he was not going to call me. I thought I should do so in order to avoid any misunderstanding. He had me to supper tonight and we had a very nice time. His wife is quite nice and their three children love American jazz. Every night they hear some from the tapes Claus makes from the radio.

Claus has been through some rough times and he looks it. His former wealth is gone but I believe he is on his feet again. His parents had to give up the big house we visited them in in 1938. They were apparently "invited out." His two younger brothers were both killed in the war. I don't think he has a car and they live in the apartment above his in-laws.

Tomorrow we visit a juvenile court and then make a tour of the city. Last night some of us slipped away from the rest of the group and watched some nude dancing in a night club. Not too bad for German women.

Love,
Bill

*Eyes and Ears*

May 8, 1956
Berlin

Dearest Lois,

I was really pleased to find your letter of May 2nd when we arrived this morning.

Berlin seems depressing to me. There are many ruins everywhere. They have done a noble job raising buildings among the ruins. The shops are loaded with merchandise.

The hotel I am in, a former monastery, is in a quiet, residential area. I love it and you would, too. The rooms are old and comfortable.

I will fly to Frankfurt on Saturday. I would not be taking the extra week here except that I now have a chance to see people and places that I may not see again.

Tomorrow we have a busy schedule.

Love,
Bill

Susan Kandt Peterson

May 10, 1956
Berlin

Dearest Lois,

Please tell Jimmy and Susan that I am very proud of their letters and Frau Keck will be happy to have a picture of Tübingen Castle. It made me feel good inside to read the letters. I love you all and will be happy to be home again.

Yesterday we had a tour of West Berlin and a town in East Berlin (yes, in the Soviet Zone) and in between we had a lavish luncheon by the mayor. I think that the members of our group were quite impressed by the contrast between the East and the West zones. My war experience gave me sufficient background so that I saw about what I expected to see. I will talk about it when I see you. If you have seen Fascist Germany before the war, and bombed out Germany after the war, put the two together and you have East Berlin. Except, there seems to be little activity on the streets.

I love you very much,
Bill

*Eyes and Ears*

May 11, 1956<br>Berlin

Dearest Lois,

Today we visited refugee camps. There are now about 600 per day coming from the East Zone. You would be proud of the assistance your tax dollars have given the camps and the work they are doing.

I still plan to rent a car in Frankfurt tomorrow and tour southern Germany. If I can get one, I will be in Heidelberg on Sunday. I'll be there anyway, if even by train.

Must rush.

I love you,
Bill

After the war Berlin – along with the whole of Germany – was divided into two zones: the East, controlled by the Soviet Union as a communist state, and the West by the Western Allies. Before the Berlin Wall was built in May of 1961, thousands of refugees fled into West Berlin. Refugee camps were established to handle the influx.[lxiv]

May 13, 1956<br>Heidelberg

Dearest Lois,

There may be four days when you will not be able to contact me for I will be in small towns.

By Thursday, after much travel on the "Romantic Road," I will make my way through the Black Forest country to visit Hechingen and then on to Tübingen.

I love and miss you,
Bill

May 14, 1956<br>Rothenburg

Dearest Lois,

   The beauty of my surroundings has been breathtaking. As I travel, the lovely scenery continues on. I have stopped to see museums housing treasures of long ago. I am staying in places like you and I stayed in, but the radiators work! The "Romantic Road" is terrific so far, not much traffic on the narrow streets and roads. The towns are lovely in their old way. It is like seeing Tübingen after Tübingen with lush, lovely scenery in between. How I wish that you were with me!

I love you,
Bill

*Eyes and Ears*

May 16, 1956
Radolfzell

Dearest Lois,

It has been another day of inspiring scenery; lakes, mountains, vivid greens, white and yellow flowers, and always the towering snowcapped Alps in the distance.

In Rothenburg I saw two kids, from above, walking below on a path along the old city wall. The girl was about three and the boy about five. The girl wore tan jodhpur-type knitted pants and a bright red, dirndl dress. Of course, she was blonde with blue eyes. She kept her hand in that of her brother. When he did break away, she cried until he took her hand again. She looked up to him with confirmation of word and act. They were apparently coming from a walk in the woods. Each had a bouquet of wildflowers. When she looked up to him, they looked exactly like Hummel figures. I walked on down and intercepted them. I heard him say, "Yes, that is right, now you have something nice to bring home to Mutti." They let me smell the flowers, but they were not open and friendly like American children would have been. And, therein, lies quite a difference. I wonder what they will do within their generation. Will the time of one generation be enough?

I will have a good time in Tübingen, but I must not let Keck get weary of me. I am spending so little money I will think of something nice to get for her.

Did you know that I love you so much and I hope we make it grow and grow.

Bill

                                        May 17, 1956
                                              Tübingen

Dearest Lois,

This will be short and also the last letter until I phone from Chicago.

I am in a hotel that is quite American. I took a bath tonight, bought a dozen red carnations and went to let Keck know that I was in town. I don't think she is well. She has lost a lot of her enthusiasm. We visited shortly and then I had to go to Hechingen to see the Hessars. We had quite a chatty time.

Tübingen isn't the same. There is much traffic, much activity, and bright lights with many shops. Also, many new buildings. It is not the Tübingen we came to know.

I am quite anxious to get home.

Love,
Bill

With humor, Dad wrote the following postcard showing downtown Wichita once he was home:

```
                                         June 6, 1956
                                         Wichita
Dear Jimmy and Susan,

   I have finally arrived home in Wichita and was
very happy to see the family. Mommy and the kids
were very nice to me and I am enjoying them more
than ever. Susan's room had been painted and we
all had a good time unwrapping presents.

Love,
Daddy
```

Following Dad's trip, a February 21, 1957 article in the *Wichita Eagle*, published the story of "Judge Kandt receiving an unexpected gift from a German soldier he had helped capture. Two bottles of brandy came from Hans Suerdieck, one of three soldiers Kandt was instrumental in capturing north of Rome during the American drive against the Germans and Italian Fascists."

> *"I hadn't heard anything from anyone connected with the incident until this year. The last I saw of the soldiers was just before they were to be transferred to prisoner of war cages belonging to the American Army. The soldiers were captured in June, 1944. Actually, the German soldiers were eager to surrender to anyone representing the American Army.*

*They feared falling into the hands of the Nazis, Fascists or Italian partisans."*

*With Kandt was Ray Daguerre, now of El Paso, Texas. Kandt said he and his fellow agent, Daguerre, who spoke Italian, were told by the German-born wife of an old Italian newspaper editor that three Germans wanted to 'give-up.' "One of the prisoners was a relative of the woman." Through a farmer, Kandt and Daguerre made contact with the Germans who were hiding. They were in uniforms when they surrendered, but they were not armed.*

*"To protect them from the partisans we placed the three men under house arrest. They were told to remain at the editor's home. They were supplied with food and other provisions. The three Germans subsequently were turned over to the American forces in charge of guarding prisoners of war. That was the last I saw of them."*

*The editor involved in the capture was Dr. Gino Brutti, who worked with several Rome dailies. He wrote to Kandt in June of 1944:*

```
                          Rome, June 13, 1944
Dear Mr. Kandt,

    I regret that ignorance of your lan-
guage prevents me from expressing how
much I esteem your respect and the con-
duct of your office. Such a conduct and
dignity constitute an eloquent proof of
```

> *your conception of liberty and life and represent the best propaganda for your country. I should desire to become better acquainted and am at your service.*
>
> *Devotedly,*
> *Dr. Gino Brutti*
> *Editor of "The Messaggero"*

Before Christmas, Kandt had sent a Christmas card to the editor and his wife. The woman subsequently sent word of the judge's whereabouts to the German soldier.

Dad kept a copy of the soldier's letter, written in German:

> Vechta, Jan.7, 1957
>
> My Dear Mr. Kandt:
>
> A few days ago, I received your address from Frau Brutti in Rome.
>
> After 12 years it is a privilege to thank you for all that you did for us.
>
> Do you still remember Via Sforza, the place where you took us and how you brought us food and cared for us? In gratefulness, I have often sung your praises.

Quietly I always thought that I might see you again to thank you for your humanity, but the war was relentless and there remained for me only the hope to bide my time. Now, after 12 years, I have the opportunity, and how often I thought about you. Haven't you sometimes felt the ringing in your ears? You must have heard it.

Upon my last visit to Rome we spoke often of you, but no one knew anything about you.

All the badness from the war has disappeared from my memory. Only the good remains, thanks to you.

It appears from the letter to Frau Brutti that all goes well with you, which pleases me from the bottom of my heart. Unfortunately, I cannot give you a very favorable report about myself because I have had much misfortune during the last five years. I have had business reversals and three deaths in the family last year. And to top it off, I have lost my voice.

Dear Mr. Kandt, why did you not make your whereabouts known sooner? I would gladly have invited you here in my better days. This would have made me happy because I have much to repay, especially to you.

In thankfulness, please accept this gift as a miniature token of my appreciation. If you have married in the meantime, then the accompanying acknowledgment is for your wife. Both come from the heart.

Your
Hans Suerdieck


Before Dad died from complications of Parkinson's disease at the age of 84, memories of World War II and the CIC would bring tears to his eyes. When Mom died ten years later, I began reading book after book after book about World War II. One could spend a lifetime immersed in that war and never peel back all of the layers. The hows and whys and what-ifs still confound me. How could the German people have allowed Hitler to reign with unlimited power?

I've wondered about Hans Suerdieck and other German soldiers. Was the brainwashing influence of the Nazi Youth program so successful that they joined the German army out of fervent desire to fight for Hitler? Or were they forced to fight for an ideology they didn't believe in for fear of retaliation? There is little doubt that the individual solider could have foreseen how Hitler's war would ultimately be responsible for claiming the lives of a staggering 70-85 million people across the globe: military deaths, civilian deaths and deaths by disease and famine.[lxv]

I was stunned to learn that in a 2018 survey, ten percent of Americans had never even heard of the Holocaust, the state-sponsored mass murder of millions of people. 66% of millennials did not know what the Auschwitz concentration and death camp was. 58% of Americans said they believed the Holocaust could happen again. Another recent survey of 7,000 Europeans showed a lack of knowledge about the Holocaust, just 75 years after the end of World War II. One in five people between of the ages of 18 and 34 had never heard of the Holocaust.

*How can this be?*

By Nazi genocide alone, 21-31 million men, women, children and babies were extinguished, both within and outside of concentration camps, through ruthless forms of brutality: hanging, beheading, starvation, disease, torture, shooting, overwork, burning alive, exposure, drowning, lethal injection, mass trench murder, medical experimentation, reprisal raids, and gassing.

*21-31 million*

Why? Simply because they were Jewish or harbored Jews. Many were Jehovah's Witnesses or Gypsies. Or disabled. Or mentally ill. Maybe they had a different color of skin or a different sexual persuasion. German Communists, Social Democrats, Slavs, Poles, dissenting clergy, and conscientious objectors were not spared. Nor were artists whose opinions and work Hitler scorned. Journalists, lawyers, judges, and editors who disagreed with Hitler were sought and killed. Even those who were overheard telling a joke about Hitler.

Democracies can, and have, fallen. By themselves, Constitutional safeguards and words on paper are not enough to secure a democracy if an authoritarian leader is given power. Designed by some of the most highly esteemed legal minds after World War I, Germany's 1919 Weimar Constitution and Rechtsstaat rule of law were deemed impervious to government abuse. However, when Adolf Hitler's rose to power in 1933, both the constitution and the rule of law rapidly crumbled.

When Hitler was appointed chancellor, there was a belief that the vice-chancellor and other non-Nazis in key government positions would contain and temper him. As one German aristocrat boasted in 1933, "Within two months, we will have pushed Hitler so far into a corner that he'll squeal."

Hitler never squealed.

Biographer Peter Longerich, one of the leading authorities on the Holocaust, says, "The life of Hitler remains one of the most incomprehensible examples of how quickly the touch of the wrong person, at the wrong time, can shatter an order that appeared stable."

Hitler slowly and effectively undermined the fabric of the Germany nation. He was very popular with the German people during the pre-war years, as Dad and Mom observed. Following World War I, the Great Depression and extreme economic instability left Germany vulnerable. With massive debts to pay for WWI reparations, Germany's hyperinflated currency became worthless. Unemployment was high. Hitler's compelling personality drew huge crowds of screaming fans, arms raised in the Heil salute, who regarded the Fuhrer as their savior. Hitler created jobs. He began a huge program of public works, which included building hospitals, schools, and public buildings such as the 1936 Olympic stadium. The construction of roads created work for 80,000 men. More jobs were provided by the removal of Jews from the workforce (whose jobs were then given to Gentiles).

Rearmament was responsible for the bulk of economic growth between 1933 and 1938, creating millions of jobs for German workers who built weaponry for the German army (this, in spite of limitations imposed on the military by the Treaty of Versailles). However, most jobs were created primarily through conscription, the compulsory enlistment of men into military service.

The German people – humiliated, desperate, and impoverished – finally felt relief.

While less than one percent of the German population in the 1930s was Jewish, Hitler made them his scapegoat and blamed them for the collapse of German society. He disregarded the many Jewish soldiers who had sacrificed their lives for Germany in WWI and the contributions of the German Jewish community to Germany culture, both economically and socially.

While antisemitism was not new to Germany before Hitler, few of the outspoken groups which existed prior to 1933 were in any position to play a significant role. In 1933 there were forces that objected to antisemitism and directly resisted it, but Hitler was a master illusionist who used lies to justify the means. His propaganda machine hammered certain ideas into the German consciousness through repetitive exposure, endlessly repeating the same anti-Jewish slogans. Jews were portrayed as apes or vermin that endangered society. At every turn, Germans were met with posters telling them that Jews were the enemy. Hitler wanted to create a nation of "superior" people and insisted that Jews – along with other "undesirable" groups – be removed to outside work camps.

But perhaps education was the greatest destroyer of German freedom, and the chief catalyst of the Nazi regime. Education, re-invented by the Germans, reinforced certain themes. Students were taught to idolize and worship Adolf Hitler, raising their right arms each day to a "Heil the Fuhrer" salute. Hitler's picture, mandatory in each classroom, stared down from the wall. Songs were sung praising their leader. Students were encouraged to wear their Hitler Youth and League of German Girls uniforms to school.

Students in the Hitler Youth were thoroughly brainwashed and had the power at times to intimidate their teachers and demand that school subjects – such as Latin – not be taught. Learning National Socialism and becoming physically fit were prioritized, and compulsory physical education training comprised several hours of each school day. This left little time for family.

Teachers urged students to inform authorities when their parents did not abide by Nazi beliefs. Children were taken away from parents who denied a belief in National Socialism. Hitler believed children belonged to the state. Mothers were reduced to being receptacles which brought children into the world.

The education system in Germany was standardized, with the same subjects taught at the same time throughout the Reich. All schools were political, and Catholic, special education, and democratic schools were shut down. New textbooks replaced the old. In each textbook illustrations of Hitler, with pages of his sayings, were highlighted throughout. Nazi beliefs were woven into math, history, art, and biology. Modern art was deemed degenerate.

Jewish teachers were dismissed from German schools and universities and non-Jewish teachers were fired if they did not support the Nazi regime. Student indoctrination further taught that Jews walked and spoke differently, with grotesquely different facial features. Students learned that Jewish people were dishonest monsters who killed babies, out to destroy Germany in their plan to take over the world.

Knowing he had the German youth and workforce in his pocket, Hitler then turned his attention to the more educated. At universities, books of higher learning were falsified to "prove" that the true German was of a superior Aryan race, and that all other races had no place in German society. Professors in the most prestigious universities gave seminars while students did research and wrote doctoral theses on the superiority of the Aryan genome. As my father attested, the education he received during his time as an exchange student was highly politicized.

Hitler lived in constant fear of being usurped as a dictator. He maintained power using the tactic of "divide and rule," creating constant competition and disruption among the senior members of his regime, especially between Hermann Goering, Joseph Goebbels, Heinrich Himmler, and Ernst Rohm.

In late June of 1934, Germans were shocked when Hitler ordered the massacre of hundreds of men in a purge called the "Night of the Long Knives." Through this series of executions, carried out by the Nazi SS, Hitler consolidated his power and wiped out men he considered political rivals. Over half of those murdered were members of the SA, the paramilitary Specialized Assault troops whose brutal tactics Hitler had once used to effectively intimidate his enemies. Chief among these was SA leader Ernst Rohm. Hitler and Rhom had been close friends, with Hitler overlooking Rohm's homosexual proclivities. To the public, Hitler justified his actions by citing Rhom and others as legitimate threats.

Not only did Hitler eliminate his perceived enemies, he now proclaimed himself supreme judge of the German people, in effect placing himself above the law. "If anyone reproaches me and asks why I did not resort to the regular courts of justice, then all I can say is this: in this hour I was responsible for the fate of the German people and thereby I became the supreme judge of the German people! Everyone must know for all future time that if he raises his hand to strike the State, then certain death is his lot!"

Nazi media portrayed the event as a preventative measure against a revolutionary, violent, and uncontrollable force, rather than the series of political murders they were. Goebbels broadcast the Nazi account of the executions on July 10th, thanking the German press for "standing by the government with commendable self-discipline and fair-mindedness" and accusing the foreign press of issuing false reports so as to create confusion. He called the coverage of these newspapers and magazines a "campaign of lies."

The Nazis took steps to ensure no one could openly opposed them in the press. In October of 1933, it was declared that all editors must be of Aryan descent. In May of 1933, Nazi students began burning books. Goebbels condemned works by Jews, liberals, leftists, pacifists, foreigners, and others as "un-German." Libraries across Germany were purged of "censored books." Censorship was heightened and any person actively publishing anti-Nazi material was threatened or imprisoned.

By 1935 over 1,600 newspapers and thousands of magazines were closed by the Nazi regime.[lxvi]

If there was resistance to Hitler in Germany, it never became a unified movement. People were not allowed to protest or march. There were loosely organized plans for a coup, but the outbreak of war made the further mobilization of resistance in the army more difficult. German citizens became afraid, always looking over their shoulder, not knowing who might report them for any small infraction, real or imagined. They feared the brutality of the Nazis. Plots to assassinate Hitler failed and the organizers of those plots often murdered.

As time wore on, members of the German public were effectively reduced to bystanders who could do little to condemn the Nazi racial policies. And it appears that a significant section of the population became completely indifferent to the atrocities committed, or the fate of the Jewish population.

Adolph Hitler unleashed the greatest evil in modern history. The war erupted on September 1, 1939 and did not end until September 2, 1945. Six years. With over thirty countries involved, World War II became the largest, deadliest, and most destructive war to date.

It would be nice to say that the end of World War II was the end of evil. But unfortunately, that isn't so. Seeds of hate and greed were sown by others before Hitler and they continue to be sown today.

We've long known of the dictatorial rule in Russia and North Korea. The same is true of Communist China, who has ruled with an iron fist for decades. One system of control the Chinese government exerts is cultural genocide, not in the form of mass killing, but in the form of attempted mass "extermination" of ideas and beliefs. This is what is happening to the Uighurs, a minority Muslim population in northwest China. In a systematic brainwashing of hundreds of thousands of Muslims, the Uighurs are separated from their families and sent to a network of high-security prisons, called "re-education" camps, where they are interrogated and often brutalized. Afterward, they are moved to cities and used as slave labor in factories, some of which make goods for Western countries. Many Uighurs flee to other countries in self-imposed exile rather than return home.

In addition, China is perfecting a vast network of digital espionage as a means of social control, with implications for democracies worldwide. The country is the first to implement a pervasive system of algorithmic surveillance which harnesses advances in artificial intelligence, data mining, and storage to construct detailed profiles on all citizens. An accompanying network of surveillance cameras will constantly monitor citizens' physical movements.

The Chinese government has long scrutinized individual citizens for evidence of disloyalty to the regime, but now it is beginning to develop comprehensive, constantly updated, and granular records on each citizen's political persuasions, comments, associations, and even consumer habits. It poses a chilling new threat to civil liberties in a country that already has one of the most oppressive and controlling governments in the world. Moreover, what emerges in China will not stay in China. Its repressive technologies have a pattern of diffusing to other authoritarian regimes around the world. Already, there are other countries on board to utilize the same technology, purchased from China.[lxvii]

We are not immune to the loss of democracy. Democracies are undergoing a decline in political rights and civil liberties. Freedom House found 2019 to be the 14th consecutive year of decline in global freedom, with elections less likely to be fair; press freedom under attack; corruption pervasive. The unchecked brutality of autocratic regimes and the ethical decay of democratic powers combined to make the world increasingly hostile to fresh demands for better governance.[lxviii]

According to a recent *Journal* paper, autocratic governments are on the rise. Autocratic rule, also known as authoritarianism, is when one leader or political party exercises complete power to govern a country and its people. Scholars say countries across the globe are experiencing a rise in autocratic rule with corresponding declines in democratic ideals and practice.[lxix]

And, a recent global poll by the *Journal of Democracy* showed an alarming decline in the number of people who believe it essential to live in a democracy. From Sweden to the U.S., Britain to Australia, only one in four of those born in the 1980s regard democracy as essential.

Winston Churchill wrote, "It has been said that democracy is the worst form of Government except for all those other forms that have been tried. Unless we want to try one of those other forms, we need to fight against autocratization, at home and abroad."

Unlike traditional dictators of the past, with autocrats coming to power through coups and violent military crackdowns, democratic backsliding today begins at the ballot box. Today's would-be autocrats typically emerge from democratic settings, maintaining a veneer of democracy while disemboweling its substance. It happens slowly, in barely visible steps. They vilify and scapegoat vulnerable minorities to build popular support and then weaken the checks and balances on government power needed to preserve human rights and the rule of law, such as a free press, an independent judiciary and vigorous civic groups.[lxx]

They demonize elections and build on the growing loss of faith in government. They distort truths, relying on a public who doesn't know what the truth is anymore. They oust critics and surround themselves with enablers who hope to profit politically or financially. Even the world's established democracies have shown themselves vulnerable to this exploitation of emotions and manipulation.

Organizations such as Human Rights Watch, Amnesty International, Freedom House and U.N. Watch monitor and track the status of democracy in today's world, and their assessment is disturbing.

Here are examples of autocratic governments in progress in 2020:

In 2018, Brazil elected as President Jair Bolsonaro, a man who—at great risk to public safety—openly encourages the use of lethal force by the military and police upon its citizens. This, in a country already wracked by a sky-high rate of civilian killings by police and more than 60,000 homicides per year.[lxxi]

In Hungary, the parliament agreed to allow Prime Minister Viktor Orbán to rule by decree without a set time limit as of March 2020. No elections can be held and the Orbán government will be able to suspend the enforcement of certain laws. Individuals who publicize what are viewed as untrue or distorted facts which could "alarm or agitate a large number of people" now face years in jail.[lxxii]

The modern, post-World War I Turkey that my parents visited in 1939, with its first elected president and reforms toward secular Westernization, is not the Turkey of today. Turkey's president used to hold a primarily ceremonial role, while the country was mainly ruled by a prime minister in a parliamentary democracy. But that changed in 2017 when a referendum, led by President Recep Tayyip Erdoğan's party, overturned the existing government structure. The prime minister's role was abolished, clearing the way for Erdoğan to extend the limits of his power. Among other things, Erdoğan now has the official power to appoint ministers, issue decrees, and make judiciary appointments. As of right now, Erdoğan will likely remain president until 2023. If reelected, he could stay in power until 2028.[lxxiii]

During his nearly 20 years in power, Erdoğan has violated human rights in his own country of Turkey and destabilized and exploited others in order to promote his nationalist agenda abroad. Erdoğan continues to commit gross human rights violations in Turkey by using a failed 2016 military coup as an excuse to silence the media. He has jailed over 150 journalists, purged 150,000 military officers and civil servants, and engaged in a systematic operation of ethnic cleansing against minorities in Turkey and northern Syria.[lxxiv]

In the Philippines, elected President Rodrigo Duterte has encouraged summary executions, supposedly of drug suspects but often of people guilty of no more than being poor young men. "If you know of any addicts, go ahead and kill them yourself," he said during his inauguration speech. It is estimated that between July 2016 and January 2017 as many as 27,000 have been murdered without due process in a court of law. There are reports that cases of mistaken identification have led to people with no connection to the drugs trade being murdered. Duterte has bragged that he has killed people himself, seemingly as means to reduce crime while he was Mayor of the city of Davao, before he became president.[lxxv]

In India, elected Prime Minister Narendra Modi's blatantly anti-Muslim initiatives are a grave threat to India's founding as a secular and inclusive nation. He has failed to halt the demonizing of Muslims, while attacking civic groups that criticize his rights record or environmental policies. Lynch mobs have popped up across the landscape, killing scores of mostly Muslim and lower-caste Dalit people.

Mr. Modi placed Hindu extremists in top government posts while putting other Hindu nationalist allies at the head of important universities and cultural institutions. Place names and textbooks were changed to play up Hindu teachings and de-emphasize Muslim contributions to India. "Supporters of the government feel enabled to commit all kinds of crimes because they feel they have political protection," Meenakshi Ganguly, the South Asia director for Human Rights Watch, stated in 2020.[lxxvi]

As of this book's publication, the world is witnessing a resurgence of white supremacy and neo-Nazi groups, with attacks on those of different religions and skin colors. The West has seen a notable and sometimes violent turn toward nationalism and anti-Semitism. Polls show that Jews feel less safe than they did a decade ago. More people are currently fleeing persecution from conflict and political violence than at any time since the end of Hitler's war.

The world can seem a messy place. People transgress. Governments transgress and veer away from moral codes and laws. No nation lives without guilt for wrongs committed. But it is through failure that wrongs can be acknowledged, histories told in truth and actions taken to rectify and rebuild. The continual assessment of the health of a democracy is essential to insuring its presence around the world.

A healthy democracy is diverse, one that respects the inherent dignity and rights of each individual. It means accepting the fact that we must share our country with people who think and look differently than we do. It insures free and fair elections and supports active participation by the people, in civil and political life.

A healthy democracy best thrives when unified by strong leaders. In challenging times good leaders seek to heal divisions, bring various parts of the country together, and summon people to a sense of common purpose. Leaders must be held accountable and political parties must be strong and fair. Dwight D. Eisenhower claimed that unless parties advanced "a cause that is right and that is moral," it is not a party at all but a "conspiracy to seize power."

I find my father's words, written in 1955, equally meaningful today:

> *Perhaps the most vital human factor of citizenship in any nation is that nation's concept of personal freedom. The glory of its civilization and the strength of its ideals must be measured ultimately by the realistic application of its concept of personal freedom of the individual, and not only upon its*

*citizens, but upon all men everywhere. The individual, in all of his dignity, is still the fundamental unit of our society.*

Defending freedom remains one of the greatest causes of our time. As we look at the past, as we look at the present, are we better equipped to look toward tomorrow? History books of the future are filled with blank pages. How will they be written? How will our stories be told?

# References

i Buck, Stephanie. "The Nazis outlawed hiking, then they turned it into a Hitler Youth travesty, Seeking awe through nature became a crime against the state." *Medium. Timeline*, Jan 23, 2017, timeline.com/hitler-youth-nazi-germany-hiking-29a3ac1c7b3d

"Members of the League of Girls Practice Their Gymnastics Routine." *United States Holocaust Museum*, USHMM, Timeline, ushmm.org/propaganda/themes/indoctrinating-youth/

UHP STAFF. "His Purest Creation: Child Soldiers in World War II." *The Ultimate History Project*, ultimatehistoryproject.com/child-soldiers.html

ii "The SS." *US Holocaust Memorial Museum*, USHMM, ushmm.org/content/en/article/ss

iii "The Nazi Olympics Berlin 1936." *US Holocaust Memorial Museum*, USHMM, ushmm.org/information/exhibitions/traveling-exhibitions/retired-exhibitions/the-nazi-olympics

"*Jesse Owens and the 1936 Olympic Games*." American Experience. PBS Learning Media, unctv.pbslearningmedia.org/resource/amex24.socst.ush.owens/jesse-owens-and-the-1936-olympic-games/

Sparrow, Sam. "Understanding the Creepy History of Berlin's Olympic Stadium." *As the Sparrow Flies*, asthesparrowflies.com/olympic-stadium-berlin/

iv Editors, History.com. "Benito Mussolini." *History*. Updated: Sept 3, 2019, history.com/topics/world-war-ii/benito-mussolini

v "Konigsplatz, King's Square." *A View On Cities*, aviewoncities.com/munich/konigsplatz.html

vi Vaughan, David. "The Master's Voice." *The Guardian*, Thursday Oct 9, 2008 06.56 EDT Radio, theguardian.com/culture/2008/oct/09/radio.hitler.bbc.czechoslovakia

vii Cavendish, Richard. "The Munich Conference." *History Today*, Vol 58 Issue 11 Nov 2008., historytoday.com/archive/munich-conference

"Munich Pact." Dictionary.com, *The New Dictionary of Cultural Literacy*, Third Edition. Copyright 2005 by Houghton Mifflin Harcourt Publishing Company, dictionary.com/browse/munich-pact

viii "The Edgar Bergen and Charlie McCarthy Show." *Old Time Radio Downloads*, oldtimeradiodownloads.com/variety/edgar-bergen-and-charlie-mccarthy

ix "Military Service." *The US Holocaust Museum*, USHMM, Propaganda, Timeline Themes, ushmm.org/propaganda/themes/indoctrinating-youth

x "Winter Relief of the German People." *Wikipedia*, wikipedia.org/wiki/Winterhilfswerk xi Ritchie, Jasmin. Certified Educator. "The Versailles Peace Conference. *Enotes*, enotes.com/homework-help/how-did-treaty-versailles-punish-germany-after-wwi-148213

"Treaty of Versailles." *History.com*, history.com/topics/world-war-i/treaty-of-versailles-1 The Editors of Encyclopaedia Britannica. "The Treaty of Versailles." *Encyclopedia Britannica*, Updated Jan 6, 2020, britannica.com/event/Treaty-of-Versailles-1919

xii History.com Editors. "The Day in History, October 30, 1938." *History.com*, history.com/this-day-in-history/welles-scares-nation

xiii A Teachers Guide To The Holocaust. fcit.usf.edu/holocaust/DEFN/volk.htm

xiv "Culture in the Third Reich: Disseminating the Nazi World View." *The US Holocaust Museum, USHMM*, encyclopedia.ushmm.org/content/en/article/culture-in-the-third-reich-disseminating-the-nazi-worldview

xv The Editors of Encyclopaedia Britannica. "New Deal." *Encyclopedia Britannica*, britannica.com/event/New-Deal

xvi History.com Editors. "Joseph Goebbels." *History.com*, Updated: June 7, 2019, history.com/topics/world-war-ii/joseph-goebbels

xvii Taylor, Alan. "American Nazis in the 1930s-The German American Bund." *The Atlantic*, June 5, 2017, theatlantic.com/photo/2017/06/american-nazis-in-the-1930sthe-german-american-bund/529185/

xviii Biography.com Editors. "Edward VII." *Biogragraphy.com*, Updated: Sept 10, 2019, biography.com/royalty/edward-viii xix "How did the Nazis Construct an Aryan Identity?" *South African History Online*, SAHO, Updated Feb 14, 2020, sahistory.org.za/article/how-did-nazis-construct-aryan-identity

xx History.com Editors. "Kristallnacht." *History.com*, Updated: Dec 6, 2019, history.com/topics/holocaust/kristallnacht

xxi "Synagogenplatz Memorial, Tubingen." *Nationalmuseums.o*rg, Information Portal to European Sites of Rememberance, memorial-museums.org/eng/denkmaeler/view/1127/Synagogenplatz-Memorial,-T%C3%BCingen#

xxii Zucker, Michael. Author of "*The Eisenhower Encyclopedia*." "What did Hitler and Eisenhower think of each other?" *Quora*, quora.com/What-did-Hitler-and-Eisenhower-think-of-each-other

"Dwight D. Eisenhower." *Wikipedia*, en.m.wikipedia.org/wiki/Dwight_D._Eisenhower

Evans, Richard. "*The Third Reich in Power*." Penguin Books, Reprinted Edition, September 26, 2006.

xxiii Simkin, John. "Education in Nazi Germany." Spartacus Educational. Sept 1997, Updated Jan 2020, spartacus-educational.com/GEReducation.htm

"The Nazi Party: The "Lebensborn" Program." *Jewish Virtual Library*, Source: The Forgotten Camps; ABC News 20/20 Special Report. "Hitler's Master Race:" Nazi Program Attempted to Create Racially Pure Children (April 27, 2000), jewishvirtuallibrary.org/the-quot-lebensborn-quot-program

Giles, Milton. From his book, "*Fascinating Footnotes From History*." Published September 24th, 2015 by John Murray Publishers.

xxiv Frankel, Heinrich and Roger Manvell. "Herman Goering." *Encylopedia Britannica*, Updated: Jan 16, 2020, britannica.com/biography/Hermann-Goring

"Herman Goering." *Jewish Virtual Library*, jewishvirtuallibrary.org/hermann-goering

xxv "Definition of 'auslander.'" *Collinsdictionary, Webster's New World College Dictionary*, 4th Edition. Copyright © 2010 by Houghton Mifflin Harcourt. All rights reserved, collinsdictionary.com/us/dictionary/english/auslander

xxvi "The Deutsches Ausland-Institut." *JSTOR*, jstor.org/stable/29780434?seq=1#page_scan_tab_contents

xxvii "*Jewish Refugees From The German Reich*, 1933-1939." United States Holocaust Memorial Museum, USHMM, ushmm.org/exhibition/st-louis/teach/supread2.html

"America and the Holocaust. Deceit and Indifference." *PBS.org*, American Experience, PBS. Aired April 6, 1994, pbs.org/wgbh/americanexperience/films/holocaust

Greene, Daniel and Frank Newport. "American Public Opinion and the Holocaust." *Gallup*. April 23, 2018, news.gallup.com/opinion/polling-matters/232949/american-public-opinion-holocaust.aspx

"The United States and the Refugee Crisis, 1938-41." *United States Holocaust Memorial Museum*, USHMM, Holocaust Encyclopedia, encyclopedia.ushmm.org/content/en/article/the-united-states-and-the-refugee-crisis-1938-41

"Requirements for German Jews Applying for US Visas, 1930-1940." *Facing History*, facinghistory.org/resource-library/text/requirements-german-jews-applying-us-visas-1930-1940

xxviii Blakemore, Erin. "A Ship of Jewish Refugees Was Refused US Landing in 1939. This Was Their Fate." June 14, 2019, *History*, history.com/news/wwii-jewish-refugee-ship-st-louis-1939

xxix Anderson, Pete. "Why did the Spanish Civil War Start in 1936?" *History Today*, Published in History Review Issue 48 March 2004, historytoday.com/archive/why-did-spanish-civil-war-start-july-1936

Anderson, Emma. "Spanish Civil War Ends, Franco Moves to Power." *The Local*, 1 April 2015, thelocal.es/20150401/spanish-civil-war-ends-franco-moves-to-power

xxx Robert M. W. Kempner. "German National Registration System As Means of Police Control of Population." *Scholarly Commons*, The, 36 J. Crim. L. & Criminology 362 (1945-1946), Vol 36/Issue 5, Article 7, scholarlycommons.law.northwestern.edu/cgi/viewcontent.cgi?article=3364&context=jclc

xxxi "Billie Burke." *Oz Wiki*, Edited Friday July 13, 2018, oz.fandom.com/wiki/Billie_Burke

xxxii "What is Fasching? Street parades, costumes, celebrations in Germany." *The Stuttgart Citizen*, Feb 1, 2018. Culture and Leisure. stuttgartcitizen.com/lifestyle/street-parades-celebrations-mark-germanys-fifth-season-2-2/

xxxiii National Carl Schurz Association. *The Historical Society of Pennsylvania with the Bach Institute for Ethnic Studies*, Records, 1709-1995 (bulk 1817-1983) MSS 167, hsp.org/sites/default/files/legacy_files/migrated/findingaidmss167ncsa.pdf

"Carl Schurz." *Wikipedia*, wikipedia.org/wiki/Carl_Schurz

xxxiv "Invasion of Czechoslovakia." *BBC*, Bite Size, bbc.co.uk/bitesize/guides/ztydcwx/revision/5

xxxv 1939: Extravagant Celebration of Hitler's 50th Birthday." *History.info*, history.info/society/culture/1939-extravagant-celebration-hitlers-50th-birthday/

xxxvi "Telegraph by President Roosevelt to the Chancellor of Germany Adlolf Hitler 14 April 1939." USA.USA*Embassy*, (Source: United States Department of State, Published 1983, Peace and War: United States Foreign Policy, 1931-1941 (Washington D.C.; Government Printing Office, 1943, pp. 455-58), usa.usembassy.de/etexts/ga3-390414.htm

xxxvii Maypole Celebration: "Welcoming Spring with Germany Maypole Celebrations." *Reflections Enroute*, reflectionsenroute.com/welcoming-spring-german-maypole-celebrations/

xxxviii "Wagner-Rogers Bill." *United States Holocaust Memorial Museum*, USHMM, encyclopedia.ushmm.org/content/en/article/wagner-rogers-bill

xxxix "Hitler's Reply to Roosevelt." *Erenow*, Military History, erenow.net/ww/risefallthirdreich/76.php

xl Editors of Encyclopedia Britannica. "Konrad Henlein, Sudenten-German Politician." *Encyclopedia Britannica*, britannica.com/biography/Konrad-Henlein

xli "The Nazi Party Rally Grounds." *Nuremberg*, Museum, museums.nuernberg.de/documentation-center/national-socialism/the-nazi-party-rally-grounds/

xlii "Gertrude Scholtz-Klink." *Spartacus Educational*, spartacus-educational.com/GERscholtz.htm

xliii Workers in German Labor Service. "Workers in German Labor Service (1939-1945)" *LAMOTH*, Los Angeles Museum of the Holocaust, lamoth.info/?p=creators/creator&id=1137

xliv "I.G. Farben." *Holocaust Research Project.org*, Holocaust Historical Society, National Archives Kew, Wiener Library, holocaustresearchproject.org/economics/igfarben.html

"The Empire of I.G. Farben." *Reformation.org*, reformation.org/wall-st-ch2.html

xlv "Graf Zeppelin History." *AIRSHIP.NET*, airships.net/lz127-graf-zeppelin/history/

xlvi "Strength Through Joy." *History*, tutor2u.net/history/reference/strength-through-joy

Land, Graham. "Tourism and Leisure in Nazi Germany: Strength Through Joy Explained." *History Hit*, July 23, 2018, historyhit.com/tourism-and-leisure-in-nazi-germany/

xlvii "The History of Modern Turkey." Wikipedia, en.wikipedia.org/wiki/History_of_the_Republic_of_Turkey

xlviii Taylor, Ann. "American Nazis in the 1930s-the German American Bund." *The Atlantic*, June 5, 2017, theatlantic.com/photo/2017/06/american-nazis-in-the-1930sthe-german-american-bund/529185/

History.com Editors. "Lend Lease Act." *History.com*, Nov 4, 2019, history.com/topics/world-war-ii/lend-lease-act-1 xlix Luce, Henry R. "America and Armageddon" *Life Magazine*, page 40, June 3, 1940

l Schul, Bill. "Judge Saw German War fever." *Wichita Beacon*, 1959

li "The Counter Intelligence Corps." CIC History, National Counter Intelligence Corps Association. *NCICA*, ncica.org/history.html

lii Sayer, Ian and Douglas Botting, *"American's Secret Army, The Untold Story of the Counter Intelligence Corps."* Grafton Books, 1989

liii "World War II Rationing." *US History*, www.u-s-history.com/pages/h1674.html

liv Schul, Bill. "Judge Saw German War fever." *Wichita Beacon*, 1959

lv "Fascism." United States Holocaust Memorial Museum, *USHMM*, enclyclopedia.ushmm.org/content/en/article/fascism-1

lvi "D-Day, June 6, 1944." *ARMY-MIL*, arm.mil/d-day/

lvii The European Post. "St. Tropaz, August 15...1944--what happened?" *The European Post*, europeanpost.co/st-tropez-15-august-1944-what-happened/

lviii Richards, R. Robert. *"Alias 'the Fox", The Wartime Recollections of Robert R. Richards*, 1994, printed by Robin Enterprises, Westville, Ohio, 1994

lix Gaskill, Gordon, "G-Men in Khaki." *The American magazine*, January 1945 lx Greene, Richard Allen and Inez Torre. "Nazi Death Camps." *CNN*, April 15, 2015, cnn.com/2015/01/26/world/nazi-death-camps/index.html

"Nazi Camps." *United States Holocaust Memorial Museum, USHMM*, encyclopedia.ushmm.org/content/en/article/nazi-camps

lxi "Crush Nazi Re-Birth." *Kansas City Star*, March 31, 1946-Sunday

lxii Schul, Bill. "Judge Saw German War fever." *Wichita Beacon*, 1959

lxiii Sayer, Ian and Douglas Botting, "*American's Secret Army, The Untold Story of the Counter Intelligence Corps.*" Grafton Books, 1989

lxiv Eric H. Limbach, *Unsettled Germans: The Reception and Resettlement of East German Refugees in West Germany*, 1949-1961, google.com/search?q=refugee+camps+berlin+1956&oq=refu&aqs=chrome.0.69i59j69i57j0l2j46j0l3.2287j0j8&sourceid=chrome&ie=UTF-8

lxv "World War II casualties." Wikipedia, en.wikipedia.org/wiki/World_War_II_casualties

lxvi "Nazi Propaganda and censorship." United States Holocaust Museum, *HolocaustEncyclopedia*, encyclopedia.ushmm.org/content/en/article/nazi-propaganda-and-censorship

lxvii Anne Mitchell, Larry Diamond. "China's Surveillance State Should Scare Everyone." February 2, 2018, *The Atlantic*, theatlantic.com/international/archive/2018/02/china-surveillance/552203/

lxviii Repucci, Sarah. "A Leaderless Struggle for Democracy." Freedom in the World 2020, *Freedom House*, freedomhouse.org/report/freedom-world/2020/leaderless-struggle-democracy

"Data leak reveals how China 'brainwashes' Uighurs in prison camps." 24 November 2019, bbc.com/news/world-asia-china-50511063

lxix Inglis, Shelley. "So you want to be an autocrat? Here's the ten-point checklist." *The Conversation*, Nov 19, 2019, theconversation.com/so-you-want-to-be-an-autocrat-heres-the-10-point-checklist-125908

lxx "World's Autocrats Face Rising Resistance." *Human Rights Watch*, hrw.org/world-report/2019/country-chapters/global

lxxi "World's Autocrats Face Rising Resistance." *Human Rights Watch*, hrw.org/world-report/2019/country-chapters/global

lxxii Bayer, Lily. "Hungary's Viktor Orbán wins vote to rule by decree." 3/30/20.Updated 3/31/20. *POLITICO*, politico.eu/article/hungary-viktor-Orbán-rule-by-decree/

lxxiii Ngo, Madeline. "Turkey's president just won reelection-and a dangerous set of new powers." *Vox*, Jan 25, 2018, vox.com/world/2018/6/25/17500772/turkey-erdogan-election-results

lxxiv Ben-Meir, Dr. Alon. "It's time to tame Erdogan." *Middle East Online*, Feb 03/07/2020, middle-east-online.com/en/it%E2%80%99s-time-tame-erdogan

lxxv "More than 7,000 killed in the Philippines in six months, as president encourages murder." *Amnesty International UK*, amnesty.org.uk/philippines-president-duterte-war-on-drugs-thousands-killed

lxxvi Jeffrey Gettleman and Maria Abi-Habib. "In India, Modi's Policies Have Lit a Fuse." *The New York Times*, March 1, 2020, nytimes.com/2020/03/01/world/asia/india-modi-hindus.html

# Other References

Friedman, Ina R, Author of *The Other Victims: First Person Stories of Non-Jews Persecuted by the Nazis* (Boston: Houghton Mifflin, 1990) "The Other Victims of the Nazis." Social Studies, socialstudies.org/sites/default/files/publications/se/5906/590606.html

"Nazi economic and social policy." *BBC, Bite Size*, bbc.co.uk/bitesize/guides/zw6s7p3/revision/1

Greene, Richard Allen. "A Shadow Over Europe." *CNN*, edition.cnn.com/interactive/2018/11/europe/antisemitism-poll-2018-intl/

Wall, Harry D. "Ignorance About the Holocaust is Growing." *CNN*, Updated Sunday, January 27, 2019, cnn.com/2019/01/27/opinions/holocaust-education-importance-wall/index.html

Freedland, Jonathan. "The 1930s was Humanity's darkest, bloodiest hour. Are you paying attention?" *The Guardian*, theguardian.com/society/2017/mar/11/1930s-humanity-darkest-bloodiest-hour-paying-attention-second-world-war

"German resistance to Nazism." *Wikipedia*, en.wikipedia.org/wiki/German_resistance_to_Nazism

Rummel, R.J. "Democide: Nazi Genocide and Mass Murder. 20,946,000 Victims: 1933-1945." Chapter 1. 1992, Transaction Publishers, New Brunswick, N.J., *hawaii.edu*, hawaii.edu/powerkills/NAZIS.CHAP1.HTM

"Germany From Democracy to Dictatorship."annefrank.org/en/anne-frank/go-in-depth/germany-1933-democracy-dictatorship/

Evans, Richard J. "A Warning From History." *The Nation*, Feb 28, 2017, https://www.thenation.com/article/archive/the-ways-to-destroy-democracy/

"Night of the Long Knives. The Triumph of Hitler." *The History Place*, historyplace.com/worldwar2/triumph/tr-roehm.htm

"Background: Life Before the Holocaust." *British Library*, bl.uk/learning/histcitizen/voices/testimonies/life/backgd/before.html

"Berlin: The Persecution of Jews and German Society." *Humanity Action*, humanityinaction.org/knowledge_detail/berlin-the-persecution-of-jews-and-german-society/

O'Shaughnessy, Nicholas. 'How Hitler Conquered Germany." *Slate*, March 14, 2017, slate.com/news-and-politics/2017/03/how-nazi-propaganda-encouraged-the-masses-to-co-produce-a-false-reality.html

"How did the Nazi consolidate power?" *The Wiener Holocaust Library*, theholocaustexplained.org/the-nazi-rise-to-power/how-did-the-nazi-gain-power/night-of-long-knives/

Ayelett, Shani. "How Hitler Won Germans Over With His 'Scientific Religion." With her conversation with Dr. Tamar Ketko who authored *Ice Creatures: The Nazi Education System*. Reisling Books, Hebrew. HAARETZ, haaretz.com/world-news/europe/.premium.MAGAZINE-how-hitler-won-germans-over-with-his-scientific-religion-1.5474185

Simkin, John. "Education in Nazi Germany." *Spartacus Educational*. Sept 1997, Updated Jan 2020, spartacus-educational.com/GEReducation.htm

Crossland, David. "Lebensborn Children Break Silence." July 11, 2006, *Spiegel International*, spiegel.de/international/

nazi-program-to-breed-master-race-lebensborn-children-break-silence-a-446978.html

Levitsky, Steven and Daniel Ziblatt. An extract from: "How Democracies Die." Viking, Jan 25, 2018, *The Guardian*, theguardian.com/us-news/commentisfree/2018/jan/21/this-is-how-democracies-die

Steven Hochstadt. "The Weakness of Democracy." History News Network, Mar 26, 2019, historynewsnetwork.org/blog154196

"Democracy in Retreat." *Freedom House*, Freedom in the World 2019, freedomhouse.org/report/freedom-world/freedom-world-2019/democracy-in-retreat

"The Nuremberg Laws. Holocaust and Human Behavior," Chapter 6, *Facing History and Ourselves*, https://www.facinghistory.org/holocaust-and-human-behavior/chapter-6/nuremberg-laws

"Life in Nazi Germany, 1933-1939." BBC, bbc.co.uk/bitesize/guides/zpq9p39/revision/7

Kyle Matthews, Pearl Euadis, Arthur Graham, Michael Abramowitz, Jeremy Kinsman. "Five human rights issues that need urgent attention in 2019." May 3, 2019, *OPENCANADA.ORG*, opencanada.org/features/five-human-rights-issues-need-urgent-attention-2019/

"Doris Kearns Goodwin: 6 Essential Traits a President Needs." *History*, history.com/topics/doris-kearns-goodwin-on-presidential-leadership

"The Nuremberg Laws. Holocaust and Human Behavior," Chapter 6, *Facing History and Ourselves*, https://www.facinghistory.org/holocaust-and-human-behavior/chapter-6/nuremberg-laws

Day, Matthew. The Telegraph. "Shocking' Holocaust Study Claims Nazis Killed Up To 20 Million People." *Business Insider*, March 4, 2013, businessinsider.com/shocking-new-holocaust-study-claims-nazis-killed-up-to-20-million-people-2013-3

"World's Autocrats Face Rising Resistance." *Human Rights Watch*, hrw.org/world-report/2019/country-chapters/global